The Case of California

The Case of
CALIFORNIA

Laurence A. Rickels

University of Minnesota Press
Minneapolis • London

The writing of this book was sponsored in part by the Alexander von Humboldt Foundation and the Interdisciplinary Humanities Center at the University of California, Santa Barbara.

Frontispiece: "Black Narcissus (The Case of California)." Photograph by Nancy Barton.

First University of Minnesota Press edition, 2001

Published by the University of Minnesota Press
111 Third Avenue South, Suite 290
Minneapolis, MN 55401-2520
http://www.upress.umn.edu

A Cataloging-in-Publication record for this book is available from the Library of Congress.

ISBN 0-8166-3878-0

Printed in the United States of America on acid-free paper

The University of Minnesota is an equal-opportunity educator and employer.

12 11 10 09 08 07 06 05 04 03 02 01   10 9 8 7 6 5 4 3 2 1

Contents

Contents

Fast Foreword

Rickeln *(Middle High German): to bind, cut off, bury*

The history-long and society-wide investment in psychoanalysis can turn out a case as specific and vast, as external
and theoretical, as that of "California." As the Frankfurt
School put it: the Californian "culture industry is psychoanalysis in reverse."[1] Investment in psychoanalysis brought
the Frankfurt School to the Coast of an exteriority which its
time done (down) in Germanic *Bildungs*-culture had prepared it to recognize: California, childhood, and psychoanalysis occupy interchangeable places to the extent that
each in turn occupies the missing place of our death cult.

This recognition of the California scene is as coextensive with Freud's first system (the one *Totem and Taboo*
brought to completion) as is the Frankfurt School's other
double take on California with the second system (the one

that takes us "beyond the pleasure principle"). Only from within the second system could National Socialism be doubled back onto California and also diagnosed as "psychoanalysis in reverse."[2] Thus on the personalizable level or label, California is a death cult; on the social, outward, happy-face level, it distributes pleasure via sadomasochism, the adolescent group, or friendship.

The Case of California excavates the places "California" occupies as concept or placeholder within Freudian psychoanalysis and within such extensions of the Freudian system as Frankfurt School thought, East Coast psychoanalysis, and deconstruction. While California is, in fact, named within the psychoanalytic corpus, much of its force goes without saying. To excavate the full range of California one must apply pressure to a series of adjacent (and often equally marginal or missing) concepts covering group or adolescent psychology, female sexuality, the haunting of music (in particular) and of the mass media at large, the charge of child abuse, and a certain convergence of religious and hysterical conversion. Such acupressure cannot but follow and release roller-coaster-like shifts of register. But archaeological excavation or deconstruction must remain nonexclusionary in the fantasies it shares. By moving to the Coast of the Freudian system, a critique of modern mass thought structures can be established—from within a master discursivity, institution, or ideology. In this way the spectral appeal of the perpetual teenager and the missing or abused child (to give two interrelated examples) will not have been surrendered to journalism or to the state. At the same time, this case study of California recovers a political engagement of psychoanalysis which emerged within Freud's second system only to be obscured by the seeming segregation of marginal trajectories—those of group psychology and female sexuality. The bisexual constitution, which organizes groups and groupies around its double repression of father, governs the bicoastal distribution of Freud's otherwise undivided political critique. The separations and out-of-phasednesses thus inhabiting the Freudian systems must gold rush appears to relatives and friends Back East only "as one dead." "Round about California in that day were scattered a host of these living dead men." The narrator, who is new to the Coast, becomes the unwitting witness to one man's nineteen-year-long refusal to accept his young wife's passing; photographs, letters, and the details of her interior decoration reserve a place for her return. The delusion or ritual of anticipating her weekend comeback is sustained within a support group of friends. At the end, when the party has gone on into morning—mourning—and the absent woman has not been beamed back, the friends drug the friend who had almost begun to grieve, but it was too late. At this end, according to Philippe Ariès, a larger scale identification has been admitted. "Henceforth, and this is a very important change, the death which is feared is no longer so much the death of the self as the death of another, *la mort de toi*, thy death."[5] For Freud this historical or hysterical change that Twain's Californian tale documents doubles as the *primal* precondition of every so-called self-relation, which must always take the detour via the dead other. The *disavowal* of the other-bound bond in turn marks a certain origin of modern group psychology.

According to Leon Altman, to "go West" is derived from an early American colloquialism, "gone West" (into unexplored territory), which meant that the person had absconded, disappeared, or died.[6] Not only in Babylonian myth does the sun descend westward into a country of the dead "from whence is no return," a "land where one sees nothing" (239). "In whatever country one asked, 'Where is the gate to the city of the dead?' the answer was always, 'In the West'" (241). Thus in 1959 Altman can claim his own treatment of the death symbolicity of "West" to be somehow unique only by dropping a footnote to a Californian colleague who, already in 1927, was able to conclude: "Symbolically, San Diego should have the highest suicide rate in the United States and the West Coast as a whole should be higher than the East Coast. Since earliest times, the sunset has stood as the symbol of death; and the West, typifying the land of the sunset, is another expression of the same thing" (236, n. 1). But Altman holds onto his claim of innovation when it comes to the role of "West" in dream symbolism. The dream Altman excavates is located, like Altman, in *Amerika* or New York. But the ship is moving Westward, an inadmissible direction from New York harbor; the dreamer is stricken with unfathomable grief. Although Altman mentions (in passing) that the recent death of one of the dreamer's good friends contributed to the dream's makeup, he brings the dream into focus against a public backdrop and phantasm: "He read a newspaper account of a man, going to California to recuperate from an illness, who took passage on a through train. When the train arrived there the man was found dead in his compartment" (238).

In increasing numbers distinguished thinkers feel the need to write about California, which they are nevertheless hard-pressed to situate (even as they pass through it) as an object of interpretation. What is it about California that places a call to thinking? And what does it mean, then, to write on location when, although we think we know where it is located, California cannot be considered (in any classical or traditional sense) as place or character.

In this study the stress on California is thus not so much upon an empirical or historical entity as it is introduced and used as a philosopheme. The decision to deploy California as philosopheme is motivated in a perhaps historical sense by the way Germany was used by Hölderlin and, in a more stressed way, by Heidegger to designate in terms of destinal promise that which is yet to come. While no transcendence can be claimed for California, it compellingly marks and situates values of postmodern technicity in relation to a hermeneutics of pain and mourning.

The desire to render California a semiotic placeholder for a vast and complex network of contemporary phenomena is not a new one: the Frankfurt School made California an essential supplement to its spookulations. One extreme example (and indeed one that has not received any critical attention) is the far-reaching dispute that Benjamin and

Adorno organized around the hyper-American figure of Mickey Mouse. Who would have thought that the profound erudition of these two distinguished thinkers would find a snag in the invention of a Walt Disney?! Yet Mickey Mouse, as jarring as this may seem, dramatizes for the proponents of the Frankfurt School the predicament of the technologization of the human subject as it is systematically deprived of secure anthropomorphic grounding. Mickey Mouse is not an indifferent or altogether innocent emblem of humanistic transformation. His voice was recruited to agitate against the Nazi regime. But whereas in 1935 the League of Nations celebrated Mickey Mouse as "an international symbol of good will," Adorno at the same time recognized in Mickey Mouse the new sadomasochistic subject of technology whose metabolism of friendship, group membership, and suicide was shared equally, he concluded, by California and Nazi Germany. With Mickey Mouse, Disney had invented not only the totally American product but also the first in that category to circulate with unequalled international appeal. The Californiaization of "the West" had commenced its countdown—and body count.

As foreign object California has most recently exerted a good deal of its manifest destiny fascinating French writers. But as Blanchot announced in *The Writing of Disaster*, fascination blinds. For these new-wave writers on "California" cannot wipe out—not without at the same time barreling the interpretation of a German text. The French have always shown the greatest distinction when interpreting Germany or its flipped-out side, California. Lyotard, for example, drifts with this divide when he lines up California and Germany against a "wall of the Pacific" thrown up by the trauma of Auschwitz. California and Germany are indeed the divided or bicoastal states of emergency and disaster. The center of nuclear sites always threatening to erupt, California is the other place of total war. California occupies the intersection between technology and the unconscious as part of an interiority lodged inside the discursivity of psychoanalysis—and shared with Germanicity. California is thus not discoverable in some place on the outside about which one might have opinions. This mode of target practice has, however, been a leading tendency among ideologues of the American university ranging from Baudrillardians or Jamesonians to certain feminists and film theorists. This trend, to which Jonathan Culler gave the headline "California criticism," finds and founds its appetizing other within a native habitat which doubles as radical simulation—or forgetting—of Freudian psychoanalysis. Only the Frankfurt School and deconstruction have countered this trendy degenerescence with commemorations of unparalleled *Leser*-precision. Not tourist-trapped by certain attractions so sensational in many discernible ways, a psychoanalytic study of California must choose instead what one might consider to be at once a mode of close reading and a mood of authenticity—namely, ambivalence.

The reading assignment California issues is coextensive with the links and limits of psychoanalysis (*the* American master discourse). Thus the excavation of California must commence with Freud's rejection of America. This reject became the first attraction of the psychoanalytic exploration of mass media culture which Adorno and Horkheimer would relocate, within the range of one philosopheme, on the Coast (whose other coast was, by then, Nazi Germany). Freud's anti-Americanism has been packaged and dispensed with as the stereotype of European self-historicization at America's expense. But unlike, for example, Stendhal's charge that Americans were incapable of love, Freud's diagnosis gains in precision the more generally and extensively it is allowed to range. "America" is the password that opens onto a complex in Freud that held the place of (and held in place) Freud's missing account of adolescent psychology. Freud's analysis of America (or California) drops alongside the emergence of the second system, which rose to analyze or withstand the advent of National Socialism. Thus the political front of psychoanalysis was originally and always formed to meet a challenge of total war issued in one place but only recognizable (as having a future or nice day) in the other place. The trajectory of exile from Nazi Germany only fast-forwarded psychoanalysis to the other front or time zone of one totally awesome war. Only within this paranoid theater of prophesied warfare does Freud's rejection of America fall into place. Thus America's very acceptance of psychoanalysis attracted Freud's ambivalence. And indeed America never could receive Freud's science without rendering it new and improved: the defections of Jung, Rank, Reich, and Lacan, among others, always found support groups in America. Genuine ambivalence (as opposed to the group-bound narcissism of outright rejection) governs Freud's humorous vision of Fifth Avenue shop windows advertising what would be coming soon: "gifts for every stage of the transference."[7] But Freud thus only confirms reservations that he himself had made when he analogized his discoveries with consumer projection. But if the integrity of Freud's science was consequently lost once it became the ideology of mass media and consumerist societies, it has also remained, for all the same reasons, the native habitat of their critique. The out-of-phasedness of these relations of analogy always renders undecidable the causal relations behind the seeming interchangeability of the Freudian system and mass media culture. Even family relations are without influence: as though without connection, Freud's American nephew, Edward Bernays, can be said to be the founder of the public-relations industry.

Although Freud wanted to keep America "on the side of Libido," his own reaction while touring what he preferred to refer to as "Dollaria" rebounded from another side—the down side of dyspepsia, "colitis," and other "embarrassing situations."[8] These upwardly mobile symptoms were the sum total of the "great deal" that America had "cost" him. In German the verbs "to cost" and "to taste" occupy one soundshape *(kosten):* the melancholic disorder America "cost" him he also "tasted" there. The melancholic reproach had to be internalized, but also shared: "This race is destined to extinction. They can no longer open their mouths to speak; soon they won't be able to do so to eat." Their mouths were already occupied with other brands of feedback: "Can an American live in opposition to the public opinion?" Thus the proposal that Freud collaborate with the edition of a "source book" of his writings specially designed for American consumption quickly ran the circuit of his nausea: "Fundamentally the whole thing is, being authentically American, quite repellent to me. One can rely on it: if such a source book were available, no American would ever go to the original." American "broadmindedness" only betrayed a serious "lack of judgement" and shortness of attention span: Americans, finally, had "no time for libido."

America thus reflected in practice the pull Freud assigned in theory to group psychology and its psychoticizing structures. Freud chose a certain Frink to head American psychoanalysis—only, then, to witness him withdraw into psychosis. But the group membership of American psychoanalysis was opting, as though via teletype with the personalized brand of the same disorder, for transfer of the democratic principle "from politics to science:" "Everybody must become president once, no one must remain president; none may excel before the others, and thus all of them neither learn nor achieve anything." What even Freud called the "American pattern of replacing quality with quantity" was thus already in place—inside the asides, implications, and exclusions of the Freudian systems. That is, America stood under the negative sign of work Freud could accomplish only on the sidelines of his two systems. America shares this margin first with Freud's theory of the technical media in terms of unmournable death or haunting and, in the second system, with Freud's enigmatic assignment of matricentricity (indeed, the female gender) to the constitution of the modern masses. The reconstruction of the case of California within Freud's science (and within its doubly exiled extensions or survivals) commences in a place of conversion: California is where unending mourning achieves its society-wide manifestation (or massification) as sadomasochism, where the death wish yields to death drive (which takes a detour via suicide), and where the femininity of mourning constitutes the group's secret agenda, gender, and desire. The psychohistory that documents the intellectual migrations to the most modern of frontiers cannot but unfold or fold out a psychology of the ultimate idol of Freud's second system: the adolescent or Californian. But the two anchorpersons for this special report on California—Kafka and Thomas Mann—have been selected, according to the bicoastal logic of this case, from among Germanicity's teenagers at heart. In between: television covers the ins and outs of this psychoanalytic investigation of a global conspiracy—the Californian (and German) invention of adolescence.

The philosopheme "Germany" has triggered rounds of association to which (as with the phenomenon of mourning according to Freud) "other obscurities can be traced back" (*SE* 14:306). But in the meantime the association of "psychoanalysis," "the body," "the media," and "adolescence" shares its Central European origins with the other philosopheme—"California"—which has superseded the manifest sense or destiny of the unconscious, the body, the media, the teenager. If postmodernity is postmarked (like the repressed according to Freud) "made in Germany" (*SE* 19:236), then California is its address and tech-no-future.

As case, this study exhibits a law—that of unmourning. But like the *Geist* or ghost of philosophical self-help programs, what can, at the end, be called "California" must, to that end and on the way, have attained and unfolded self-consciousness. That quest must first pass through the relays and delays of *The Case of California*.

Let the Children Kodak

*S*ince I became aware of this phenomenon, I've found
that at least seventy percent of my patients were possessed and it was this condition that caused their
dis-ease. Most of these people were relieved—through de-
possession techniques—of more than one entity. Occasional
patients were unwitting hosts to as many as fifty or more!
Possession is a relative condition. When it is complete—which
is rare—the original personality seems to be gone and is replaced by that of the earth-bound entity. Usually there is a
vacillating balance between the two; at times, the spirit exerts
only slight influence, while at others, he or she can be ex-
tremely dominant. In some cases, there is an ongoing inner
battle for control, replete with mental dialogues—even insults
and commands!

The spirits that possessed my patients were once people
from all walks of life, who—after death—remained in the
physical world and became "displaced persons." They had not

made the proper transition between the earth plane and the "other side" at death. Sometimes years later without bodies of their own, they merged accidentally or intentionally with people whose lives thereafter were never the same. For these spirits, there was no worse fate than sentencing themselves to residing in other individuals' bodies, for they thereby postponed their chances to enter the spirit world where they belonged.

—Edith Fiore, *The Unquiet Dead: A Psychologist Treats Spirit Possession*

Freud's analogies between media technology and the malfunction of the psychic apparatus are circuited through psychoanalysis's inside-out coextensivity with mass-media society. By the time he advanced his first theory of the technical media (which doubled as a theory of haunting), Freud could reserve for the analogues forged with media technology exclusive "endopsychic" status. Those delusional formations which featured the incursions of the mass media were the hallucinatory projection onto an outside of an internal ("endopsychic") scan of psychic disturbance. And these delusions were endopsychic perceptions or projections precisely to the extent that they reproduced *and* modeled Freud's *theory* of the psychic apparatus.[1]

The endopsychic cables of this inner/outer trajectory were originally laid via analogy with archaeological excavation—which was set up, in the *Gradiva* reading, as endopsychic perception of the return of childhood recollections from the repressed. The excavation of mummified childhood thus dug the place that media technology coincided with and superseded in *Totem and Taboo*. The theory of projection introduces the media-technologization of an archaeological dig redirected from repression to the burial ground of identification.

(The archaeological project of Sir Arthur Evans which excavated ancient Crete also dug "California": up front a bungalow-and-pool culture; deep down, it turned out, death cult precincts. The funereal perspective was rediscovered via the underlying Westward axis of the palace Evans re-opened: only cemeteries open onto the West. Mortuary palaces, which Hollywood film sets and Disney amusement parks have syndicated, first undertook the simulation in flimsy materials and in slightly reduced scale of the everyday life everywhere else.[2] The processes of representation in the work of mourning which have ever extended living to the dead—reduction, simulation, and, via the funereal logic of specularity, reversal—have always also reserved a place for a double invention: technology and the unconscious.)

By 1912, then, Freud's endopsychic analogizing had shifted from externalization of the "psychology of the unconscious," which myth was said to represent (SE 6:258–59), to the media-technological outside of what is, as psychic apparatus, also already inside. Henceforth competing claims to the understanding or ownership of the unconscious would themselves be part of the endopsychic perception. What Freud kept apart in theory—the projection of death wishes or haunting and haunting's station identification (which the inward, vampiric turns of melancholic preservation install)—was already conjoined in practice within the endopsychic orbit of his science. Thus Ludwig Staudenmaier's 1912 treatise *Magic as an Experimental Science*—which right away invites comparison with Schreber's autoanalysis—could be officially recognized by psychoanalytic reviewers as confirmation of theories which, in Schreber's case, had still required reservations: "His experiments confirm the experience of psychoanalysis. The hallucinations that he describes are in a certain sense photographic, that is, cinematographic recordings of the unconscious."[3]

Following instructions he would bring to the completion of a system within his own "how to" book on the science of magic, Staudenmaier began his research project by putting himself in the ready position: the spirits he had, in his state of concentrated preparedness, invited to possess him, soon teleguided an impulse to write not under his conscious control.[4] An urge he first felt in his finger tips began dictating the messages he wrote down letter by letter; as he wrote down one cipher the next in line already appeared with total clarity on his internal scanner; then the next complete word also announced itself, but as a vaguer intuition. In time the anticipation of whole words achieved amplification as the advance audition of the sound shapes he could not help but record; soon pencil and paper became superfluous. Recapitulating a concise history of the technical mediatization of representation, he developed from an occult "writing medium" into that which writes without writing:[5] a "listening medium" (24) for which Staudenmaier can find only media-technological analogues.

Although Staudenmaier at first takes his transformation into an audio device to mark a kind of progress, he soon discovers that the inner voices which keep growing in number tune in too often, pointlessly, and against his volition. What's more: they lie (25). Out of this jamming of the voices that possess him emerge what Staudenmaier designates as "personifications," which embody the regular recurrence of contact between certain hallucinatory visions and their corresponding audio portions.

Staudenmaier's personifications—featuring "Highness," "Child," and "Round Head"—are his personalized versions of centers of the brain which under normal conditions silently advise the conscious ego. But in Staudenmaier's case his personifications often converse only among themselves and behind his back: "not unlike the way in which two or more telegraph operators within a complex network of telegraph stations can work together without the knowledge of the other operators" (70). These demonic personifications, which double now as telegraph operators, now as African tribesmen (82), are soon enrolled in the double analogy Staudenmaier ultimately chooses for his system: the conscious ego serves as ruler (or head librarian) in charge of a subconscious populated by highly specialized bureaucrats, who are in fact on their own, on automatic (143, 155).

But as true gadget lover, Staudenmaier attempts to bring this Kafkaesque bureaucracy under the direct control of his own body ego, which would be incomparably strengthened, Californiaized. And to secure the control panel of his bureaucratized subconscious he needs only observe the "law of reversibility" (43), which states that the process or apparatus that receives impressions can also produce and project them on the outside.

Staudenmaier discovers this law by observing on his own person the formation of hallucinations which he can only compare to the regular functioning of camera and telephone: the telephone membrane that hears also speaks at the other end of the line. "In like manner one can, via the ear drum, 'speak' and in general produce tones and with the eyes produce light" (47–48). Whereas when you speak the stimulus runs down from the brain to the vocal cords, tongue, and so on, when you hallucinate the auditory apparatus is turned on to receive directly (and transmit) the stimulus that drops from the brain to the ear drum. "Hopefully in the age of gramophone and telephone, which both speak via membranes and produce tones and even music, the moment is no longer so far off that one will cease viewing the production of speech, tones, and music through the ear drum as a form of haunting, but rather as a natural art form, which however requires training" (49).

But the law of reversibility exorcises and explains occult phenomena only by not relinquishing haunting to the outside:

> The visible and photographable ghost phenomena of the Spiritists are thus in my view nothing other than real hallucinations stemming from the subconscious. . . . And even when the phantoms speak, move, and become tangible—this too is nothing more than an artful and uniformly created combination of real optical, acoustical, and other hallucinations, comparable to some degree to the combined performance of cinematograph and gramophone. (91)
>
> The belief professed by Spiritists that one comes into contact with the dead according to some vital principle independent of the body would be tanta-

mount to claiming that there is in cinematography, and independent of the material apparatus, an invisible principle simply because the shapes projected onto the screen dwell and act outside the apparatus. (107)

There is nothing outside the apparatus or the body except projection, which builds and fuels the apparatus by divorcing the body from itself. He leaves outside his science that which rules it absolutely: projection, which *is* the law of reversibility. That is, the schizo aspires to be able to project any number of personas or personifications without each time knowing, consuming, or recognizing them as identifications.

Staudenmaier rejects—onto the projection track—the independent vital principle only in order to realize, in isolation from an "invisible principle" which lies above and inside him, what had all along been his ultimate and close-range research goal: the prevention or reversal of the aging process which control of the subconscious apparatus would achieve within his own corpus (230).

Since the psyche is media-technological, always and already sending and receiving wireless communications across air waves, it surpasses the occult mediations of telepathy or Spiritist photography (182). Therefore, rather than rely on photographic reproduction of hallucinations, future researchers should be able to store and play back the projections right on the retina screens of the possessed (190–91).

But when Staudenmaier turns up the volume on this amalgam of ghostly, psychic, or technical media he discovers that the ambivalent backfire of identification, which makes the mass-cultural proximity of love and identification so dangerous, destructive, and hot, blazes its trails only on the outside. Thus a personification playing the role of dead Dr. von D. protests, when Staudenmaier tries to convince the specter that D. is dead and gone, that the role he now plays he had earlier rehearsed inside Staudenmaier. Since at that time Dr. von D.'s thoughts had been unable to turn up the volume on the internal speaker, he could only go—without saying.

Staudenmaier thinks he's still in the projection-and-identification precincts of relations with father. Thus he tries to reintroduce, on rewind, literacy requirements: he trains his subconscious to communicate not only silently and directly but via articulations in which he can intervene: he can instruct and admonish his advisory centers and they in turn can counsel him in their respective areas of expertise (159).

But it's too late. His personifications may be players or deceivers, but the "art of the actor" which they observe—to the point of treating Staudenmaier as their subject and servant (168)—tunes in on sitcom sets or mirror stages and not in the theatrical space of Oedipalization. Like the patients and projects of Jung and Lacan, Staudenmaier cannot go "neurotic" without in fact advancing a psychotic case.

To down his endopsychic perception and get off too, the psychotic must share the perverse, perpetually adolescent, or group fantasy. Sadomasochism, as law of transformation of "nerve energy," thus dispenses and disperses the gadget-love bond with one's own technologization and reversibility. "It is furthermore well known that pain triggers pleasurable feelings, that pain allows itself, as it were, to be metamorphosed into pleasure" (50).

"In a certain sense this compares to the progressive development of a cultural state, in which enlightenment and education *[Bildung]* penetrate to ever wider and deeper circles of people" (227). These are the circles of consumerism that will demand more say in government, which will thus increasingly decentralize. The role of the unconscious is growing. Not only the "upper consciousness" and its functions await extended development, therefore, but, in the future, "also those of the lower-standing psychic and psychophysical agencies of the subconscious" (227). The future man, whose arrival Staudenmaier has been building up to, will no longer represent a strict psychic unity, but will participate in and exercise greater control over the whole governable body through increased decentralization. "That is the counterpart to the . . . transitional phase of increased centralization during the exercise of particularly intense and psychophysical functions" (227).

But while Staudenmaier's frenzied research project or projection produces ghosts, nowhere does it include disciples. Staudenmaier concedes, there's simply no time (230). Staudenmaier's realignment of apparatuses along the trajectory of projection stops short at the separation between psychoanalysis and every other psychology. In the place of the rejected independent vital principle, Staudenmaier's proper "Death" issues the limit concepts of his psychological speculations. But this invisible principle or force, to which Staudenmaier would forever defer submission, has been relocated within psychoanalysis as the conscious injunction that opens up access to the unconscious: ghostbusting (which psychoanalysis sponsors) legislates and commences with the inconceivability or unrepresentability of one's own death. Psychology's limit is thus turned around: inside this limit (on the side of identification) we encounter a relation not to death but to the dead which remains a necessarily projective rapport with the death wishes we addressed "live" to the other, who is always the first to go. As in the film and book *The Hunger:* the culture of media technology, like or rather as the "vampire" Freud uncovers in *Totem and Taboo,* compensates for displacements of narcissism through a belief in immortality vouchsafed by scientific search for the cure of aging. Death has dominion in *The Hunger* to the extent that there is only eternal youth, but then, in catastrophic fashion, sudden but equally eternal aging.

Staudenmaier must treat the whole body and not just the cortex if he is to keep his developing hallucinatory-projection skills under direct conscious surveillance (143). At the same time he must, since he's on his own, embody the discoveries of his research. The credits of this unacknowledged projection of his body announce mother, with whom he still lives. It turns out that mother had, right from the start, been the witness and operator inside the projection booth of her son's science. Staudenmaier's mother, who was there, alone bears witness to his successful thought transferences, both the telepathic communication between them (184) and the apples he was able to knock down from a tree via remote control (233).

His ultimate achievement—just ask his mother—was his hitherto unheard of ability to sing with total precision (97). The apples Staudenmaier knocked down he sought to preserve for several weeks on the outside but then ate them instead. Another inward turn was taken by the rubber ball which had first come into his mother's possession. This hand-held caricature of an adolescent prankster's head, which, once squeezed, stuck out its tongue, became, after Staudenmaier had completely forgotten the game his mother had given and played with him, the life-size personification "Round Head." The personification that thus bounces back from the mother's ball alone succeeds in taking control of Staudenmaier's body. But "Round Head"'s sadistic humor dares Staudenmaier and even the other personifications to crush his ball.

Staudenmaier introduces "Round Head" as another example of personification immediately following the description of "Child," the personification that causes him to hallucinate dolls and visit toy stores. In the toy department of one large store the little inner voice cried out: "How wonderful! This is heaven!" (35). But "Child" springs from "children centers" located inside anyone who likes little ones; these child-care centers are the basis even of a parent's pleasure in offspring (164). Staudenmaier's "Round Head" follows his introduction or invention of "Child" as the adolescent and cartoon reanimation of a childhood, which remains missing. Thus "Child" represents a perfect—and posthumously born—childhood which the death-cult accoutrements for sale in toy stores commemorate. In place of ego ideal and childhood, Staudenmaier must follow the bouncing ball of mass-friendship or suicide: "ghosts . . . are our neighbors in our own brain" (94).

As soon as Staudenmaier senses his tongue twisting and his expression grimacing under the personification's direction, he dismisses "Round Head." But although he destroys the ball, the delusional backfire of the science of magic has already transformed the researcher's whole body into an elastic, plastic instrument of manic gymnastics and music (138). Like Schreber, Staudenmaier secures group membership as the exquisite unmourned corpse that comes—Michael Jackson style—in the one size (nation, god, race, and gender) that fits all.

At this end the primal antibody has already been rejected. Thus Staudenmaier can argue—and thus admit the point of breakdown which organizes his science—that the ghosts of dead fathers indeed believe they are telling the truth when they proclaim their visitation rights (127). Subconscious personifications do not lie to the conscious ego when they announce their ghost appearance: they don't know any better. Personifications, like the hypnotized, tend to believe that they are in truth what they, as hallucinations, only seem to be: it is their "completely characteristic and general defect" (33).

Staudenmaier busts the exteriority of the returning dead only by connecting up every medium, whether media-technological, psychic, or occult, via projection—which he however leaves outside his disciple-less (and father-less) science, or, in other words, in maternal control. Staudenmaier's body building, like his media-technologization, turns on melancholic identification, which is always a maternal legacy.

The Disappearance of Childhood Is a Rerun

The technological cabling systems of psychotic delusion are not only effects of viewer participation in mass media society. They are also the exteriorization of a technologization of body and psyche that goes down in the work of identification or mourning (during a station break, in other words, that announces the coming event of psychosis or group membership). This inward turn or origin of the technological has been brought to us, moreover, by the historicization of the era of media technology's (and childhood's and psychoanalysis's) invention.

The first society-wide effect of a technical medium—the literacy requirements which the printing press introduced—installed between infancy and adulthood holding patterns of initiation or instruction. The new being created to inhabit this liminal state was the pupil or child. But if at our end childhood can only be found missing among the perpetually childish consumers of the culture industry, this today show is but the rerun of the first appearance of childhood—always and already in the wake of the child's disappearance.

According to Philippe Ariès, in the eighteenth century the new focus in the work of representation in mourning covered not some image of the living person but the moment or monument of his individual death. "Children were the first beneficiaries of this new desire for preservation."[1] But Ariès miscalculates when he argues that the eventual decrease in infant and child mortality rates contributed to this representability of children.[2] A decrease did go into effect, but only a century later. The child thus attained ontological status too soon, only in time to deliver a massive occasion for and challenge to mourning.

In 1912 *Totem and Taboo* announced the interchangeable carriers of melancholia, haunting, or gadget love: children, so-called savages, and the unconscious. How could we have overlooked it! The unmourned dead put through the connections which media technology proffers. Hence adolescence, the next invention, impulse, and problem of the growing culture of education or *Bildung,* comes complete with its own technologization and phantomization. Ariès nominates Wagner's Siegfried as model of teen self-esteem. Through body *Bildung,* friendship, and group membership the adolescent redistributes and socializes the personalizable effects of loss and hauntedness. A crowd of losers identifies with Siegfried's teen appeal. Hanging out at his favorite haunt, Staudenmaier, the perpetual teenager, works (out) to survive the suicidal impulse, which remains coextensive with his coconstituted immortality. That the eternal is thus the internal follows from a fact of life: the other is always the first to go. In California there's only perpetual adolescence and then, suddenly and forever, limitless aging.

On the outside the Round Head or Happy Face; on the inside suicide. In terms of primal scheduling, the first unknown ancestor to become self-aware or adolescent (whom myth casts as eater of fruit from the tree of knowledge, and the culture industry as fast-food consumer) was the first to contemplate suicide.[3] Adolescence thus busies the circuits of the suicide hotline (which was the first support group—of friends):[4]

> In order to determine how frequently a teenager might be the recipient of a suicidal message, the author surveyed 120 high school students asking them whom they would tell if they should ever consider suicide. . . . "Friend" was selected as first choice in 91 percent of the responses.[5]

Best Friend or Worst Enemy: the constituency of the adolescent suicide pack corresponds, as though via teletype, with Staudenmaier's personifications or ghosts.

In *Totem and Taboo* Freud presented and refereed the close encounter between projection of ghosts and media-technological projections which Staudenmaier's eternally teen magic embodied. Phantom remote control, which the teenage suicide pact (like Staudenmaier's body-building contest) observes, was, in theory, busted. Haunting henceforth belonged in the movies: ghostly visitations present the projective recycling of death wishes which the survivors of the dearly departed cannot acknowledge up close but only in long shot as the vengeful impulses harbored by the dead loved ones who, thus reanimated, must follow out the projective beam of otherwise inadmissible hostility.

The death wish is the premier application of "omnipotence of thoughts"; according to Freud this omnipotence underlies every detour taken by narcissism via yet another extension of the senses, ranging from belief in magic to media technology (*SE* 23:113). Because omnipotence of thoughts first comes into focus as death wish, even the first occasion for exercising this omnipotence must be shared with a dead person—a "vampire" who, via projection, haunts the one relieved in exchange of any responsibility for his death wishes.

The cinematic device or incursion first associated with the 1974 movie *Earthquake* lends its tremors to what can henceforth be referred to as endopsychic (or projective) "sensurround," which achieved its fullest projection with the 1912 advent of the Melanesian Cargo Cult.

Once you have the mourned dead where you want them, leave them there. In Cargo Cult they are in Australia, building the techno-devices which the white man, the unmourned phantom, keeps to himself, just as he thus intercepts the messages from the ancestors which the telecommunications devices were designed in the first place to forward. The disruption of the work of mourning is always the origin and onset of technologization. Thus in Melanesian legend the white man's interference flows from the quake and surf of a child's unmournable loss:

> In the northern region of New Guinea, among the Tangu people, there lived a woman who had to make do without a husband's protection. One day her child remained alone at home. A stranger came, killed the girl and buried the corpse. But the woman had a dream which showed her the location of the grave. She found the corpse, placed it in her bag, and wandered from village to village until she found a suitable site for its proper burial and, at the same time, a man, the younger of two brothers, who married her. By her new husband she had two sons. Occasionally she visited the grave of her daughter. Once as she was separating a few coconut fronds she saw flow out of the grave salt water in which fish were swimming. The woman took some water and a small fish as nourishment for her family. The results were stunning. Over night her son grew into manhood. The older brother of her husband gazed with envy upon this son. So the woman directed him to the grave in order that his son too could be miraculously metamorphosed. But instead of taking a small fish the fool seized a large one which was as long as an eel. Whereupon the earth shook, water gushed forth and the ocean came into existence and divided the brothers. After a while they

could once again communicate with each other. They let leaves drift across the sea conveying the messages they had written upon them. In the course of this exchange it soon became clear that the younger brother was able to invent and manufacture marvelous things, steam-powered ships, for example, umbrellas, guns, and canned goods, while the older brother could only imitate these products. That is why there are peoples which have black skin and eat yam roots.[6]

Before the emergence of Cargo Cult, the Melanesians had centered their ancestor worship on legends of voyage and homecoming. The first Cargo monuments erected in place of these ancestral trips were flagpoles and telegraph poles, in each case analogues or citational props of the media-technological range of the white man's sensorium. In his retechnologization of Stoker's *Dracula*, Friedrich Kittler has analyzed the phantomizing shift that the telegraph introduces into every reception of the new media.[7] First the occult, hysterical, and, indeed, technical medium that Mina Harker becomes or functions as once Dracula has breastfed her and then, finally, the actual network of telegraph stations that confirms which harbor has received the "terrible cargo" keep the fleeing count in the range of his hunters. Confined to his "earthly envelope" on the return trip to Transylvania, the vampire cannot, during daytime programming, outdistance in movement or communication the transportation medium that holds him. Thus Dracula remains bound to the age-old images of Death that convey him along a trail of mortality occupied both by the voyage and the postal circuit.

Upon impact with the new media, the modern aborigines (Stoker's citizens or the Melanesians) turn around to face an attack by vampiric ghosts. To bust these ghosts, they must plug into their own technologization—a desperate act of identification that is always the only alternative to licking them. Once the telegraph introduces the "live" broadcast, the aborigines of technologization drop the ancient mediations and place direct calls to the dead. They trash the ancient religious beliefs and death cults featuring, on the inside, round trips of self-searching and initiation into Death and, on the outside, hierarchical distinctions segregating men from women and children. Under the direction (or on the wavelength) of Mina, the so-called new woman, the vampire hunters record their own thoughts, opinions, and sentiments at the same time as they include every relevant newspaper clipping or train schedule. The result: an archive that, via a series of inner/outer coextensivities, leaves no gap through which the vampire king could escape. But this openness that flushes out Dracula also hides the new improved vampirism which the mass-media archive of thought control contains.

The feedback of his thought control gags Staudenmaier with a tune. The phantom Muzak jams the superegoical playback. The heard or herd instinct of Cargo Cultists will not admit the return of the mournable dad. "Virtually without any contribution on my part, my chest *[Brust]* began to expand and I started to sing with a voice that was fundamentally more beautiful, more voluminous, and stronger, and in a way that had never before been in my control, so that it instantly struck my mother. My aim and range increased at the same time by imperceptible degrees. Moreover I occasionally heard distant magical singing. I only had to listen and push back all disturbing thoughts" (97).

Kalifornien

Kafka was the survivor of a regime of abuse which claimed two brothers who would henceforth be missing. He was a perpetual child destined at the end to skip a beat and slide directly into a grandparent's place (see the conversations with Janouch). But Kafka reserved the group grope bond of adolescence, which he had never undergone, as the model of his late desire to affirm life. Wanting to feel good about himself, Kafka placed his writing second to his belief in "nature cures," which included vegetarianism, nudism, gardening, and chewing some forty times before swallowing. Kafka charged modern medicine with the negligence or abuse that killed off his brothers. Thus he swore that if his belief in nature cures could be proven wrong then he would have been "wrong about everything else." Kafka's nature-cure bond with his dead brothers promoted a pattern of relations that every biographer would judge sadomasochistic. But through the commitment to writing which guaranteed that only the phantom would get off at the prospect of Kafka blowing each date and engagement, Kafka attempted entry into that adolescent circle of friendship and group membership which he had decided to call Life.

Kafka, the total Californian, wanted only teen self-esteem. Thus he joined Max Brod in a teen writing team that competed, went on field trips, and kept diaries. Kafka began his diary late in life: usually the side effect of adolescence and group membership, Kafka's journal writing was a triumph of deliberation or affirmation. The diary was finally closed off by the ghostly hands that always dialed only the father's collect call (on lines that had in fact been deregularized by melancholia and which originally put through the "song" of phantom siblings).

Kafka not only invented Amerika—in the original place of one declared missing *(Der Verschollene)*—but, moving Westward within Amerika, he also projected California, the goal of his futuristic but unfulfillable vegetarian desire. At *The Castle*, which doubles and projects the Westward move (for example already in the Count's name, West-West), Kafka hears at his end of the line both the songlike white noise or roaring of a sibling connection and, once taken off hold, the paternal blast from the past. Together with sex and philosophy, music belonged to the target area of Kafka's desperate, doomed affirmations. He gagged on something which (like diaries) has nothing to do with culture, but which, like California, is the surplus of everything.

The hits of popular music supply the inspirational and habit-forming source which twentieth-century literature or transference downs in order to come up with its success stories.[1] Listening to the radio beat teaches one to write. But those catchy tunes and phrases keep on tuning in on automatic in a manner Frances Hannett, for example, would consider as "haunting."[2] Hannett, who specializes in straightening out homosexuals by constructing a mother transference out of snatches of song haunting her patients, is able to locate, case by case, the primal source of these popular tunes:

> The foregoing examples support the thesis that the haunting lyric is a "voice of the preconscious" and must be understood in the same way as a dream fragment, a fantasy, or a repetitive act. Such lyric fragments have both manifest and latent meaning. The manifest meaning restates the defensive surface position. The latent meaning, referring to the impulses and wishes and their genetic origin, is revealed only by analysis of the lyric as if it were a dream. The first case cited provided the opportunity to discover this. The persistent analysis of his song lyrics as a form of resistance made it possible to follow through, in this patient, the evolution and eventual resolution of the mother transference. (237)

But if this channel of identification is at once maternal and American, Hannett argues, then a certain perpetually adolescent shortness of attention span and lack of patience (though not of patients) has also been turned on.

> It has been inferred that this culturally enforced position of American mothers has resulted in the infantilization of their children, especially the sons. From this, the central conclusion is that songs preferred by the children of these mothers express that unresolved anaclitic relationship in its many ramifications. (267)

But the American mother is listening too—not to the refrain of incestuous or homosexual relations but to the unacknowledgment of another child's loss which the sibling's "haunting lyrics" also secretly record. In Gilbert Rose's case study of music appreciation, the grieving mother seeks shelter in the dislocations and "slow time" of modern music. (The surviving child who grows up in such a shelter or crypt becomes the haunted transmitter of the dead sibling mother could not mourn or let go.)

I wondered if she might be turning every moment into a kind of shock and surprise, ripping each moment out of its context in the flow of time, and in this way perhaps continuously repeating, actively, the traumatic moment when she was informed of Nancy's death. . . . We might speculate that it was a way of dislocating time—in order to correct and master it—of saying, "If only it had been an hour earlier, or later, Nancy would be alive now."[3]

When it is enjoyed, music releases one, according to Heinz Kohut and Siegmund Levarie,[4] from "the original fear evoked by sound" (70). But soon silence as the threat of aloneness or death leads one to "whistle in the dark" and create "the illusion of a supporting group" (71). The pleasure taken in music is thus the measure of one's ability to withstand sound under the group protection of, for example, Walt Disney's *Fantasia*:

> Other listeners were pleased with the aid given by the simultaneous visual "commentary" which the film provided and which made them tolerate complex musical stimulation that could otherwise not have been mastered by them and would perhaps have created an unpleasant tension. (74)

Group-supported pleasure comes with repetition—with recognition of the tune the second time around (80). The repeated act of identifying a tune represents a form of mastery interchangeable with that attained through drug use (76). Thus music must be taken repeatedly to preserve, as always with drugs, the direct hit—the direct connection with the body:

> In identification with the music, the listener has reached the final mastery of an external task. He has reached it by regression to a primitive ego state which permits the ecstatic enjoyment of music. To this ego state belongs the most primitive form of mastery by incorporation and identification. At this moment the

ecstatic listener does not clearly differentiate between himself and the outside world; he experiences the sounds as being produced by himself, or even as being himself, because emotionally they are what he feels. (84)

Pact Rats

When part one of Maus *. . . hits America's shopping malls this month, folks are going to wonder what to make of a comic book from a major publisher whose subject matter is the Holocaust and which portrays the Nazis as cats and Jews as mice. . . . Maus's cats and mice are not without precedents. Orwell used a talking-animal story to anatomize totalitarianism, and the "mouse-folk" in Kafka's "Josephine the Singer" have much in common with the Jews. Equally to the point is the wartime animated cartoon "Der Führer's Face," in which Donald Duck gives Hitler the rasp-berry.*
—*Newsweek*, September 22, 1986

In the winter of 1917 Kafka faced the music: the tuberculous deterioration, which his physician's diagnosis had given in long-range forecast, previewed at close range.[1] Field mice invaded the Bohemian farmhouse in which he had taken ambivalent refuge from the diagnosis (which he ignored by choosing as a kind of last resort such an unhealthy vacation spot). The suicide trip comes complete with earphones: the noise of the invisible, secretive mice—as they "undermined a hundredfold all the walls"[2]—turned up the volume on Kafka's lifelong hypersensitivity to sound.

Although it was his own opinion, Kafka saw it first in Jan Cerny's notion that sound waves inaudible to the human ear crowd around our range of hearing; they comprise the hidden "sounds of silence" which music recovers within an ever-expanding sensorium. Kafka read up on the research, which already demonstrated "that insects communicate with each other by sound waves inaudible to the human ear."[3]

But listening in on these bugged wavelengths, Freud made out the model and constitutive possibility of telepathy's broadcasts; thought gets automatically transferred within groups along the same telepathic channels of communication that keep bees in touch (*SE* 22:55–56). But the group recycles only certain relations to loss: insects represent (in or as the shadow of a dreamer's death wishes) small children, in other words, younger siblings (*SE* 5:357).

Because the herd was thus bugged, it was up to the remote-controlling double, or, as Kafka put it (through), the "artefact" or "daemon," to transgress and expand the "established frontiers" of mankind's standard reception. Cerny picked up the airwaves of this internal (eternal) expansionism, phantomization, and autotechnologization:

> Everything that lives reverberates. Everything that lives emits sound. We only hear part of it. We do not hear our circulation, the dying and growing of bodily tissue, the sounds of the chemical processes. Nevertheless, the cells of our organism, our brain, nerve and muscle fibers are inundated by these inaudible sounds. They resonate with our environment. The power of music results from this.[4]

According to Kafka's voice-over, music, since it thus "animates silence," cops only "dangerous pleasures": "Music is the multiplication of sensuous life."[5] This multiplication of the senses falls back upon and withdraws within music's primal or techno background—the noise or white noise that grows and goes down on automatic: "every noise once overcome is followed by a new one still to be overcome and thus on and on in an infinite series."[6]

In a letter to Milena, Kafka describes from the losing side of the finish line the race or contest that noise fuels: on the fast lane, transportation media, and, on the invisible, invincible track, media technologies.

> Mankind has invented the train, the car, the airplane in order to exclude to the extent possible that which is phantom-like between people, . . . but it will not help anymore, . . . the opposing side is so much calmer and stronger; after the postal service it invented the telegraph, the telephone, the radio-telegraph.

Following the headstarts transportation takes, each advance in telecommunications encircles with a "phantom hand" every new takeoff. As Kafka concludes: "The phantoms will not starve, but we will be destroyed."[7]

Kafka addressed these phantoms at the end of his own contest, which he was losing, the terms of which belonged to the pact he had sealed under his mother's superintendence, which had come due. Kafka referred to this pact with ghosts as a game—of attending his own funeral. He always tried to get in a game when he was doing fiction. But in the first place he did a round with his mother.[8] One attends one's own funeral only as an other; one must, in short, have already identified with, and thus reanimated, the corpse. Those attending, with Kafka, Kafka's own funeral are his unmournable dead—his ghosts—who must mourn in Kafka's place in advance of his passing.[9] Once the tuberculosis diagnosis got out, Kafka recognized what he had tried to write *down:* the aborted outcome of his "childish-disgusting but successful game."[10]

The game seemed over in 1924 when Kafka retreated from his failed "Russian mission" to his father's house.[11]

The first time he let go and shared the fantasy of "The Judgment" (he referred to the story as excremental birth and as the ghost of a single night),[12] it was a Russian friend who doubled as phantom address and embodiment of Georg's writing. Georg, the name Kafka assigned to his writing pact with a phantom, belonged to one of his two younger brothers, both casualties in infancy, according to Kafka's charge, of abuse or neglect. The game of mourning he played with his mother, the game that helped preserve and conceal the missingness of the brothers within a writing pact with their ghosts, replaced the work of mourning mother could not undertake. But in "The Judgment" Kafka read loud and clear that a father's authority can tap into and usurp a son's rapport with phantoms: according to father, the phantom friend in Russia both does not exist and writes only and ultimately to the father. What remains is the superegoical command from which the son cannot swerve since he carries inside illegitimate Cargo, which the superego, as Freud makes clear in *The Ego and the Id*, is programmed to abort.[13] Thus the condition of the pact or game with the encrypted brothers—that both parties either stay or go—is transformed into terms of a suicide pact: the melancholic son, at the close of "The Judgment," fulfills the terms of the contract (which, according to the father, he put out on himself).

In his diary entry of September 25, 1917, Kafka wrote: "I could thus entrust myself to death. Vestige of a belief. Return to father. Great day of reconciliation." By its transformation into return to father, the Russian mission opened onto the suicide mission it had contained. At the end of the double mission which "The Judgment" first projected outward and which the mice in 1917 zoomed into close-up, Kafka conceived inside his father's house the testament of two stories. "The Burrow" plays back full blast the noise of mice devouring from within the walls around and in Kafka. In "Josephine the Singer or the Mousefolk," the rodent's solo panic achieves popular appeal within a culture industry that places a phantom at the center of group identifications advertising the father.

Josephine's song is part children's piping, part silence; her spectacular disappearance—which was already always in place—doubles the absence of childhood in a culture where everyone at the same time remains childish. The babbling child to whom the "paternal group" turns a "deaf ear" is missing—neither living nor dead—while, in her missingness, Josephine continues to represent a primal object of mass identification.

According to the Hamelin legend of piped music, rodents and children occupy interchangeable places on the road to their disappearance. In his case study of Ratman, Freud admits that rodents are chthonic creatures conveying the souls of the dead and, indeed, often those of missing children. But the rat economy or conveyer belt still features as star and model the dead father (for whom rats are totemic stand-ins). But the rats scurrying from the original record of the case through the published study's footnote underworld convey the death of Ratman's sister, which the father's death cannot replace or cover over. The condition of the sibling pact? "If you die," Ratman's sister pledges to him before taking her departure, "I'll kill myself" (*SE* 10:264).

In 1917 Kafka retreats from the mice into his sister's room, where they soon reemerge. He compares mice to cannibals but brings their smallness into focus as the focus of their dread effect upon him: "the thought, for example, that there could be an animal that would look exactly like a pig, in other words, as such amusing, but would be as small as a rat and would emerge noisily from a hole in the floorboard—that is an unbearable thought." The "terrible mute loud" sound of these miniaturized—mediated—animals refines and tunes in Kafka's aural sense, which soon broadcasts only scratching, piping mice. Thus putting on his ears, Kafka, panic-struck by a sensurround of mouse noise, invites radical intervention: on the one hand he calls the exterminators, on the other he calls in, as he did when conceiving "The Judgment," Freud. "Discovery of where the fear comes from is the business of psychoanalysts," Kafka allows; but he closes this sentence with the spectacularly unfitting appendage: "I am not it" *(ich bin es nicht)*.[14] At the tail end of mouse and noise control, we find denial—not by Kafka but by his doubly slipping ventriloquist.

According to psychoanalysts all music is background music on station identification. As a hebephrenic schizophrenic described this encroaching background to Géza Róheim, music approximates the sound in the back of one's head as one eats and chews. What rebounds as Muzak is the death-wish noise in the background of identification or of, as the schizophrenic called it, "eating the wrong way." The wrong turn leads down to the anal underworld where a missing sister has been conserved. When little sister died of stomach cancer she entered the schizophrenic's belly which, via her pushbutton control, filled up with "hot air." At the internal end of this ventriloquized relationship, the sister assumed the undercover role of "bug" or "teethy": on the outside her schizo brother was "hungry, but hungry inside."[15] Ghosts—or, in Freud's transposition, recycled death wishes—can be channelled as "haunting melodies," fragments of song that Theodor Reik discovered tuning in independently of any matching context in the auditor who cannot help but hum along.[16] Stuck on the scratch of a death wish, the personal record becomes part of the group activity which music has forever been. Thus with so-called haunting melodies one has shifted in fact from wish to drive, from the first to the second system. The dimensionality of this shift opens up a background that music and sociality have come to cohabit. As Freud puts it, the death drive, because it joins in "silently" (*SE* 21:119), backgroundizes the "melody of the drives" (*SE* 14:62)—and with it, or within it, all music. But like everying else Freud valiantly faced in his second system, music did not in fact spook him; rather its unanalyzability (which music shares with TV) set an uncanny limit (that of nontransference) to Freud's therapeutic interventions.

While his "thoughts were occupied with questions of priority" (*SE* 6:107), Freud, stumbling over a lapsus, admitted myth or music into his system. The haunted melody's Westward migration skips between a German beachtown and a Classical scene of exhibitionism of mythic proportions. Read Freud's slips:

> I was sitting in a café, turning over the pages of a copy of the *Leipziger Illustrierte* [an illustrated weekly] (which I was holding up at an angle), when I read the following legend under a picture that stretched across the page: "A Wedding Celebration in the *Odyssee* [Odyssey]." It caught my attention; in surprise I took hold of the paper in the proper way and then corrected my error: "A Wedding Celebration on the *Ostsee* [Baltic]." How did I come to make this absurd mistake in reading? My thoughts at once turned to a book by Ruths (1898), *Experimental Investigations of Music Phantoms*, . . . which had occupied me a good deal recently since it trenches on the psychological problems that I have been concerned with. . . . In Ruths' work on music phantoms I found at the beginning of the list of contents an announcement of a detailed inductive proof that the ancient Greek myths and legends have their main source of origin in phantoms of sleep and music, in the phenomena of dreams and also in deliria. Thereupon I plunged into the text to find out whether he also realized that the scene in which Odysseus appears before Nausicaa was derived from the common dream of being naked. . . . I found nothing on the subject in Ruths' book. (*SE* 6:106–7)

What *can* be found is a technologization and phantomization of music's reception which admits the unconscious but leaves out repression, and releases projection while at the same time unacknowledging identification. Ruths' reliance on analogies with the photochemical process to explain the one-sided (or one-way) projection of music phantoms is a trademark of background music: "Muzak," which was at first invented to play on the phone while the caller was on hold, was modeled after "Kodak." Originally "printed" through "progressive substitution" of stronger for weaker images, music phantoms are subliminally or telepathically beamed from composer, conductor, or some ancient past to the listening observer. In the place of projection, mental images and associations recompose themselves into alien bodies by reversing light and dark, front and back. The result: background music. "To our observers," Ruths writes, "music often appears only as an accompaniment to their phantoms."[17]

Grin and Bury It

Following a performance of *Hänsel and Gretel*, "especially sharply developed" phantoms of children mobbed one of Ruths' observers. Suddenly the face of the deceased Mr. G. pops up on one of the tiny ghosts. This collision of *revenants* in the place of mixed reception strikes the observer as disturbing, even uncanny. Mr. G.'s phantasmic return is the rerun of his live performance as moving target on the range of the observer's ambivalence.[1]

Ruths leaves this turn in his theory of phantoms on the sidelines of the argument proper; and yet it is the line along which every music phantom can be folded back onto the unconscious. In the place of the unconscious, Ruths advances a theoretical conjunction of the hypnotic reach of music and the cartoon caricatures with which it populates its projective trajectory. Thus in one example doubly registered in what Ruths calls the unconscious, an "unconscious" musical accompaniment switches, according to a progressive comparison also lodged in the "unconscious," the recollection of a dentist's office to the more intensely received precincts of Dr. B. Another switch turns recollection into phantom: the bandaged state of his waiting patients has been transferred to Dr. B.'s person. The listening observer's thought upon recognizing the phantom: "Oh poor Dr. B." (125, 221–22).

Giving more personal space to the other side of the convergence marked by loony tunes, Ernst Kris rides out a psychoanalytic theory of caricature which presupposes the interchangeability of comic and manic effects. Down in the footnote to this conjunction we find, following it into the underworld, a reference to the popularity of Mickey Mouse. Since what "was feared yesterday is fated to appear funny when seen today," comic phenomena, which on occasion even cause displeasure or pain, cover a zone between pleasure and the warding off of fear.[2]

What Ruths develops into music phantoms, Kris advances in terms of the grimace, the autoplastic ancestor of cartoon caricature. On the satisfied infant's face the smile represents the first mental contact between one human being and another (227). But at the disturbed end of face value, the grimace pops up when a repressed tendency interferes with the sequence of an intended expression—as when a smile disturbs an expression of condolence, only to be distorted in turn. As false smile and harbinger of death wishes, the grimace is received as a break in the "pathognomic melody": Kris can bring this break into focus only as the difference between photography, where the false smile remains hidden, and film, which lets roll the grimacing lack of pathognomic melody (236). The grimacing withdrawal of the smile marks the breakdown of a melody the infant's smile originally struck up.

Smile and grimace suspend lines of defense which push back the convulsions of laughter. To keep from laughing, either the laugh impulse must be muted into a smile or the complete range of bodily and physiognomic expression must be shut down. In this case (it's a different way) the grimace places itself (cryonically) in charge of the imitation of a corpse. Group laughter, says Kris, is a tame descendant of the primal orgy (226) which always combined pain and pleasure, mourning and mania in—on—the face of human sacrifice and its musical accompaniment.

The break in pathognomic melody gives rise to grimaces and, as in Ruths' reception, to ghosts: those animating caricature and those (the same ones) haunting an eighteenth-century psychotic sculptor named, as always to the point, Messerschmidt. At the mass-cultural end the caricaturist and his audience cause—in thought and effigy—the model's features to become twisted in grimace; but this pleasurable liberation of aggression also results from the underlying comparison, the likeness in deformity, for which the resemblance between humans and animals has been a model. Doubled over with laughter, the caricaturist's audience takes a turn in becoming animal: by rendering the whole body an "apparatus for expression," laughter approximates the animal's sole means, in the absence of any index finger, of pointing something out (224).

In fun—in making fun—one looks aggressively and libidinously for a companion (211). But the laughter of the group discards the butt of the joke; the laughter itself becomes the sole content or, in Kris's words, the sealing of the pact (221). On the psychotic's scanner: the contract of group laughter covers a pact sealed with phantoms. The psychotic identifies with the butts of mass fun by turning into a grimacing caricature; at the same time, however, he has turned the other way—toward the phantoms—to resist their penetration into his opened mouth under cover of the attack of laughter released by group identification.

On the psychotic, ribbing builds the grimace as the cryonic separation from the body that would otherwise be convulsed with laughter. The psychotic sculptor studied by Kris touches his rib while carving grimaces to prove, in the context of castration anxiety, that the rib—from which God created woman—is still there. Kris quotes Nicolai's eyewitness account:

In the exact required relationship to the pinching of his flesh [under the ribs], . . . he . . . made grimaces in front of the mirror, and believed thus to have achieved miraculous control over the demons. While he was working, he looked into the mirror every half minute and made, with the greatest exactitude, precisely that grimace which he just needed. (137)

Hence the grimace, which is always and originally rehearsed over and against one's own mirror image, represents for the psychotic an attempt at self-recovery; he "struggles before the mirror for a genuine facial expression in order to retain the rapidly vanishing contact with the environment" (144). The psychotic saves face by making faces which, like apotropaic masks, also ward off the demons (235).

Follow the Bouncing Ball

T *he delusions of patients appear to me to be the equiv-*
alents of the constructions which we build up in the
course of an analytic treatment.
   —Freud, "Constructions in Analysis" (1937)

The psychotic hauntedness featured in the eighteenth-
century dossier on Messerschmidt returns in 1938 (and too
close for comfort) in the case of a schizophrenic architect
treated by Kris one on one. The case was, right from the
start, not personalizable. He was hospitalized together with
his landlady who claimed with equal conviction that the
architect was chosen for a special mission. Both agreed that
Hitler was his representative on earth (154–56).

   Christians "are praying to a dead body" (157), the body
of Christ lying in the mother's lap; the architect compares
himself, in his own pieta position, to this corpse. But if he
speaks of himself as being dead, it is also because he has one

immediate precursor: his mother who died of poison administered by the secret organization (of Jews and Catholics) which continues to persecute him. Skipping (a) generation, his fiancée Josephine bears in her absence (an absence doubled by the hysterectomy the Cardinal of Vienna forced on her) the maternal bond. Only the reversal of the womb's removal, Josephine's return from Germany, could redeem Austria. In the schizo architect's cartoon drawings, the psychotic redemption of Austria and the reversal of psychoanalysis are guaranteed by the figure of "God mother" or "God containing the mother," which is placed above the figure of "God" (162). The reversal of removal will, through his reunion with Josephine, save marriage (which "has been destroyed by the Old Testament, by the Jews") (161).[1] This newly restored wedding bond, now named "holy wafer," will slip the Oedipal through the edible (the identificatory, nice, or violent).

> Every conception is through the holy ghost. *God sculptured semen and egg and united them.* The male semen enters the woman and pervades the blood. It is the holy wafer. Marriage is the holy wafer permeated with rays or semen. (161)

This mass identification in the place of marriage represents the psychotic solution (which has in 1938 political ingredients) of the couple within the group. The pieta, as group mascot, which replaces a piety originally based (for example, in Vergil's *Aeneid*) on the father function, advertises the body (the maternal body) as the off-limits limit of a pleasure sadomasochistically recircuited through the group, the phantom, the prophecy. From Christian mass to the masses, from the wafer or host to the music ghosts, the psychotic or group member has by 1938 retained from the father function only the signature which, retrograded to its primal status as magic, now gives prophetic power to not only the architect's mythico-musical programs (pogroms).

The architect's incessant production of writing and drawing—Dr. Mabuse style—closes in, in each case, on his signature, which validates pages that have more the status of statements than representations in need of authentication. The content of each drawing is read as prophecy of what will soon happen or as document proving the already directed course of events. Thus on a roll the schizophrenic continues to reduce his representations to hieroglyphs or musical notation: since magical thought requires only the notes to catch the beat, the schizophrenic architect is able to represent each new angel within the progression of his prophecies with yet another outline of the letter "M" (168). A certain magic sword (of "mother God"), like the bouncing ball in musical cartoons, follows the score by settling it; the names of those touched or dubbed must go (158–59). These prophetic scores, which ultimately project Josephine's return, were first—fast—forwarded to Hitler, his double and god. "When Hitler actually invaded Austria, the patient was beside himself with joy. He was seen for the last time on March 13th, two days after the occupation, when he said triumphantly: 'Now it is done; I accomplished it all with my sword'" (157).

Demons persecute Messerschmidt and God is the architect's rival because, in each case, a certain kind of knowledge has slipped magically into mortal possession. Thus: "Interdicts of imagery to protect the divine from magical practice prevail over centuries in many cultures. . . . Painters conclude pacts with the devil in order to compete with God, while builders, heirs to the builder of the tower of Babel, commit suicide" (166). The crime of acquiring secret knowledge is always (as in the Adam and Eve story) one of consumerism. But as Byron put it in *Manfred* before Nietzsche put it to music: "The Tree of Knowledge is not that of Life." Already at this syncopated intersection, one case of encryptment swings open three others: the story of Manfred's dead sister, who alone can put him and herself to rest, loans its props to Schreber's delusional system because of the affinity between Manfred's secret burial plot and the suicide pact of the Schreber brothers, which the Oedipal context only covers over. Freud makes allowance for funereal sibling connections between *Manfred* and Schreber from a perspective which opens onto his own case of haunted rapport with an encrypted brother. But this case is open and shut: Freud returns to the familiar turf of mourning for the dead father just in time to overlook, while pointing out Nietzsche's yearning for his father, the effects of Nietzsche's dead brother Joseph.

The contract or bond of identification comes complete with vigilance, preparedness, and proofing against disarming laughter: the guffawing mouth allows the divine or phantom penetration which the psychotic cannot admit—having desired. Sculptor and architect must protect and project their brand of consumerism, zombieism, or "eating the wrong way" in place of the paternal corpse or primal antibody. To eat his secret and have it too, the psychotic must keep both ends of his internal relations from appearing; entry always represents departure. The basis of caricaturist praxis—resemblance to animals—is equally Ratmanoid in its constitution and calculation: it shares the fantasy of father's penetration or internalization with an encrypted child or sibling. Caricaturist abuse libidinizes the jocular conjunction of human and animal physiognomies. The exaggerating charge *(caricare)* reverses itself: on the other side of caricaturist and totemic ambivalence, we also find animated the anthropomorphized animal or adorable pet. At the caricaturist and cartoon end of totemic standards—in the place of the ego ideal—paternal comeback also turns on a child's return. Since according to classical studies of physiognomy the form of the lips bears association with the heads of animals, Messerschmidt draws the lips of his grimacing busts inward (138). The break in physiognomic melody breaks the pact or track of group laughter which, according to the psychotic, attracts ghosts and gods in search of open but cute orifices.

The psychotic sculptor and architect operate at the extreme end of music phantomization, which otherwise remains within the normal range of the senses. According to Ruths, phantoms regularly emerge as part of any public reception of music. And yet only the listener capable of self-concentration tunes in the projections on the composer's original wave length; the mob, which is ruled by distraction, scatters and blurs a mix of phantasmic impressions. This "psychotic" disposition, which, in its unprotectedness and unsublimatedness, must resist and follow all the phantoms, is "the signature of the group" (341).

The Endopsychic Sensurround

By beginning with phantoms (rather than, say, with ambivalence or identification) Ruths does not so much anticipate as simulate, in the phantom mode, discoveries which Freud would relocate in the convergence of delusional formation, the regular functioning of the psychic apparatus, and the psychoanalytic theory of its breakdown. Media technology, which gives currency to the tubular experiences of the delusional psychotic, supplies analogue connections with the psychic apparatus which it, at the same time, puts through. From *The Psychopathology of Everyday Life* to the Schreber and Ratman case studies, this point of convergence goes by the name "endopsychic perception," which Freud first gave within the context of "psycho-mythology":

> The dim inner perception of one's own psychic apparatus stimulates thought illusions, which of course

are projected onto the outside and, characteristically, into the future and the beyond. Immortality, retribution, the entire beyond are all reflections of our psychic inside.[1]

Around this first sighting of the psychic apparatus, the endopsychic equation or projection swings back, already in *The Psychopathology of Everyday Life*, onto the theoretical frame, which also gets into the picture:

> The obscure recognition (endopsychic perception, as it were) of psychical factors and relations in the unconscious is mirrored . . . in the construction of a *supernatural reality*, which is destined to be changed back once more by science into the *psychology of the unconscious*. (*SE* 6:258–59)

The designated delusion in this "construction" and "seduction of an analogy" (*SE* 23:268) is, as always, paranoia (*SE* 6:259). Paranoia's gadget love of the other's unconscious (which gets fine-tuned) is without access to its own unconscious programs. It shares this disposition or structure with the instant of endopsychic change- or play-back of "supernatural reality" or "psycho-mythology." The unstoppable music playing in the background is in fact the unanalyzable (since nontransferential) center, origin, and screen of endopsychic operations. Thus the replacement of myth with music in the target area of pre-post-Freudian spookulations (from Ruths and Staudenmaier all the way to Adorno and Attali) represents the slide from the myth complexes of the first system into the group identifications of the second system. "California" is the endopsychic reflection of this shift into another theoretical format—that of the group *inside* the death cult which has doubled (on contact with) the surrounding outside which is thus also internally (eternally) groupified.

In the background of an aside, Staudenmaier addressed the "world historical significance of hallucination" (79), which recasts Luther, Saint Teresa, and Goethe as mediums. He finds one contemporary pop-psychological outlet of the genealogy of hallucination (which turned personifications into myths) in the familiar phenomenon of melodies that one cannot get out of one's head (77).

According to Ruths, myth recorded the ancient phantasmic hallucinations which happened only to recur. Although only part of the musical accompaniment, these hallucinatory or haunting impressions were taken for real at the time they were first saved on the myth program. Via the light show of "color phantoms" which musical sound releases, the hallucinated spirits and gods originally shredded wavelengths belonging to specific types of music (which afterwards, once the hallucinations were taken for divinities, could be counted only among the gods' accessories). Thus Apollo was the video portion of the high notes of his lyre (257) and the sirens were set off by the color phantoms which bird song animates (263). Flute music charged the self-flagellations of Marsyas and the teen passion of Adonis (258). In the passion play starring Adonis, the flute music accompanied the final departure of a youth or child (261).

Whether as omen or reanimation, music phantoms are brought to us, ultimately, by the exigencies of corpse disposal. The spirits that carry off youths killed in battle were released by the trumpets of warfare's musical accompaniment (259). But the remainder also lies within the range of phantomization. While listening to a Haydn symphony, one of Ruths' observers witnesses the stately flotation of youthful music phantoms that take Adonis as role model. But these phantoms take off from ancient burial ground. The melancholic feeling which the symphony inspires also always overcomes the observer—at the acme and onset of the military-literary recasting of myths to the beat of their scores—whenever he watches children dancing in the street to march music (87).

In the Schreber case Freud applied to psychotic delusions (and borrowed from their endopsychic makeup) a model of projection without yet formulating its theory, which he announced as forthcoming. In his next major work, *Totem and Taboo*, Freud let roll on the alternating fast tracks of identification and projection an inside-out theory of ghosts which, doubling on contact, was at once Freud's theory of aberrant mourning and, via the series of endo-psychic analogies Freud advanced and followed, also the analysis of the primal contexts of modern technical media. Freud recast telecommunications as communication with ghosts; what the technical media project as haunting is, simply, projection: projection of death wishes which cannot be acknowledged up close but only in long shot and in re-verse as an alien menace coming from without.

In place of this projection of mass media culture onto the secret site of our missing death cult, Freud introduced in *Civilization and its Discontents* a model of sadomasochistic distribution and administration—via group identifica-tion—of what had accordingly accelerated beyond death wishes: the death drive. Between 1930 and 1960 psychoana-lytic busters of mass culture watched the primal scene of consumerism—cannibalistic identification with the dead father—on bicoastal sets toning teen passion and tuning in wavelengths of exile. Thomas Mann's libido rides out this transfer to Venice Beach; the media-blitz of the Nazi rise or high was fast-forwarded, via a kind of repress release, to the Coast; the cultural rereading program loaded in Frankfurt switched to hard drive in Disneyland and Hollywood, the theme parks or death cults of the future. This always local (lo-cal) encounter with total war created a shrink of dis-tance between Germanicity and "California." The war against war (the mass suicide trip) enlists instant analysis, which works out on the Coast, the place of the shrink. In the first analyses styling with "California" Freud's Frankfurt School followers rereleased primal consumerism across the bicoastal divide as a dialectic of sadomasochism which swings out around public opinion and Christian love and back in as suicide.

From Mark Twain and Thomas Mann to Adorno, Hork-heimer, and Lyotard, literature, psychoanalysis, and philosophy have returned to California to address the crises crowding out the future. Californian popular culture has always inspired—almost prophylactically on the part of its witnesses—the reinterpretation of media technology and its cult contexts (Hollywood burial rites, racism, and body building) which Adorno and Horkheimer undertook in Santa Monica. On this first time they went all the way to the sadomasochistic ends of the pursuit of happiness.

It was on the Coast of the Freudian system that Benjamin and Adorno agreed to disagree about the meaning of Mickey Mouse. Benjamin linked and separated Freud's projection and sadomasochism models via both laugh tracks of this cartoon figure's appeal. In notes scattered around his Karl Kraus essay, Benjamin attributed a new "kind of experience" called "incorporation" or, interchangeably, "cannibalism" to the satiric rapport with the other shared by Kraus and Mickey Mouse. The new cannibal replaces the old creature concept—according to which man's relation to his fellow man was purified concurrently with the satisfaction of the sex drive—with a new creature concept which permits purification of the relation to one's fellow man at the same time as primal hunger is satisfied. For Benjamin it follows that the cannibalism of Mickey Mouse or Kraus covers a new relation to technology, which sides this time around with nature's destructive aspect. What is thus "materialistically" overcome is "mythic man"—Faust, for example—who erected (in place of new technologies to which he couldn't relate) the fetish of creative labor. Mickey Mouse is the anti-hero or hacker of user friendliness. His single slogan or caption: Only destructive labor is worthy of man.[2]

Benjamin was thus already cheerleading Mickey Mouse across the connecting drift between the satiric ego and group psychology. In the first version of "The Work of Art in the Age of its Technical Reproducibility" Benjamin brought the sadism already attending satiric cannibalism to the forefront of mass cultural tensions, where it is put on fast forward. According to Benjamin, the interchange between projection and introjection has accelerated, in the contest of doubling between the technical media and the psychic apparatus, to the point of inducing or reproducing mass psychosis. Films featuring "figures of the collective dream such as Mickey Mouse orbiting the globe" inject balance into this doubly internal/external trajectory by detonating therapeutic "explosions" of group laughter:

> If one takes into account the dangerous tensions which technical mediatization and its consequences have engendered in the vast masses—tensions which, at the critical stage, take on a psychotic character— then one cannot but recognize that this same technical mediatization has created as protection against mass psychoses psychic inoculations via those films in which a forced development of sadistic fantasies or masochistic delusions can prevent their natural and dangerous ripening in the masses. . . . The monstrous mass of grotesque events which is now being consumed in film is a drastic indication of the dangers threatening mankind from the repressions which civilization brings with it. American grotesque films and Disney films effect a therapeutic detonation of the unconscious.[3]

It was at this point of injection that Benjamin and Adorno developed different reactions. Adorno pursued, against Benjamin's active affirmation of Disney hygiene, a funereal reading of Mickey Mouse culture and its sadomasochistic phantasms. At the tail end of Mickey Mouse's orbit around the globe, Adorno concluded that both fascism and the culture industry were "psychoanalysis in reverse." Adorno and Benjamin thus give the bad and the good news surrounding a united front of psychoanalytic criticism which turns both with and against institutions of thought control.

The "Uncanned"

Your dig at Werfel gave me great pleasure. But if you take Mickey Mouse instead, things are far more complicated, and the serious question arises as to whether the reproduction of every person really constitutes that a priori *of the film which you claim it to be, or whether instead this reproduction belongs precisely to that "naive realism" whose bourgeois nature we so thoroughly agreed upon in Paris. After all, it is hardly an accident if that modern art which you counterpose to technical art as aural, is of such inherently dubious quality as Vlaminck and Rilke. The lower sphere, to be sure, can score an easy victory over this sort of art; but if instead there were the names of, let us say, Kafka and Schönberg, the problem would be posed very differently.*

—Adorno to Benjamin, March 18, 1936

The projective circuitry Freud developed in the Schreber case and in *Totem and Taboo* went around as haunting and telecommunications and came around, via telephathy's transference-compatible hookup with hypnosis, as group formation. Tuning in the hypnotic channels of group formation—even one-on-one hypnosis embraces in the single medium a group of one—Freud pushes aside any direct "influence" claimed for music in bringing about suggestion. In the background, music in fact channels the subject's concentration, as though on the phone, to the hypnotist at the other end of the line. At this end, says Freud, the hypnotist or "leader of the group is still the dreaded primal father" (*SE* 18:127ff). But in hypnotic relations, this primal father serves the actively engaged medium only as a prop onto which the psychic performance carried out inside the medium can be outwardly projected. The hypnotist or leader of the group is thus—in Fritz Wittels's words—"employed by the medium as a phantom."[1] According to treatises on haunting, from Burton's *Anatomy of Melancholy* to Freud's *Totem and Taboo*, the unmourned dead have always been destined, in theory, to return as ghosts. Thus from the cult of Isis to psychoanalysis, the mournable death of the father has been injected or introjected into the grieving body to abort the unmournable deaths of mother, child, and sibling. But from cartoon caricatures and music phantoms to the leader of the group or hypnotist, we find in the place of projection—interchangeable and yet radically non-superimposable—both the mournable death of the father and the unmournable death of the child.

The cult of Isis was shot up into primal Egyptian genealogy on the occasion of the first death, which was a murder. Before the death of Osiris, perpetual teens lived forever. The only prior rupture had been the curse one teen bride laid on another from the next generation: she could not conceive any month (that is, once a month) in the year.

Osiris was murdered: in the aftershocks forms of preparedness were introduced. Horus, who was originally one of Osiris's siblings, was reconceived as the son. Osiris was remade as father through a ritual reconstitution that left out the penis so that nothing can come between us (father and son). The murder (or the surgical reconstitution) becomes the requirement of mourning. Osiris was the first stiff to be stuffed into a mummy: the work of mourning maternalizes the dead and makes dad good to eat. Isis fashions a symbolic substitute or phallus through which, in the wake of the unmournable death of child or teen, father and son transmissions and insurance policies can be introduced. The child is "father of the man:" the unmournably dead is called dad and, hence, always already (mournably) dead or dad on arrival. But the group bond that had shared its omnipotence with this primal requirement of double occupancy for the dead (every dead person becomes Osiris) now shares, via the identifications that go down in a Christian mass, its fantasy of purely peer relations (with the dead).

Freud wrote the manual on identification overload which he appended within *Group Psychology and the Analysis of the Ego*. In military organizations, which reflect the most ancient form of group psychology, the members of the group identify with one another while setting up their commander as ego ideal; but they never, except to the point of becoming geeks, nerds, dorks, identify with the leader. The Christian church introduces modern group psychology by doubling group identity back onto its identifications. The church not only brings about group identification among the faithful and establishes Christ as ego ideal but also enforces identification with Christ: every Christian must love the other Christians just as Christ loves them one and all. Identification has thus been added where object choice has already occurred, while on the other side, object love has been commanded where identification is already in place. The categorical demand that love be thus extended, via identification, to everyone else, represents for Freud a radical devaluation of love, which counts a late arrival in American mass culture (*SE* 21:115–116).

The command to love one's neighbor as oneself is one of the punch lines of *Civilization and its Discontents:* it names the sadomasochistic program of pleasure's sacrifice to and installment alongside aggression. Thus—Lacan adds by at the same time giving his rereading of melancholic identification in terms of drive and principle—the Marquis de Sade's law of sexual pleasure, which decrees that every body be at everybody's disposal, guarantees that the pleasure to be had will be enjoyed only by the Other or by what Lacan also calls, in the essay on Hamlet, the phantom.[2]

According to Adorno, group identity's depositing of animosity to pleasure within pleasure, which is always kept in some other place, represents the institutionalization of that reception of music Freud tuned in by turning the pleasure principle around to its other side. Music as such, Adorno summarizes by keeping in a separate time zone the very measure of mass culture's degenerescence, was at once the most direct expression of drive and the intersection where it observed limits.[3] But in modern mass music—for which Adorno reserves the single signifier "jazz" since he recognizes in its grimacing shape the syncopated shortcut of castration (J 102)—this primal function of music has been shortcircuited not so much by the music as by what Adorno calls regressive or infantile listening. In primal precincts, consumption and production are one and the same. Thus regressive listening "coincides via advertising with production," just as its audio portion "begins as soon as advertising turns around into terror" (F 33). In addition, regressive listeners "display their enthusiasm only as advertisement for the product they are consuming" (F 41). In short, regressive audition turns only on identification: the regressed auditor identifies himself with the popular song "by identifying it and thus incorporating it as part of his property" (F 36). The differentiating standard of taste no longer applies in precincts crowded with incorporations; to like a song "is the same as recognizing it" (F 14–15).

By charting mass culture's return to primal structures as the circumvention and rebound of Christian identification (hence the secret connection Adorno announces between jazz and pogroms [J 101]), Adorno turns, following Freud, on America: "In American parlance having a good time means: to be bystander at the pleasure of others, a pleasure which in turn has standing by as its sole content" (F 26). Like "the man who must kill time, because he is not allowed to direct his aggressivity against anything else," the regressive listener succumbs to what Adorno also calls "auditory masochism"; not only in the sense that substitutive pleasure is offered and withdrawn through identification, but since the safety zone of identification turns out always to be a condemned site, regressive listening is destructive only to the extent that its pleasure is on autodestruct. Regressive auditors can only "parody and destroy that which excited them the day before in order to seek vengeance for their recognition that this excitement could only be feigned" (F 44–45). "It does not go without punishment and hence not without inhibition that the depraved productions of music culture are subjected, at the receiving end, to disrespectful fun and sadistic humor. Through regressive listening music as a whole begins to assume a comical aspect" (F 48). Within the culture industry music thus commands sadomasochistic parodies of affirmation: dancers take sexual excitement as a model only in order to deride, over and again, the spasmodic rapport of a doubly feigned fulfillment.

This metamorphosis—into jitterbugs—flips to the reverse side of the psychoanalytic categories of thought to which it owes its broadcast. Thus "drastic allusions to sexual consummation" cover over—by keeping sexuality and sexual repression on interchangeable tracks—the underlying unconscious process of identification which Adorno calls social. Contrary, then, to what psychoanalysis may lead one to suspect—Adorno cautions while remaining on this side of the Freudian system—the symbolic representation of sexual union should be designated the manifest dream content of jazz, which receives amplification rather than censorship. At the social or latent end of identification: verse and chorus, couplet and refrain evoke the ancient relation of lead singer or dancer to the collective (J 94). "The individual in the audience experiences himself primarily as couplet-ego, then feeling himself lifted up and cancelled out in the refrain, identifies himself with the refrain collective, enters dancing into it and thereby attains sexual fulfillment. As far as it goes this is the well-known dream level of jazz" (J 95). But what remains under dream censorship is the sacrificial sense and function of what Adorno designates as the jazz subject who, as lead singer or dancer, "is hardly anything other than a—perhaps detached—human sacrifice" (J 96).

Since he remains under dream censorship, the jazz subject, as object of sacrifice, is weakened or blurred to the point of embodying an impotent clown-self who must nevertheless go the rounds of the eternal rebound of his sacrifice. On account of his weakness, as though he were being rewarded for it, the jazz subject becomes assimilated within the collective that made him weak in the first place and which continues to administer norms that his weakness cannot satisfy (J 98). The dream thought that underlies the jazz subject's sex appeal or commando: if I allow my emasculation only then am I potent: "in learning to fear the social principle and to experience it as castration threat—directly only as impotence anxiety—the jazz subject identifies with the very principle he must fear, but now, in exchange, belongs to to the point of dancing along" (J 98).

According to Adorno, then, assimilation within this collective—down to the bodily integration of each member—requires and brings about castration and, in exchange, incorporation. At or on this stage the jazz subject occupies a double track. At one end he embodies the limit of sadomasochistic pleasure, offering affirmation only to the extent that in becoming "identified with the social principle" he "can identify . . . with it and enjoy—come to—his own mutilation." At the other end the jazz subject doubles or contains his own genitally decentered, and hence resurrected, corpse. Adorno concludes that jazz represents the "ritual consummation of this mutilation of the genitally centered subject" (J 106).

Jazz syncopation produces hot music which, however, as coming attraction, promotes "mere coming too soon, just as anxiety leads to premature ejaculation, just as impotence expresses itself in premature and incomplete orgasm" (J 98). Jazz syncopation is thus "ambivalent": "It is at once expression of protesting pseudosubjectivity, which resists the measure of time, and of regression prescribed by the objective principle, which suppresses the historical experience of time the dancing body might otherwise attain and holds the powerless body in timelessness—in the past—and mutilates it" (J 102).

The social or unconscious function of jazz can thus be "observed most clearly in the relation of the dancers to the music:"

> They follow the objective rhythm without ever dancing out the break: it is the key to the success of Mickey Mouse, that he alone precisely translates into visual terms all breaks. The pride of the dancers with respect to the syncope, however, is only that of not allowing themselves to become confused or sidetracked. If this is achieved, they are accorded the pleasure gain of identification with the objective principle together with the pleasure of suppressing the jazz subject. That they themselves are this subject, remains as unconscious as the rhythmic shape of the breaks remains unrecognized. They identify with him only by keeping open the possibility of straying or stumbling; . . . The originally improvised element of protest is received now only as contest with weakness. (J 105)

Thus the jazz subject, the rubric Adorno reserves for every star and sacrificial victim of modern group formations, is ultimately, in 1936, Mickey Mouse—who gets all the breaks by embodying them.

"Grateful Dead"

This comic strip-down of sublimation conjugates castration and incorporation: on the libidinal scanner the star attraction, in the place of the ego ideal, is the identificatory double or friend. According to Freud, what has been thus desexualized through identification can, as "moral masochism," be resexualized, reanimated in turn. The consequences and conditions of moral masochism are at once resistance to psychoanalysis and the loan of feelings of guilt (*SE* 19:166). To sponsor group identification moral masochism must borrow from the interior monologue of identification: melancholia. Borrowed feelings of guilt are the result and remainder of identification with an other whom one had at one time chosen as erotic object; the loan of guilt feeling is often the only (secret) souvenir of the abandoned love relation. The cure: the analyst must assume the position of the patient's ego ideal which, Freud stresses, remains off limits as far as psychoanalysis goes; such a takeover is precisely what saviors and dictators accomplish for groups (*SE* 19:50, n. 1).

Taking music as primal mass medium, Jacques Attali recasts group formation, from classical music to jazz and rock and roll, in terms of socialization of melancholia. Headsets plug into a scene of sacrifice which doubles as primal past and repast of music. From the first symphony concerts to the "live" performances of jazz or rock (which are only replicas of already released recordings) Attali observes in musical culture beginning with the Enlightenment a sadomasochistic dialectic which shifts from representation of the work of mourning to mediatized models of repetition; primal aggression comes to be phantasmatized, internalized, and, at the same time, autoeroticized. Thus music "has become a simulacrum of the solitary spectacle of the sacrifice. The spectator has become an accomplice to individualized murder."[1]

Freud advised Fliess in a letter dated May 2, 1897, that primal scenes referred to things heard, not seen. From primal scene to primal scene of sacrifice and cannibalistic mourning, the culture of musical accompaniment—or indigestion—has already exchanged the body for the corpus which comes in the one size or age that fits all. Only the dead die young: "Music thus fashions a consumer fascinated by his identification with others, with the image of success and happiness. The stars are always the idealized age of their audience, an age that gets younger as the field of repetition expands" (110). The sacrificial crisis, which music, as noise control, originally managed, ultimately asserts itself as relations of friendship and suicide among childish mascots whose childhood has already withdrawn into commodification.

> This channelization of childhood through music is a
> politically essential substitute for violence, which
> no longer finds ritual enactment. The youth see it
> as . . . the mouthpiece of their dreams . . . when it is
> in fact a channelization of the imaginary, a pedagogy

of the general confinement of social relations in the commodity. (110)

Thus it is not so much music that has become fetishized, canned, or commodified as childhood itself which, as within Josephine's mousefolk, can only be found missing.

This juvenilization or "individualization of the sacrificial relation," which counts the missingness of childhood in the body count of "distinctive cultures" it has caused to disappear (111), takes the form of a "stockpiling of sociality": the consumer piles up recordings with which the time left over for their audition will never catch up. This escalation of unconsumable commodities—which are merely placeholders for social relations—has the nuclear stockpile as model and aim. Hence the only way out of the confinement of social relations inside commodities: society-wide installation of "suicide motels" in which individuals would, on their own, carry out what the arms race between states could no longer accomplish for them: "individuals would relieve the states of having to make the final extension of the field of repetition—the collective stockpiling of death would become individualized" (126–27). From the single Bates motel to a chain of suicide motels, the melancholic would have achieved socialization. His music: rock and roll.

Rock music was first rehearsed as the beams that guided Nazi bombers and missiles to precise spots of detonation.[2] Rock and roll recalls when the *Blitzkrieg* raged; on its own side of recollection—inside total war—rock counts among its stars spectacular casualties of suicide missions.

But the genealogy of rock music also shows Attali the way mass culture advertises not only one "new" age and one gender, but also one race. The group identification of happy-faced suicides outblasts the melancholic's recognition of his haunted state by plugging it into the massive coupling, beyond any pair of individuals (dead or alive), of sadism and masochism. This teen-age race (to the finish line), which already left the body behind among the phantom effects of identification and audition, turns on the other race. Rock represents the careful filtering or vampirization of "black despair" which fuels the commodification of (white) childhood (105). From jazz to rock, the white race pretends to be the black race, which must go (or pretend to be the white race, as in disco). The body that has been lost can only be reanimated: at the same time, revenge is taken against the body despised for departing. Indeed, when anybody or everybody can turn zombie—according to *The Night of the Living Dead*'s scan of sixties culture—this body, the exploited body, can die. Thus the film's only living target and casualty remains the black man who, at the end of the projection, is shot by the posse which takes him to be (in the other sense that gives the group license to kill) the survivor of living death.

Mickey Mouse Club

At the canned or internal end of music's projective target range Adorno finds that even the "disease" of regressive listening has "conserving significance" (F 35): within the death-cult sensurround of amusement parks it "mummifies" leftovers of distinctive cultures and epochs (F 45). Thus in Mickey Mouse culture all music is background music to the extent that it occupies interchangeable places with silence. Adorno would make this occupation of one zone of audition by its exclusion the datable effect of silent film, or rather of silent film's continued existence within sound film. This double time zone shifts to primal time. The first sound films originally ventriloquated only two stars: the Jazz Singer and Mickey Mouse. "Music indwells the gaps of silence that emerge between men malformed by anxiety, bustle, and unprotesting submission. It assumes everywhere and unnoticed the deadly sad role which it had in the era and specific situation of silent film. It is now apperceived only as background" (F 15). But Adorno's countdown of the emergence of Mickey Mouse as the corpus of technology slips out of sync with contemporaneity over the issue of children's songs, the inspiration or target of their citational counterparts on hit parade. Adorno acknowledges that a "synthetized jazz children's song" also played in the era of the other: even at the turn of the century mass consumption popularized and libidinized—abused—children's songs. The difference that does remain for Adorno is the society-wide sadomasochism that in the meantime attends the broadcast:

> But the configuration in which such a children's song appears: the masochistic derision of one's wish for lost happiness, or the compromising of one's own wish for happiness through retroversion to a childhood, the unattainability of which guarantees the unattainability of happiness—this is the specific accomplishment of the new listening, and nothing that strikes the ear is spared inclusion within this scheme of appropriation. (F 35)

Constrained only by the orbit of their reversal, the drives go into reverse. The "mutilation of the genitally centered subject" which jazz orchestrates "releases, in the moment of regression, the partial drives. They are of course at the same time repressed through the false integration they undergo and thus become dangerous; homosexuality turns into a collective of conspirators, sadism turns around into terror" (J 106). In turn, the mascot of false integration—the break-dancing jazz subject—plays back, on both sides, a certain return of the pogrom. The fun that issues in pogroms makes victims dance with pain: between not being able to stand—the pain—and spasmodic shrugging of shoulder blades, the dance steps of jazz are exchanged. "Benjamin says," says Adorno: "in jazz we see the gestures of individuals who might make an appearance in pogroms: clumsy people who are forced to be dexterous" (J 101–2). But Benjamin has been forced to agree with Adorno's Freudian, consumerist perspective in an essay Adorno composed in radical disagreement with Benjamin's affirmative and active reception of media-technologized culture. According to Benjamin, spectator identification with the camera or projector—apparatus to apparatus—has substituted the exhibition values of distracted testing for the cult values of concentrated absorption. The popularity of Mickey Mouse refers to an inside-out alliance with the machine; the stereo-eared caricature was, after all, modeled after the projector framed by two reels of film. But the cult and occult values of melancholic absorption nevertheless return (Benjamin refers to the "retrenchment" of aura) even within the Disney projection booth: according to Disney, Mickey Mouse reanimated his own childhood.

Thus Mickey Mouse could only grow, as Adorno somehow knew in advance, into the fetish of childhood at the dead end of—or in the wake of—destrudo. In Disney's case, Mickey Mouse was the repository of a double lack which relinquished childhood at one end and the ego ideal at the other. Mickey Mouse was created as the once-and-for-all replacement of Oscar the Rabbit—lost to the "false friend" and plagiarizing competitor Back East; with Mickey Mouse, Disney for the first time placed one of his creatures under copyright protection. Only the cartoon figure thus shaped on all sides by effects of melancholic incorporation could be charged with playback of Disney's own childhood which, however, as abused child he always and already lacked.

Mickey, first named Mortimer, first borrowed Disney's adult voice, which instantly met with ridicule and rejection. Mickey Mouse subsequently received from his ventriloquist the other voice that elicited the laughter deposited not only inside Disney. Mickey Mouse's desexualized squeak belongs to an incorporated laughter, a laugh track that bonded not only Disney to California; it was with "Laugh-O-Gram Inc.," which he founded to shelter his creatures, that Disney went West. The cartoon animals mouthing this laughter animated what is otherwise "trained out of" children, namely, the "spontaneity of animals," in which "the entire body comes into play."[1] On the train back from his disappointment with plagiarism or incorporation Back East, Disney invented the mouse following the bouncing ball of train sounds: "m-m-mowaouse" (93). Upon conception followed execution: Disney gave the mouse big circular shoes that would "give him the look of a kid wearing his father's shoes" (95). Thus wearing the swollen feet of Oedipus, Mickey Mouse is at the same time grounded with a certain pre-history of psychoanalysis—of the Oedipal—which overlaps with child abuse and overtakes the father's contribution to neurotic symptom formation. But Disney quickly brought the complex full circle when he improved upon another extremity: "Five fingers looked like too much on such a little figure, so we took one away. That was just one less finger to animate" (95).

In "Ghost Exterminating Company," when Mickey and his friends get splashed and splattered with batter and flour the ghosts are thus scared away—by the other ghosts. The other occult exercise, "Skeleton Dance" (which was at first shown only to LA morning audiences) gives the X-ray of Mickey Mouse's premier in "Steamboat Willie" as sadistic music maker: Mickey started out his career ferociously squeezing, banging, twisting, and tweaking the creatures who were forced with their entire bodies to make music. This kind of nonsentimental energeticism (which E. M. Forster, for example, found scandalously relaxing) did not yet realize Disney's ambition to make Mickey Mouse a kind of popular hero or alter ego: "Rather than a caricature of individuals, our work is a caricature of life" (145). The rest followed: Mickey Mouse was fixed. Henceforward he doubled on contact within every group membership.

Thus Disney created the ghost of a childhood he had never in fact shared. As one of his fans put it: "Many, many years from now when this magical Pied Piper of our time wanders from this imperfect world which he has done so much to brighten and adorn, millions of laughing, shouting little ghosts will follow in his train—the children that you and I once were, so long ago" (298). And yet while creating the mascot of piped music and little ghosts, Disney was afflicted and disturbed "almost as if it were his own personality that was being tampered with." Once Mickey Mouse's character became unalterable (in 1931) Disney had a nervous breakdown (a "collapse"). Schickel dates Disney's obsession and rat race with death from this time on fast forward. It was as though the future (even the desire for the future) had been lost.

Borrowing from Konrad Lorenz, Stephen Jay Gould argues that Mickey Mouse embodies those features of juvenility which "trigger 'innate releasing mechanisms' for affection and nurturance in adult humans."[2] Mickey Mouse progressively received from Disney those "releasers" which attract "an automatic surge of disarming tenderness" which likewise disarms the libidinous urge to abuse children which their helplessness—according to Freud (*SE* 13:33)—otherwise attracts.

On his own Gould argues that, at the furthest reach of his orbit, Mickey Mouse encircles mankind's evolution all the way to the tail end of his own metamorphosis. The neoteny embodied by a cartoon figure remains the identifying trait of humans over and against their precursors and fellow mammals; human beings alone retain into adulthood youthful characteristics. The slowdown of developmental rates which underlies our neotenous species takes the form of long periods of gestation, extended childhoods, and the longest life span among mammals. That we are always in a state of development we owe to our neotenous nature. Mickey Mouse, too, developed up to a point—of perpetually adorable youthfulness. From the Mickey Mouse Club to MTV, neotenization is the chosen channel: to become what one is becomes the other—nihilistic—program of child hoods. A certain backfire of adolescence fueled by MTV has required inclusion of educational spots within the ongoing music-video show since countless addicted "children" are tied, like their teen models, only to the tube.

The always transit state of institutions corresponds to a neotenous schedule: within the prolongation of childhood, culture is transferred through education. But as Nietzsche and Freud already cautioned, the various holding patterns that extend childhood institute, in sync with Mickey Mouse's development all the way to nondevelopment, a state of paralysis in which only the mutilation, replacement, and exchange of body parts and organs produce the effect of (while closing off) development. Thus the educational apparatus, which Nietzsche already saw as consisting of isolated prosthetized bodily parts—reading mouth, listening ears, transcribing hands—assumes, in mass culture, the compact shapes of the preferred Disneyland souvenirs: Mickey Mouse ears and the hands of Mickey Mouse watches.

S-laughter

T *he body cannot be remade into a noble object: it re-*
mains the corpse however vigorously it is trained and
kept fit.
—Adorno and Horkheimer, *Dialectic of Enlightenment*

The superegoic converter "awakens an echo in the id" whenever "the present is changed into the past": "not a few of the child's experiences will be intensified because they are repetitions of some primaeval phylogenetic experience." The superego gives birth to institutions out of the spirit of "a childhood which is prolonged so greatly in human beings by a family life in common" (*SE* 23:206–7). The ego, which counts on being the sole beneficiary of its own life insurance policy, practices body building to catch the feedback of its superegoic institutionalization. No institutionalization (or neotenization) without body building; no body culture, therefore, without anorexic or cryonic separation from the body, which is packaged and dispensed with in favor of spiritual pursuits (such as New Age and support-group activities).

According to Benjamin,[1] gadget lover, body builder, and cameraman alike have acquired a surgeon's ability to penetrate deeply into the "natural distance from reality" (which was maintained in pretechnological times) and, beyond that, into the very "web" of "reality" (496). Benjamin reopens the inoculation argument which, in the case of Mickey Mouse, was organized around a laugh track (which tracked back to horror). The superintendence of the surgeon, which Benjamin admits into his reading of media-technologized culture, guarantees the connection between Mickey Mouse films and slasher and splatter movies, which let roll their cartoon afterimages and sequels on the same internal and global track which Disney films first installed and encircled. Once special effects caught up with cinematic penetration and cutting, the "live" body (instead of the cartoon double) was surgically opened up on screen.

> The surgeon . . . greatly diminishes the distance between himself and the patient by penetrating into the patient's body, and increases it but little by the caution with which his hand moves among the organs. . . . The surgeon at the decisive moment abstains from facing the patient man to man; rather, it is through the operation that he penetrates into him. (496)

The physician remains proximate to the primal murder which he reenacts up to the point at which he reverses himself and turns his hostile penetration into the cure. The physician, every child's first candidate for the father-god position, embodies and enacts the antidotal supplement of identification that our technologization has ever required. Film technology emerged to coincide or collide with train transportation, which was regularly featured in early cinema and, indeed, frequently used in film making to extend the range or motion of the camera (the "tracking shot" tracks back to this primal cohabitation of film and train-travel technologies). But trains also contributed the first public form or forum of psychic trauma when the shock of real or anticipated accidents was recognized as the cause of psychocultural disorders ("railway spine," for example). Amusement parks and films thus contributed to catastrophe preparedness by injecting doses of train wreck into the sensorium to absorb future shock.[2] We withstand shock by getting wired: we learn to get a blast out of being terrified by the culture industry's simulations of catastrophe.

Splatter and slasher entertainment, from Grand Guignol to Brian DePalma, has been brought to us by sons of surgeons. Grand Guignol gave owner-manual instruction on the latest advances in surgery and psychiatry in the course of splatter shows that also featured the use of new media technologies. In the 1902 play "On the Telephone," a husband must listen on the phone to the brutalization and murder of his wife at the other end of the line. André de Lorde, who was the son of a physician, attained his greatest success on the Grand Guignol stage (measured by the number of playgoers who fainted) with a realistic blood transfusion. The proximity of terror and laughter (which fixes the half-life of horror entertainment, which ends up laughable) was control-released by Grand Guignol: on a given night one-act comedies and farces alternated with the horror plays. The technique, called "hot and cold showers," lubed the audience's intake of the "slices of life" or death.[3]

DePalma's celebrated "cut," to which he began giving a cinematic twist when at age seventeen he saw his first Hitchcock film, was first practiced and prepared in anticipation of pursuing his father's medical career. In *Blow Out* the same techno capacity that permits a penetration of phenomena that gets behind every cover-up or conspiracy also leaves behind a recording which, however, since always capable of having been engineered, tampered with, simulated, is no proof whatsoever. The sound engineer splices his recording of the actual screams of the woman he had failed to keep from being murdered into the soundtrack of a slasher film. This insert rewinds to the origin of *Psycho* (and thus to the trauma that slasher films work through), which lies in mass murder, which, as epidemic, is at once random and selective.[4] In *Blow Out* we witness the psychic/cinematic mechanisms of mourning insert the sonic trace of a loss they have penetrated and proven but then, through their simulation backfire, also again lose: the dead woman's scream withdraws into an empty and artificial corpus (the slasher film) which the work of mourning and inoculation builds. The insertion of her wired and taped death into a shot of catastrophe preparedness is a tribute to the resilience of the sound engineer's gadget love or group bond (he's a group of one). Since she was the casualty of a surveillance and election-engineering conspiracy, which was coextensive with *Blow Out*'s every cinematic penetration, cut, and splice, her loss is not traumatically bound to an epidemic of mass murder but instead gets absorbed by the catastrophe that contains itself.

Once it becomes evident in *Night of the Living Dead* that the dead can be killed, the work of mourning, which is thus in the ready position, does not kick in. Instead, the reception of the zombie invasion (announced originally as an epidemic of mass murder) shifts to another channel of unmourning and tunes in, on TV and radio sets, as the news of natural disaster. Unlike death or the dead, catastrophe befalls everyone at the same time and thus gets absorbed by its product: the group, which never mourns.

The first zombie had popped up in the place of the dead father; the dead walked because they were no longer superimposable onto and contained by Dad. When the father function or the work of mourning is out of order, the relation to the dead is based on the relation to one's own body, at once the exquisite corpse and the greater body of the group. Melancholia and group identification are the two recognizable forms which narcissism (since it must take a detour via the other) can take. In the Pausanias version, which has Narcissus take his reflection to be his dead twin sister, narcissistic identification is shown to preserve a missing person. The same identification serves the mutual admiration of the adolescent group. The teenager isn't narcissistic simply because he thinks he's cute or friendly. Rather his others or objects are interchangeable since supplied and recycled within a group (of friends) that gives his sexual impulses a larger range of externalization or release than if they were overloaded on his own person.

Body Master Machines

The neoteny program brought to us by Disney reintroduces the body-ego (and feeling good about oneself) via the playful mastery that Mickey Mouse exercises over anthropomorphized machines.

> Hanns Sachs . . . notes that the last time machines were used for play and not work was during the time of the Greeks and Romans. He explains that one of the main reasons these machines were used solely for amusement involved that culture's value of the human body.[1]

Narcissistic investment of interest in the body protects against submission to the machine. According to Sachs, the wish to gratify narcissistic impulses by demonstrating omnipotence led man back to the machine, conceived no longer as plaything but as his own prosthetic extension. The return in Mickey Mouse films to a Greek rapport with the body can only be accomplished by repressing the machine—which, however, holds the place of the body.

Thus to release repressed relationships with the body, Freud runs the charge of child abuse through its transferential/translational machine or grammar. "A child is being beaten" refers to the third phase or phrase in a series of translations which opens up under analysis only at this end and in the first formulation ("My father is beating the child, whom I hate") to conscious thought. The middle phase or phrase—"I am being beaten by my father"—remains, Freud argues, central and inaccessible, primal and constructed:

> It is the most important and the most momentous of all. But we may say of it in a certain sense that it has never had a real existence. It is never remembered, it has never succeeded in becoming conscious. It is a construction of analysis, but it is no less a necessity on that account. (*SE* 17:185)

This sheer construction is thus, at the same time, the "original fantasy" (*SE* 17:199). As Laplanche comments:

> *What is repressed is not the memory but the fantasy derived from it or subtending it:* in this case, not the actual scene in which the father would have beaten another child, but the fantasy of being beaten by the father. And yet it is clear that the repression of the fantasy can drag along with it into the unconscious the memory itself, a memory which after the event takes on a sexual meaning: "My father is beating another child—he loves me (sexually)."[2]

But the process of turning around which releases the masochistic pleasure of the second phase does not cover content alone: it parallels and propels, in Laplanche's words, *"the very movement of fantasmatization"*:

> To shift to the reflexive is not only or even necessarily to give a reflexive content to the "sentence" of the fantasy; it is also and above all to reflect the action, inter-

nalize it, make it enter into oneself as fantasy. To fantasize aggression is to turn it around upon oneself.[3]

But the repressed fantasm of one's own abuse cannot, as such, enter consciousness—to the point, in fact, of never having taken place at all.

Guilt, the currency of the father function, is the exchange rate on which the translations, which turn around by fantasizing all the way to autoerotic rebound an originally and ultimately sadistic fantasy, are based (*SE* 17:191). When a boy's fantasy includes himself being beaten by his mother, the additional turnaround of activity into passivity keeps the fantasy out of reach of repression; the standard of guilt can be applied and satisfied in this case through regression alone (*SE* 17:190). But only at those ends of translation or transference accessible to consciousness can the boy's fantasy focus on the punishment a mother delivers; the middle term, the construction of analysis, remains the paternal p-unitive measure, the penetration by or incorporation of father (*SE* 17:198).

Both genders are, at the beginning, phallically aggressive when it comes to mother (*SE* 22:119). But as fantasmatization and autoeroticization succeed this pursuit—which withdraws into its unavoidable repression—little boy and little girl alike must come to father at the other end of detours which the sadomasochistic session orchestrates.

Kafka and de Sade despised the body for its limitations and boundaries; they knew that the alliance between imagination and language which alone supports the pursuit of pleasure lies beyond the corporeal analogues of sexual excitement. In other words: the body—which is always also the maternal body—comes only to its mutilation, rebuilding, and reanimation.

The body has been left behind in the wake of its mediatechnical range, which has escalated on automatic to the point that it can no longer be plugged back into any socalled sensorium or corpus. But when it comes time to dispose of the dead, the genealogy of media reverses itself: from the point of view of (identification with) the dead, every medium acquires its only prosthetic aim on a target range of projection and haunting. Work on the remainder refastens each new medium to a sensorium which, as Schreber realized, takes cognizance only of corpses.

The unprecedented escalation, on parallel tracks, of military and media-technical innovation turned the American Civil War into the preview of the twentieth century. Thus Gertrude Stein could declare that America was the oldest nation of the twentieth century. The Civil War launched the technological advance which, according to a sheer logic of acceleration and escalation, cannot be made to fit the Freudian or consumerist model of warfare based on the sensorium and its prostheses. But the sensorium returns (together with the Freudian system) in the course of mourning or unmourning the dead. In the wake of the Civil War new modes of disposal of the dead (and thus new modes of haunting) rebounded from the furthest reaches of a sensorium which mourning had, after all, reinstalled and extended. Ever since the Civil War the group identifications or corpse-disposal systems that have grown to absorb the catastrophic status of modern warfare are new and improved; but they are not on the side of life. Modern wars have taken increasingly total (and inward) turns: the suicidal impulse is growing.

Ariès documented the shift (back down to ancient Egyptian models in the American work of mourning and representation) which coincided with the Civil War:

> Today's "morticians," whose letters-patent go back to that period, give as their ancestor a quack doctor expelled from the school of medicine, Dr. Holmes, who had a passion for dissection and cadavers. He would offer his services to the victim's family and embalmed, it is said, 4,000 cadavers unaided in four years. . . . Is there an American tradition going back to the eighteenth century, a period in which throughout Europe

there was a craze for embalming? Yet this technique was abandoned in nineteenth-century Europe, and the wars did not resurrect it. In 1900 embalming appeared in California. We know that it has today become a very widespread method of preparing the dead, a practice almost unknown in Europe and characteristic of the American way of death.[4]

Holmes embalmed the Civil War corpses piling up at the front to keep them from decomposing during the train trip back home for proper burial. The trip (and the telecommunications which always parallel even while, beginning with the telegraph, they also exceed transport) extended the reach of mummification. Thus to this day in Forest Lawn every corpse is embalmed—"made friendly"—within the context of an entire scene in suspended animation which delivers the hardened survivors a parting shot or "memory picture"; the corpse can be forgotten, lost within the unmarked sites of the neoclassical (and, hence, German) layout of Elysian Fields. (At Forest Lawn there are large-scale tributes to Lincoln, who was the first president to be embalmed.)

Just as the current phantasm of the missing child covers for the hidden loss of the Vietnam War which remains, as loss, missing in action, so during the nineteenth-century period of modern military and techno-mediatic expansion it was increasingly the dead child which one saw featured. Portraits depicting the living semblance of children were painted from their corpses; on anniversaries these "mourning portraits" were used to beam back "live" commemoration of the departed. It was again the attribute of "liveness" which photographs of dead little ones sought to capture: these shots mark the origin of the memory pictures which Forest Lawn sets up as *tableaux vivants*. Beginning in the seventies, Forest Lawn has hosted Valentine's Day parties especially for children who are thus encouraged, as they romp around the tombs, to dedemonize their growing rapport with the dead.

In neotenized culture there is no childhood; there is only the retrofashion and charge of child abuse. The charge is the antidotal dose of the recurrent shocks of their technologization, massification, teenagerization. Supported by their childhood missingness or abuse, teenagers are totally S/M: friendly, cool, and into being popular. They're unbeatable.

Gag Me with a Tune

In 1933 (in a speech composed by one of his ghostwriters) Disney sought to share his own internal rapport with Mickey Mouse with his friends and enemies alike:

> Mickey Mouse pictures are gauged to only one audience: the Mickey audience . . . that audience is made up of parts of people; of the deathless, precious, ageless, absolutely primitive remnant of something in every world-racked human being which makes us play with children's toys and laugh without self-consciousness at silly things, and sing in bathtubs, and dream and believe that our babies are uniquely beautiful. You know, the Mickey in us. . . . Mr. Mussolini takes his family to see every Mickey picture. . . . Mr. A. Hitler, the Nazi old thing, says Mickey's silly. Imagine that! Well, Mickey is going to save Mr. A. Hitler from drowning or something some day. Just

wait and see if he doesn't. Then won't Mr. A. Hitler be ashamed![1]

By 1940 psychoanalytic culture criticism from Benjamin and Adorno to Kris and Moellenhoff had scanned, by recircuiting the Freudian system through its media-technological analogues, the group identifications that had installed this "Mickey in us" and around us. According to Fritz Moellenhoff:

> The symbolic meaning of Mickey's figure is obvious. Symbolically we should have to call it a phallus but a desexualized one.
>
> Nothing persists but the somewhat painful statement that our hero is unable to love, that he is someone who, from the point of view of genitality, makes no decisions because he does not need to. . . . We know that when Mickey Mouse appeared with a man's voice he met with ridicule; with the eunuch's voice he met with laughter. . . . When Mickey appeared with his "apt" voice, he became definitely the representative of a lively, though neutral sex. . . . Identification is now established without effort and would be one of the explanations for his popularity.[2]

It is thus within Mickey Mouse's development from vampiro-sadistic rodent with a man's voice into eternal child or pet endowed with a desexualized squeak that psychoanalysis uncovers an open invitation to identify which must be conjugated, via Disney's own history, with the impact—or charge—of abuse in childhood.

The puzzling case of Mickey Mouse's popularity rehearses questions that psychoanalytic criticism in the eighties tried to answer with regard to the abused or missing child, another curious object—within pop culture—of mass identification.

According to Freud's genealogy of group identification and regression, the Christian terminal in the recycling of group identity—from mass to mass to mass—slides the unmournable death of the child beneath the corpse of the primal father which in turn slides to the side of that which it cannot cover over or bury. Christianity marks both "a cultural regression" and, ironically, and advance "as regards the return of the repressed" (*SE* 23:88); in other words, the murdered primal father makes his ghost appearance as child in the place of the father (*SE* 23:90). But Christianity "has not escaped the fate of having to get rid of the father (*SE* 23:136).

Christianity introduces the child that exists only to exit also by extending undead status to the unborn whose equal rights have all along been the primal part of the church's platform. The equally primal charge—against the Jews—of child abuse continues to haunt not only popular culture but also, with each return of the seduction theory, psychoanalysis itself. Freud wagered that anti-Semitism, in his day, had become interchangeable with rejection of psychoanalysis.

Freud thus counters phantasms of child abuse with what he calls "the constructions of psychoanalysis." With our Freudian ears on: it proves necessary to give a closer hearing to both ends of ongoing preoccupation with the abused child. In his 1986 article "False Accusations of Physical and Sexual Abuse," Daniel Schuman uncovers in a series of cases the automatic transfer to children of imagined charges of abuse which are, as Schuman puts it, "canned."[3] And then, at the popular end of group identification, we find the nine-year-old Sharon Batts piping up with a hit that covers in shortcut the Freudian reception it cannot help but tune in:

> Sharon Batts is an unlikely candidate for pop stardom. But at age nine the brown-eyed third-grader from the Fort Worth suburb of Bedford has successfully bypassed the music-industry moguls with a hit single about a subject few would pick for Top 40 playlists. "Dear Mr. Jesus, / I just had to write to you," Sharon's tinny voice sings plaintively. "Some-

thing really scared me / when I saw it on the news. / A story about a little girl / beaten black and blue." After imploring Jesus to come to the rescue of abused children, the song concludes, "Dear Mr. Jesus, / please tell me what to do. / And please don't tell my daddy / but my mommy hits me, too."[4]

Good Mourning America

*R*etired West German fire equipment inspector Klaus Schreiber channels in a very literal way. Mostly, he does it with his television set. Schreiber was quaffing a few beers with his friends one spring day in 1982 when talk turned to a radio program about messages from other dimensions. Half in jest, Schreiber suggested trying to contact a recently departed friend, Peter, with a tape recorder. "Hello, Peter, where are you?" Schreiber asked into his machine. "Come on over and have a drink." After about ten minutes of silence, Schreiber switched off the recorder, rewound the tape, and hit the replay button. He and his friends heard his invitation, then nothing but a long, low hum. He was about to turn the machine off, when suddenly a voice said, "Hello, friends." All present identified the voice as Peter's. Shortly thereafter, Schreiber's cronies left his house. Shaken by the experience, most never returned. Schreiber, meanwhile, got busy turning his basement into a small-scale laboratory for further experi-

ments in electronic contact with the dead. He worked first with tape recorders, then, supposedly at the behest of spirit voices on the tapes, he moved on to video recorders and his television set. The result was a collection of videocassettes of what Schreiber calls his "new friends." The friends' faces are fuzzy and washed out when first captured on the channeler's video camera. But by transferring individual frames back and forth between video recorders, then superimposing the images and finetuning them with a special amplifier, Schreiber often brings the hazy shapes into focus as faces. Many of the faces belong to Schreiber's dead relatives or to deceased celebrities. The latter group includes King Ludwig II of Bavaria and film star Romy Schneider.
    —Spirit Summonings

The filmy orifices into which psychoanalysis first plugged a double device—at once psychic apparatus and cinematograph—have withdrawn into the concealment cast around the new improved Freud of semiological provenance. Another way to describe the safety zone Freud has been made to occupy—and this is Stanley Cavell's way—is to expose it as "counterfeit happiness" or "insurance."[1] Cavell has moved to cancel Freud's insurance coverage by returning psychoanalysis, beyond the dialectic of desire and recognition, to the origin it shares with the techno-media and consumer projection. The coordinates of this reclaimed ground of Cavell's thinking in fact mark a series of returns: "Psychoanalysis and cinema share an origin as responses to the suffering and knowledge of women"; film's declaration of itself is in turn "understandable only in taking the position of woman, say a position in which one allies oneself with the feminine in one's character, whichever one's gender"; directing (which when represented within the films Cavell explores in *Pursuits of Happiness* also represents psychoanalytic intervention or treatment) proceeds "from an alliance with the feminine"; the narratives and themes of cinema thus "may be seen to declare that the knowledge of the existence of others, hence of oneself requires, as from a perhaps datable event in human history, the capacity for the experience of horror and of mourning."[2]

Cavell follows Derrida in locating the trajectory of return to Freud around the unconscious of Freud's discovery of the unconscious: woman, philosophy, and film.[3] But these precise precincts are already crowded with returns to Freud: it is around the Lacanian notion of a phallicized gaze that film theory, feminism, and psychoanalysis have continued to move in place within the range of this shared focus. The gaze, which marks a double takeoff (of vision and phallus), remains the leftover shard of a mirror stage to which the triad of theories (summoned to meet the gaze) cannot but return as though to the "datable event" of film's primal constitution.[4]

These ocular/specular readings of identification double on contact on both sides of the reception (or repression) of psychoanalysis. Thus on the threshold of Lacan's banishment, psychoanalysis welcomed a syndication of the mirror stage when Bertram Lewin found rebound from the nursing breast every primal moviegoer's "dream screen."

> As it approaches the sleeper, the breast seems to grow; its convex surface flattens out and finally merges with the sleeper, often to the accompaniment of mouth sensations. . . . The dream screen is the representation of the wish to sleep. The visual contents represent its opponents, the wakers. The blank dream screen is the copy of primary infantile sleep.[5]

Lewin's breast reading recasts the complete range of psychoanalytic insights (all the way to the meaning of suicide) by dropping from this mirror stage the other of identification. Thus Lewin can argue that suicide represents "a breaking through in a distorted form of the primitive wish for infantile sleep": "The prototype of this wish for death is the wish for the undisturbed, blank sleep, that is the probable state of mind of the satiated sleeping infant" (431). At this outer limit of his reading we find Lewin's conjugation of oral and visual senses as the two sides of cannibalistic identification turning, paradoxically, only on self relations. But identification, according to Freud, guarantees that suicide, for example, will always be a pact with an other: both must either stay or go.

Lewin's manic or one-way conception of identification accelerates beyond identification all the way back to auto-cannibalism. "The sleeper has eaten himself up, completely or partially, like Natalija A. or Dr. Schreber, and becomes divested of his body—which then is lost, merged in its identification with the vastly enlarged and flattened breast, the dream screen" (427). This psychotic dissolution is regularly broadcast in dreams and in sleep: ego boundaries are lost to the extent that dreamer or sleeper remains in unified contact with the breast or dream screen (426–27). The return to the womb that sleep provides—and preparation for sleep ritualizes—is the phantasmic effect or aim that advertises another repeat performance: the first occasion for going to sleep is when the nursling has drunk his fill at the breast (419). Both the phantasm of return to womb and its placeholder, our media-technological sensurround, only cover, as feedback, the always primal triad of eating, being eaten, and sleeping.

Freud's analysis of Schreber's memoirs and Victor Tausk's case study of Natalija A., which Lewin remakes for his dream screen, develop the test case study of film as already prosthetic part and portrait of the psychic apparatus. This double apparatus can only be conceived—*Psycho*-style—as the projective haunting of an internal crypt built by melancholic identification. The crypts in the cases of Schreber and Natalija A. are overlooked not by Lewin alone. But in the corner of each case Lewin includes—autocanni-balistically—as testimony in support of his rereading of primal relations we find the countertestimony of identification leftover. On his own Lewin brings into focus melancholic attachment to dead mothers only to reverse the borders of alterity: identification with the other is reducible, owing to Lewin's special logic of identification, to one's own property. But the gap of ambivalence, the defective cornerstone of identification and, as identification, of projection has thus been foreclosed. It is in the place of ambivalence, then, that

Lewin promotes the oral fantasy of autocannibalism or, interchangeably, the psychotic delusion of total world destruction. But as Freud makes clear in his study of Schreber, the world or "wealth of sublimations" (*SE* 12:73) destroyed by the unchecked upsurge of repression and the matching massive withdrawal of libido is replaced, via projection, with another world of paranoid provenance in which media-technological attachments and controls are no longer subliminally veiled. It is at this point that the analogy of psychic apparatus with film finds application.

On Tausk's psycho-scanner, Lewin charges, object regressions alone come into focus, though only to the extent that the enabling background of screen and stage—breast and orality—have been overlooked. According to Lewin the study of Natalija A. does not observe the proper scheduling of stages or phases. Whereas for Tausk the patient's delusions treat body parts as love objects at every stage of the psychoticizing regression, Lewin counters that at bottom the downward course of regression guarantees that the patient in fact occupies the oral stage. She comes full circle within the course Lewin sets for identification by simultaneously devouring her mother's breast and her own body (425). Lewin thus overlooks the melancholic identification which, with its usual staying power, has swallowed the mother whole, intact and undisclosed. At the same time Lewin displaces or loses, with respect to his all-encompassing dream screen, every precise reference to media technology built into psychotic delusions. The cryptological and the technological are always excluded together and at once. Lewin's "dream screen" cannot tune in the connections between the patient's at once cinematographic and Egyptoid-funereal delusions or projections and the cryptlike identification she finally becomes. (In the end, when her "astral body" collapses back onto her person, she can "project" herself only two-dimensionally as the cover of a mummy's casket.)

Lewin's oral triad was swallowed by Joseph Bierman, who in his study of Bram Stoker assimilated it to the conjunction of the infantile lack of motor coordination (which kept *Dracula*'s author in his own coffin bed for seven years) and the phantasm or dream of the living dead Count who rises from total sleep only to engorge himself or nurse one of his victims. But Dracula is also *Dreckula*, the maternal superego that toilet training builds.[6] By fixing vampirism exclusively as oral/sexual fantasy—and thus forgetting the whiff of the vampire's blood stench—Bierman deletes from his reading the media-technological mother tongue inhabiting Stoker's *Dracula*, a novel as much about typewriter, dictaphone, and the "new woman" as it is about the undead. The multiplug connection with the new-found maternal fits only techno-outlets of unmourning.

Lewin's dream screen supports readings of film that never graduate from the mirror stage of autocannibalism. By excluding the other of identification these specular readings also fall short of their projected moment of triumph: accession to a capitalized notion of the Other, which, however, must be sniffed out. Dog trainers (who still subscribe to the Freudian system) achieve command and control over their charges by first holding and closing in on the gaze of a dog only to glide, just before collision, next to its head; the sniff behind the dog's ear proves and guarantees mastery.

The Other serves as "fourth wall" of a stage on which primal relations put on a drama of desire and recognition. Thus boxed-in this mirror stage tunes in a digestible mourning after show: "the Oedipus complex goes into its decline insofar as the subject must mourn the phallus."[7] But desire, which is not a Freudian concept, does not cover the alternation between identification and projection into which, as mourning for the phallus, it has been inserted. The work of mourning does not plug into the mirror senses of desire; the psyche or "mirror," which mourning and unmourning observe, opens onto that which it cannot reflect back: the continued existence of the deceased within a reversed or anal underworld. Back in front of the rearview mirror: mourning practices put on reversal—black in place of lighter colors— to represent the griever's entry, via identification and according to the logic of the backside, into the reversed world of the dead. But dream screen and mirror stage don't cut the shit. Their oral and video appeal—to purity or autocannibalism without leftover—belongs not to the anal and cryptological technologies of photography and film. Dream screen and mirror stage open up a new technological era no longer plugged up into the anus.

Cute Buns

B ut Lacan already covered the funereal route back to Freud when he dropped on Boston audiences the speculation that basic definitions of civilization can be found within the range of our anthropomorphizing control over animals. We do not know what to do with our excrement; the animals closest to us, our pets, are in turn marked by difficulties attending disposal of their waste— from kitty litter to pooper scoopers. Outside this anthropomorphizing range, the problem does not seem to exist: otherwise the elephants alone would by now have buried us alive.[1] Where it does exist the problem asserts itself symptomatically (complete with implications and exclusions) as ideologies of purity. This is where Janine Chasseguet-Smirgel's reading of friendshit belongs:[2] the perpetually adolescent or perverse group response of idealization ("best friend") is tied to self-esteem, not to guilt, to pregenital anality, not to paternity. "The pervert attempts to project his

Ego Ideal onto pregenital instincts and objects instead of projecting them onto his begetter in order to identify with him" (70).

The lean and clean (and mean) machine practices good hygiene: Save a Whale/Spear a Fat Impurity. The unconscious becomes a toilet that must be kept totally flushed and scrubbed clean to protect against and project infection. The rebellion against the excre-mental, which remains profoundly anal, groups teenagers around counter-paternal models of totalization. Relations of substitution and reproduction are lost in the total equality and interchangeability of all group members before (and when it's One's turn, as) the leader. The leader, best friend, or bro always embodies, as father-hood, a fraternal not a paternal ideal:

> The leader is not the father's substitute; on the contrary, he is the man who implicitly promises the coming of a world without any father and a correlative union with the almighty mother, the one before the breaking up of primary fusion, even with the one before birth. (61)

But the lean machine running the group's metabolism is nothing other than the digestive system, which totals the different items that come out at the end as One:

> In the universe I am describing, the world has been engulfed in a gigantic grinding machine (the digestive tract) and has been reduced to homogeneous (excremental) particles. Then all is equivalent. The distinction between "before" and "after" has disappeared, as, too, of course, has history. (128)

The One is the anal alternative to father culture. The impure, which, via the same logic of equalization, becomes the double of the pure, can be offed only suicidally. From Goethe's *Faust* to Jonestown, paternity comes down to the impurity or poison (the paranoid interpretation of mother's milk) we might as well, to get it over with, go ahead and swallow. The principle of nothingness was the anal alternative to Faustian striving. And yet both souls were cut off from paternity. Faustian striving is on the side of life only so long as the single subject lives—and Faust's life has to be magically and technologically extended to create the life-span long enough for one individual to get off on life (in spite of everything). But usually life is short, and only covert operations of narcissism get one off living on via others, via, that is, one's own death, which, since one cannot recognize it, always means the other's death, the dead other.

But it is too late for Chasseguet-Smirgel's prescriptions. Relations of paternity and the work of mourning are out of order. Perpetual adolescence has taken hold—and put life (as father knew it best) on hold. The experiment is on in California, where the culture of the body ego is also a *Bildungs*-culture in which, from support groups to New Age beliefs, the body (or feeling good about oneself) has been interiorized, technologized, and intellectualized. The Californian is a product of Faustian desires and contracts negotiated within institutions, laboratories, and fitness studios. He can only have relations with his body via the suicidal rebirth that plunges Homunculus, the test-tube spirit in search of a body, into the sea, literally into a Nautilus setting.

On the bicoastal set we still watch reruns without station break of phantasms as ancient, timeless, or unconscious as the pogroms of the Middle Ages. Today the same mid-life crisis follows from shifts in the genealogy of media. Identification and projection were the two lines of defense (and the two live wires of the subject's concurrent technologization) that were brought to us by the work of mourning. Their last stand gives us psychotic delusion. Both the Schreber case and *The Ego and the Id* advertise that sublimation has only a half-life, which it owes to its origin in melancholic identification, and a limited warranty, which reflects its guaranteed withdrawal into repression. In the wake of sublimation's wipeout, the alternating alterations of identification and projection can still, if you're fortunate (like Faust), construct a narcissistic object for the libido cut loose from the world and breaking over the ego. Via hallucination, which is a symptom or sign of self-help (the other beat psychosis can follow is catatonia, fade out, regression without remainder, unbirth), the subject's technologized interiority gets extended to include the outside. The perverse or adolescent group structures of anal-sadistic regression—"the levelled and heavenly world of equivalence, homogenization"—which Chasseguet-Smirgel penetrates amount, however, to a defense against psychosis, against the limit-concept of Freud's first system (129). While the culture of (having) the right look is, at bottom, as anal as psychotic projection, its playback and record functions—idealization, imitation, make-believe—belong to group-bound denial and acting out. Identification is thus new and improved. But that which nevertheless keeps the connection between psychosis and adolescence open is not transference.

Boobs Tube

In his remake of Lewin's 1948 suggestion that the "nothing" which a patient on occasion volunteers during free association represents the female genitals, Samuel Abrams, bringing up the rear in 1974, groups support for this association around his case material. One patient, a housewife, referred to the current view of housework as menial labor as itself amounting to a mere "flatitude." This lapsus recalled her deep disappointment whenever she only passed gas while trying to move her bowels: whereas feces would have been worth the effort—flatus was "nothing." Thus she leaned toward concrete issues when weighing them against abstract principles. "'Everything' was the omnipotent mother, the valued feces, and the envied penis, while 'Nothing' was the helplessness of separateness, flatus, and the absent phallus."[1]

But Lewin's brief turn to what sounded like sexuality or difference—at least when it inadvertently turned on the projector—is in no wise the rule of his screening. According to Lewin, the cases of Natalija A. and of Staudenmaier (whom Tausk included as demonized counterpart to Natalija) reveal that "the dormescent ego loses itself and becomes a blank."[2] But these blanks are drawn at the end of a class or progression of "vague" dreams which Lewin was the first analyst to write about and ride out.[3] (Freud, who had first sighted them, dismissed them as the small-time surf of resistance.) Vague dreams display imperfect optical projection "because the dream screen is not sharply externalized":

> Sometimes the whole dream remains unprojected and feels to the dreamer as if it took place within him or inseparably from him rather than somewhere before him in his visual field. (488)

In the fifties American analysts joined Lewin in the discovery of dreams they designated now as "sleep dreams," now as "narcissistic dreams." But by introducing the concept of narcissism into dream theory, Freud himself had made possible Lewin's reception of the screen of primary narcissism:

> The dream was treated in theory as if it were a variety of psychosis; sleep was an expression of primary narcissism to which the libido had regressed, while in dreaming the ego expressed itself regressively in hallucinations. The dream is evoked by and attests to the fact that there is a certain amount of leftover waking libidinal or ego interest. (487)

Hence the more that fine tuning of the manifest dream shows only a blank screen, the nearer the sleeper is to the state of consciousness commensurate with primary narcissism. Wipe out: "the blanker the dream, the fewer impurities are there in the narcissism of sleep" (488). But Freud inaugurated Lewin's screen theory only to leave it unplugged; instead he connected narcissism, via the work of mourning, to depression and manic elation. This single direction which psychoanalytic theory has followed out is at the same time a detour around dream theory (which went unmentioned and unconnected in "Mourning and Melancholia").

Lewin finds a way back for dream theory via the obscurity or vagueness washing over Freud's first formulation of mania: the frenzied state is declared independent of any conflict between ego and superego, which in fact must be absent. Lewin's aside: "It is not clear offhand why this should not represent mental health" (490). Sándor Radó's influential followup (and cleanup) operation, which restricted mania to the state of sated oral bliss, remains for Lewin, while latently correct, manifestly off-screen. Radó's notion covered only the first state of ecstasy ("the 'kick'") which, issuing in blank dream and orgasm, represents union with the breast and the superego. This druglike rush is the other side of another one-sided account of mania or hypomania: active cannibalism shows up alongside the violent defensive positionings of denial and projection. Lewin proposes bringing the two phases together in simulcast:

> For the eroticized blank dream was so much part of
> the ecstasy, and the ecstasy and ensuing hypomania
> were so much part of the dream . . . , that neither of
> them could be interpreted fully without the other.
> Both ecstasy and blank dream had to be formulated
> in terms of sleep; the mover of both of them was a
> special variety of a wish to sleep—that is, the wish to
> enjoy the narcissistically blissful sleep of the satiated
> nursling. (491)

Just as one part of the manifest dream text denies the latent thought, so hypomania succeeds the dream as the denial and disguise of a wish to sleep.

On Lewin's program, the superego is an arouser or waker that opposes blissful sleep at the breast. In dreams and in myths the loud noises and bright lights which disturb sleep are circuited through channels of superegoic broadcast (496). Even if it is only the alarm clock, the superego announces: "Get away from your mother's breast! Wake up!" (498). This is one of the roles of the analyst to which, Lewin admits, analysis cannot, however, be reduced. Just the same, Lewin charges his critics with preferring to forget that psychoanalysis began by "putting the patient into a sleeplike state, and encouraged the dreamlike productions of the talking cure" (501).[4]

An analyst's interpretive remarks and interventions are often received by patients from "a musical standpoint" as arousing or soothing (507). Thus the "analytic split" emerges between sleep and vigilance, between praxis and theory.

> In psychoanalytic technique the wish to sleep plays a role which bears an interesting similarity to its role in dream formation. In both cases, it is a silent *sine qua non,* for there is no dream-formation without a wish to sleep and no analysis without its weaker counterpart, the wish to associate freely. (508)

Analysts have ignored the split: outside Lewin's circle, the wish to sleep never receives interpretation; the extent to which the patient is asleep is not brought to his attention. Following Lewin, Joseph Kepecs overlooks any resistance underlying the patient's claim that he is thinking of nothing, that his mind is a blank, and asks instead what the mental blankness looked or felt like. One answer: "Like a curtain—the iron curtain—impossible to get to what is behind the curtain."[5] This curtain, veil, or screen can be first suspended when a father shuts the bathroom door on his infant daughter who wanted to see his penis. What comes between us is a wish, henceforth sealed from consciousness, to see it (72). But at bottom, the screen that has come between a patient and the adult world is "a phantom of the mother's breast."[6] At bottom the veil is torn whenever Wolfman, for example, defecates following an enema's inducement. In Freud's reading, the tearing of the veil or caul is analogous to the opening of the window in Wolfman's primal-scene dream. But Lewin adds: the closed window of this dream represents the dream screen. This dream screen (the breast) represents the wish to sleep which the superegoic impulses to act (the wakers or intruders) cover over in the manifest dream; in the waking state action tends to comply with wishes while the "waking screen" (again: the breast) represents intrusion or disturbance. Intrusion drops as screen or scream between the subject and what is wished (170). "It is quite likely that many people are unable to perceive the real world clearly because between it and themselves they interpose a phantom of the maternal breast through which everything else is seen" (171). This dual, maternal relation covered by the dream screen admits no third term, anal input, or cinematic projection. The opened window or torn caul is an anal projection; in turn, the closed window or dream screen is not circuited through the anus.

The open and shut casement contains two screens which, as in Lewin's analysis of a patient's error in auto-interpretation, cannot be superimposed: in her dream she enters a motion picture theater "where she saw the most terrifying things on the screen (she did not know what), and she rushed out to keep from seeing them." The dream, she reported, represented her reaction to beginning analysis, the screen held the place of her unconscious. But she is (almost historically) a beginner in her choice of analogue. Lewin points out that the movie screen was not her unconscious, nor a movie screen, but "her dream screen and it showed her fear of dreaming."[7] Angel Garma's patient locates more precisely the place in the home of "the ghost of a breast." The patient's dream plays back the different epochs of reading separating Freud's account of Wolfman's dream from Lewin's rapt attention to the screen:

> A Mr. Wolf, whom I don't know, was at table with
> some other people. As I was half awakened from this
> dream by the sound of a passing tram, I realized that
> my dream was becoming flattened, turning into
> something like a photograph and then disappearing
> upwards, like a curtain. Only a white milkwhite back-
> ground like a television screen remained. [8]

Freudian resistance to Lewin's innovations in theory refer in practice to the model analogue, TV. Lewin notes Robert Fliess's resistance which "questions the existence of the dream screen and by implication that of the blank dream too."[9] These analysts are on one side, that of the superego, the arouser or waker that opposes blissful sleep at the breast. The wake up call that orders the sleeper away from mother's breast is issued by the analyst or father who instructs his charges to get away from in front of the tube, get out of the house (and off the phone). In analysis, accordingly, the couch becomes a set of contention: "with many patients the couch as bed and hence an early substitute and symbol for the mother, enters into the transference situation, for the analyst's remarks become the equivalent of the noises and wakers, and are equated with the father's or superego's wakening and weaning injunction" (504). Thus Lewin must take seriously the emergence of the "blank 'analytic couch' of the transference sleep": "the background 'couch' of the analytic situation, ordinarily as inconspicuous and as subordinate practically as the background dream screen, may dominate the manifest picture" (509).

In their study of Donald Duck, Armand Mattelart and Ariel Dorfman call television "the bible of contemporary living."[10] The remake of Freud's "screens"—from Jung to Lewin and Lacan—is not Graeco-Judaic-cinematic but Heideggerian, Binswangerian, and New Testament. The *Lichtung* or clearing within which the post-Freudian screen situates itself participates in a perpetual openness (or concealedness) which only TV—as that which is always on (especially when it's off)—realizes.[11] The pre-TV era is transferential; it travels via ear and anus (the two orifices of film): television is totally on, "live," and, hence, nontransferential. Its reception is that of acting out in front of a set (of responses) which perpetual adolescence and perversion equally share.

TV Führer

*I*n only four years, . . . Emma Freud, great-granddaughter
*of the legendary psychoanalyst Sigmund Freud, has fast
become one of the country's most immediately familiar
and increasingly popular TV faces, hosting a score of live or
"as-live" magazine and current-affairs programs. . . . In August 1987, when London Weekend Television started its late-
night youth magazine program, . . . Emma Freud was an obvious choice for one of the program's more outré features. And
Freud undoubtedly will find herself hitched for many years to
come to the talk show she hosted every weekend for* Night
Network, *taped "as live" in the afternoon ("absolutely no cuts
whatsoever") and broadcast to the nation at 2:30 A.M. Which
is not to imply that the improbably successful* Pillow Talk, *in
which she interviewed her guests in bed, should be anything to
be ashamed of.*

     —*European Travel and Life*, July/August 1989

Freud felt ripped-off by a prevailing Marxist "world view" that only socioeconomic relations determine the course or cause of human aggressiveness and oppression. And Freud was skeptical not only because this party-line had cut off desire but also (and more importantly) because its program could never deliver the group from the auto-destruct course set by unconscious remote control. Ideology to ideology: Freud countered that even under the most benign economic conditions the psychic inside of socialization would disrupt, on the outside, global achievement of "mutuality."[1]

Identification and consumer projection keep class membership in line with what stays on the line: the primal, Oedipal past. The Marxist take on socioeconomic or class relations does not take: the superego has been left out of the picture.

> Mankind never lives entirely in the present. The past, the tradition of the race and of the people, lives on in the ideologies of the superego, and yields only slowly to the influences of the present and to new changes; and so long as it operates through the superego it plays a powerful part in human life, independently of economic conditions. (*SE* 22:67)

With the superego in the front of the line, the inventions and installations of at once media-technological and military provenance have over and again, Freud insists, determined historical events. The range of superegoical thought control has ever expanded, on automatic, from combat zone to combat zone. And in the wake of each military expansion: the work of mourning—of analogy—plugs the automatic course of media technology back into a prosthetized and consumerist sensorium. From the outer limits of this newly extended sensorium rebound the ghosts (that is, the recycled death wishes) that continue to exercise within mass media culture the remote control which jams the lines of class war. And while Freud allowed that the Marxist experiment might be realizable under the improved conditions that new inventions (and wars) would create—and here we find Herbert Marcuse's post-holocaust and California-bound utopianism already advertised—Freud nevertheless wagered, for his money, that even within new improved types of social community "human nature" would continue to assert itself as out of control (*SE* 22:178ff).

Freud thus forecast that the new front of total war would challenge Marx-based views of social change by installing itself deep down and for keeps in the relation of self to other. Since the declaration of total war no one can be trusted; complete loyalty must be required and enforced. When the other speaks of love and respect but will *not see* (Nazi) you: take no prisoners and never agree to be friends. The political front of psychoanalysis re-emerged in the Frankfurt School's realignment of its Marxist commitment with the Freudian rereading of mass culture. The Frankfurt School was p.c. It began working out (on location) the delegations and phantasms conducting total war within a mass media culture ruled, on two fronts, by the (forgetting of the) "ideologies of the superego."

According to Freud, the very classes that Marx had enrolled for his dialectical materialism were the competing hordes in primal time zones that triumphed or lost out depending on the power and range of one side's inventions. More recently, World War I was already in or on the air with the first takeoff of an airplane. The battle for control of the airwaves had commenced. By World War II the battle lines of thought control had shifted along an inner topography of propaganda. According to Nathan Leites and Ernst Kris, the highly charged or hot involvement of World War I populaces in sensationalist propaganda shifted down, during World War II, to cool audience participation in propaganda broadcasts of information programmed for the gadget lovers of total war. Between the wars institutions of propaganda had changed the direction of their appeal: the first time around the headlines bore the address of id and superego; the second time, second by second, the ego was the rapt receiver of the news. In other words: "the first World War was 'less total' than the second. On the other hand, the media of mass communication were less developed; radio . . . had hardly been tested."[2]

Kris and Leites argue that, in sync with the development of mass media, group psychology has taken a turn toward "privatization," that retrenchment of family and individual comparable, in its open invitation to phantasms of deprivation, to narcissistic regression. Since via "projective distrust" the privatized individual can retrench himself far enough away from any threatening appeal, totalistic propaganda must attract participation through informative broadcasts rather than through fear. Even Nazi propaganda filled prime time with the statistics of war; its terrible myths had to be readdressed to future generations. On the outside: the World War I cult of cinematic projection (and hallucination)[3] was installed in the home where the bond of total war has turned everyone into participants in front of radio or TV. On the inside: totalization from war to war has led to the mastery of an ego constitutively perverse, that is, all-powerful, allied to an immortality plan or insurance policy that Freud called the death drive and Jim Jones called White Nights—the synchronization of death. The "live" participation of the entire population in total war fulfills a phantasmatic wish (of the ego): to fastforward beyond the aloneness of one's own death to the death of all at the same time.

Freud's ultimate model for the unconscious—as it keeps always in some other place—was to be on the phone. But for Freud these calls belonged to the deregularized competition of long distance carriers called transference (at one end of the line) and at the other telepathy. But what remains outside Freud's reception: the phone call also contributed to and participated in TV's invention of "liveness" (which one of television's first names, "seeing telephone,"[4] indeed commemorates).

The question of television is the rerun of the debates between a Freudian focus on ideologies of the superego and a Marxian adherence to socioeconomic developments. Raymond Williams, for example, divides the theoretical reception of television into two approaches, one deterministic, the other symptomatic. Both accomplish, under the cover of the narcissism of their small differences, the ideological decontextualization of TV (which in fact remains, Williams claims, in a complexly mediated relation of dependency on social processes). By implication—and this inward turn is conveyed up front by Williams's rejection of McLuhan's recasting of technical media as psychic functions—the Freudian consumerist perspective is condemned as ideological (indeed, idealist): it schedules the broadcasts of the psychic apparatus prior to the time zone of capitalism's social effects.[5] But when Williams reminds us that it "is especially a characteristic of the communications systems that *all were foreseen—not in utopian but in technical ways—before the crucial components of the developed systems had been discovered and refined,*"[6] he unwittingly slides psychoanalytic rereading (which alone can theorize this constitutive delay in the invention of techno-media) into the first place he had reserved for social context in the contest with the psychic apparatus.

The metaphoricity of noise and waves had to go to no lengths before finding an outlet in technical media;[7] it reserved a place within discursivities for the invention of devices that matched on the outside the psychic apparatus Freud built on both sides. But media-technology was already in place inside the unconscious only to the extent that Freud discovered and constructed it via analogies with techno-media. The postponement or repression of the advent or invention of machines (which were already in the ready position within discursivities) thus yielded, coconstitutively, the unconscious of the same psychic apparatus it had also assembled.[8]

In *The Interpretation of Dreams* the unconscious, preconscious, and conscious were modes of "attention" determining the reception of one apparatus. But Freud's first theory of dreams, complete with a premier analogue with a technical medium (the telescope), ruled out the prospect of conscious reception of the inner workings of the apparatus.

There are, then, systems at work—"like the lenses of the telescope that project the image"—that we must assume, but since they are in no wise psychic, cannot perceive (*SE* 5:610ff).

Thus the media-technical apparatus is, irreducibly, the psychic inside. But already in this early mediatization of the psyche in terms of primal television, Freud's installation of censorship between systems, which he compares to the "refraction of rays upon transition into a new medium," in fact announces the switch on of another medium, newer than the telescope but older than TV. By the time Freud discovered within the delusions of Ratman and Schreber endopsychic perceptions of the functioning of the psychic apparatus, only analogues of projection or haunting—at once media-technological and archaeological—crowded "screens" Freud had already set up in the *Project for a Scientific Psychology*.

The work of metaphor—of mourning—remains the motive force driving psychoanalysis and the mass media society it discovered into interchangeable places. The contemporaries of this drive who chose to resist psychoanalysis while developing their own scientific research project(ion)s could not but repeat Freud's analogical hook-up of technology and the unconscious. Hugo Münsterberg interpreted cinematic techniques—close-up, cut-back, and cut-off—as the externalization of mental processes (attending, remembering, and association via suggestion). "It is as if reality has lost its own continuous connection and become shaped by the demands of our psyche."[9] Staudenmaier developed in competition with psychoanalysis his "science of magic" which he based on auto-induced possession or hallucination. He concluded that hallucinations simply reverse the process of reception—which is how the sensorium regularly functions—and render it in turn a process of production: that which can receive impressions can also produce them. And Staudenmaier's proof or model for such a production of hallucinated impressions: telephone, telegraph, gramophone, and cinematograph. The enigmatic force of endopsychic projection continues to this day to fastforward every departure from or return to Freud to the most modern of frontiers. Transference shrinks or expands into this mediatized transfer. Beyond the Oedipus/Hamlet couple psychoanalysis discovered the group—whose reliance on techno-media switched on the identificatory friendliness it advertised. The politicization and remediatization of psychoanalysis admitted modern mass culture: its prehistory was covered by the Christian mass, its invention (and denial) was hailed in Nazi Germany, and its primal future was already on the line—in America.

The Lang Goodbye

Fritz Lang, who considered his own role as film director comparable to the one landed by a psychoanalyst, framed his double oeuvre (both the German films and those of his exile in California) with the Mabuse phantasm, which consists of the underworld or gang, unmourning, and media-technologized thought control. Lang was a medium that sleepwalked and sleeptalked with the same assurance that Hitler boasted of when it came to forecasting trends. But by the time Goebbels invited Lang to be official director of Nazi propaganda films (while at the same time banning *The Testament of Dr. Mabuse* for *not* including reference to the Nazi takeover), Lang was so freaked by his equal access to the same wavelengths that he split the scene. (World War I traumas inspired both Lang and Hitler to become mediums or media; while Lang was pushing painted postcards to support his pursuit, against his father's wish that he become an architect, of the art of painting, Hitler sold hand-painted postcards to finance his own artistic vocation; while Lang's turn to film would achieve a displaced following or negative representation of the paternal order, Hitler's eventual career did the same to his own father, who was on the Austrian border patrol.)

The film that sent Lang off to California *(The Testament of Dr. Mabuse)* was the synchronization of Siegfried Kracauer's Californian thesis (in *From Caligari to Hitler*). The relations of phantom teleguidance which German Expressionist film put on display converged in 1933 with the political rebound of their paranoid prophecy. The traumatic shock that shut down Mabuse—an encounter with ghosts designated comparable by the psychiatrist in charge of the case to the impact of an earthquake—releases (Staudenmaier-style) a seismic re-eruption of gadget love. The incessant writing which locks Mabuse—like Kris's 1933 schizo patient—onto the beam of remote control, reanimates a "dead brain" and places in charge of the energized braindead a name which is cut off around the good or bad breast *(Buse)*.

After the war Lang slides back to Germany to make another Mabuse movie—and his final film. He was asked to do a remake of *M.* or of *The Testament*. Instead he made a new Mabuse film which he circuited through more current technologies while at the same time modeling it on a 1940s Nazi plot of hotel surveillance. The end of his oeuvre, which he left in Germany (he died sixteen years later in California), shows his 1933 prophecy to have, by 1960, survived and outlived its self-fulfillment, at which point it lives on (in *The Thousand Eyes of Dr. Mabuse*) via TV monitors and atomic bombs. Lang keeps the live transmission of TV directed at its primal function: surveillance. TV achieves what was only projected in films; Soviet avant-garde film and Lang's own Expressionist cinema *(Dr. Mabuse the Gambler*, for example) had aimed at TV simulation through and in spite of the sutures and lines of defense brought to us by identification and projection which, on the silver screen, still remained legible and hence still within range of substitution and mourning. Thus in the midst of multiple coverups of every exchange and substitution that goes down in the counterfeit economy of *Mabuse the Gambler*, the four-part scan of some crook's exemplary biography includes a gap of noncoverage (between 1912 and 1919) which releases, by metonymy and absence, the encrypted loss of World War I.

If life is a gamble—as the 1922 *Mabuse the Gambler*, which Lang advertised as a total representation and surveillance of society, proclaims—then the cheating and counterfeit which the criminal/funereal underworld would realize under Mabuse's direction, aim at a simulation of life, an insurance against death which devalues the life that must be risked in the game of living. Freud warns against the consequences of overinsuring life against the losses and dangers that are risked with invention, discovery, or inheritance. Adolescent group protection and preparedness—or "American flirtation" (*SE* 14:290)—replaces the gamble of living with a dating game of interchangeable parts. Even the more European approach—of date rape—runs up against what Lang in 1920 entitled "tired death."

In *The Thousand Eyes* television installs in the encrypted place of cinema—in the alternation between identification and projection with which the 1933 film was still coextensive—the "mosaic" penetration to every disparate space. Lang's pre-war, pre-TV Mabuse legacy had already disbanded the linear hierarchical arrangement of control or surveillance but at the same time still borrowed from its economy in the search for some hidden place that had before (before the film's projection) remained hidden, out of view (the catacombs in *Metropolis*, for example, or, in *The Testament*, the behind-the-veil or crypt dimension of the basement room where Mabuse's orders are communicated). Within the pre-TV economy and technology of work of mourning, it still proved necessary (or possible) to uncover the arresting place of an unacknowledged loss and thus bust the ghosts for which it was the (internal) medium. In the race sublimation loses to repression, the baton is passed to simulation (or complete surveillance) which wins the speed race against identification/projection (which was heading the same way). "Electric speeds," McLuhan writes, "create centers everywhere."[1] But, as in Staudenmaier's decentralization of his own psychic unity, the "speed up in communications always enables a central authority to extend its operations to more distant margins."[2]

The Mabuse figure always held the place of the body lost to technological extension and acceleration. In *The Testament* the media-technological underworld or death cult embodied the enigmatic force and automatic course of the (maternal) Mabuse name. When the law discovers the secret name, it at the same time finds it on the tag of a corpse: but the name's body lives on as the cinematic underworld. No one gets out of the gang—alive; which means that the gang keeps alive. Thus the greater or pumped up body of the gang or group, which comes complete with maternal association, is the social form of living in the sensurround which, primally speaking, Mabuse's embodiment of unmourning at the same time founded.

The TV monitors of *The Thousand Eyes of Dr. Mabuse*—which penetrate not only various spaces or rooms, events or scenes, but even the different points of view into which each take can be broken down—bring us to the dream screen on which one can no longer properly distinguish between eating and being eaten, watching and being watched. Lewin was right to schedule autocannibalism for his dream screen. But if we are eaten at the same time as we eat (since, for example, we swallow our own saliva), excreted at the same time as we excrete, smoked as we smoke, then the property boundaries Lewin would uphold cannot hold. Thus Lewin's attempt to preserve a one-way identification symptomatizes a refusal that a certain inability to swallow or breathe also shares. On the screen beyond transference omniscience is redistributed via a "live" surveillance from which any single perspective or centralization must recede to accommodate, at the same time, the vaster range or body to be controlled. The greater body of the group, pumped up in the work out of unmourning, shreds the wake of pre-TV paternity's withdrawal.

1936–1958

In his 1958 report on the links and limits of transference—"The Direction of the Treatment and the Principles of its Power"—Lacan makes fun of American ego psychology as personified and subscribed to by Ernst Kris. It was the day following Lacan's address on the mirror stage at the 1936 Marienbad conference. "I took a day off, anxious to get a feeling of the spirit of the times, heavy with promises, at the Berlin Olympiad. He gently objected: '*Ça ne se fait pas!*' (in French), thus showing that he had already acquired that taste for the respectable that perhaps deflects his approach here,"[1] namely, in the case study Lacan has just realigned according to a transference Kris had overlooked.

One feature of the 1936 Berlin Olympics to which Lacan traveled as though on some tour of the collective unconscious ("spirit of the times"!) beams back the telecommunicative origin of a new improved kind of transference. The Berlin games were the first televised sports event, the first in a series of primal time broadcasts that counted a late arrival in the moon landing. Thus in the interview entitled "Television" Lacan assigned the moon walk to the place "where thought becomes witness to a performance of the real, and with mathematics using no apparatus other than a form of language."[2]

Largely forgotten beneath the monumentalism of Leni Riefenstahl's cinematic projections but also set up at the games were, as another eyewitness put it, "far more bulky cameras. Some looked like long white cannons. . . . All this photographic apparatus was intended to channel electronically devised pictures into eighteen new television halls *(Fernsehstuben)* in Berlin."[3] But this historian of the Olympics misses the historical change or chance that television introduced when he refers to its apparatus as "photographic." As a scholar of television put it in 1953: "there may be advantages in television's claim to immediacy: namely, that what is being viewed at the receiver is occurring *now* at the transmitter."[4] In contrast to the photographic and cryptological analogues through which Freud routed transference, an element of live transmission had thus been introduced.

At the intersection of discourses and forms of language that launched "the advent of the real, that is, the moon landing" Lacan places television on the side of every other audience he has addressed, thus including television's "liveness" within the transferential sense of audience that his seminars demand: "there's no difference between television and the public before whom I've spoken for a long time now, a public known as my seminar. A single gaze in both cases: a gaze to which, in neither case, do I address myself, but in the name of which I speak."[5] Thus sliding from the video to the audio portion, Lacan must alter, indeed, animate (in the name of that which appears as dead as "live") the answer which the TV interviewer's question had already preprogrammed:

> That's a question that might well be understood as being about your wanting to be able to answer it,

yourself, eventually. That is: if you were asked it, by a voice rather than by an individual, a voice inconceivable except as arising from the TV, a voice that doesn't ex-sist, because it doesn't say anything, the voice nonetheless, in the name of which I make this answer ex-sist, an answer that is interpretation.[6]

The funerealization of TV that flickers even in Lacan's reception is symptomatic of its untenability and inconceivability within psychoanalysis. TV must be assimilated to filmic phantomization if its broadcast is to tune in on transference (or telepathy) sets. But what is instead accomplished is the Lacanian takeover of the endopsychic sensurround which current (standard) theoretical reception recasts in terms of TV structures of desire and the gaze: "for it is a derivation of the signifying chain that the channel of desire flows, and the subject must have the advantage of a cross-over to catch his own feed-back."[7] The decade of spectacular exclusions from psychoanalysis—the fifties—covers the period of television's society-wide installation. The cases of Lacan, Wilhelm Reich, and Jung (whose work on flying saucers earned him a second exclusion) must be reevaluated in terms of the ongoing rejection of television by psychoanalysis.

It met with this total rejection because, again, psychoanalysis had already reserved or admitted a place for TV. The recycling of contents and persons among sets or sitcoms, the closed-circuit coextensivity of what takes place on and in front of the tube—the way one sees oneself being seen or finds oneself in situations that might as well have been programmed—could all be analogized with Freud's original (telescopic) conception of the dream as the rerun of daytime trivia thus openly and simultaneously displayed or repressed. TV alone realizes the "timelessness of the unconscious" which had been otherwise inconceivable within the available discursivities at the time Freud was forced to keep it a mystery and unconcept. TV's constant pull into a self-reflexive interior that is at once its topological surface realizes as "liveness" or "timelessness" the self-conscious paradox which the novel endlessly talked about from its origin on and which film would get around only to document. ("The Jack Benny Program," for example, often pretended to represent the rehearsals for the episode being broadcast.) But the analogues Freud chose to turn to and turn on belonged to the photothanatographic register.

It is as though TV attempted to conduct transfer without transference or without translation. Philo T. Farnsworth, whose contribution to the invention of TV was the dissector tube which to this day replaces the original scanning device in the receiver, was raised as a member of the Church of Jesus Christ of Latter-Day Saints. Perfected by 1936, Farnsworth's dissector shares an origin with the shredding device that guards the Mormon faith: the original Bible which Joseph Smith discovered untouched by translation was, once he transcribed it, lost without remainder. The dream guiding Farnsworth's invention tunes in his faith's "live" broadcast—via the at the same time repressed detour of recording:

> He believed that thought was a manifestation of electricity and that if we had electrical recording instruments of sufficient sensitivity, an accurate record of human thought could be made. He went on to visualize how whole libraries would be electrically recorded; young people would be put to sleep by some drowsing process; . . . they would then be given a liberal education in the course of a week or so of sound slumber, during which facts would be recorded in the subconscious mind for use in the art of living.[8]

Siding with psychoanalysis, Adorno rejects TV's "art of living" as the cover its programming of the unconscious assumes. At the living end of "liveness" Adorno sees only a norm of killing time in front of the television set. Constant, addicted viewing corresponds to the unceasing expenditure of unconscious psychic energy accompanying the effort to keep that which must not enter consciousness in the unconscious (the unconscious being, on another side of analogy, the all-pervasive TV medium).[9] Thus, Adorno continues, the belief that TV achieves the "authentic impact" of the emergence of the collective unconscious confuses that which has been sighted or brought into focus with the accent brought to bear on it. TV programming presupposes that America's completely open reception of psychoanalysis (in which Freudian, Jungian, or Lacanian thought structures are most amiably conjoined or collapsed) is already in place ("in reverse") inside and around consumers (513). Psychoanalysis was all along the only theorization of consumerism, of knowing in the self-reflexive mode: having consumed or known our (consumption or knowledge of our) environment psychoanalytically, we inevitably recycle this psychoanalytically organized knowledge back into the environment. In the endopsychic sensurround, only psychoanalysis gets consumed.

Within the primal one-on-one of consumerism—in front of the tube—dreams of omnipotence turn around, Adorno advises, into realized impotence: although utopias appear to tune in on the tube, the TV screen's sadomasochistic and miniaturist share in the funnies realizes utopias only by aborting any genuine and full-scale utopia in fact cherished by the viewers who have been bonded that much more closely to the curse of the status quo (516). In short, there can be no illusion of the "life-size" on TV. To abstract from the real size of a phenomenon, that is, to view it aesthetically and not naturally, requires a capacity for sublimation which cannot be presupposed for an audience which has in fact been weakened in this precise capacity by the culture industry—which issues sublimation requirements that cannot be met (509).

On TV we watch ourselves trying to conform. Thus assimilation literally renders us "like," "similar," or, indeed, the double we already are from the point of view of the one who controls us. Thus, following Schreber, we would be made over into or according to that which transference resists but transference-love propositions: the One.[10] At this absolute end of transference we will become what One thinks we are: the cute corpse that only comes (or goes) generic.

But TV reduces to repression in Adorno's account only because its "live" transference cannot be tuned in within the Freudian system. According to Beverle Houston, the maternal promise of endless, sourceless supply that television incarnates not only renders TV watching feeding time but also slides the viewer into the "mother position."[11] The multiple identifications, the slide from station to station, from fiction to fiction, assign the television spectator the place of the feminine subject as theorized by Freudian psychoanalysis. Television displaces models of succession by modes of simultaneity just as femininity—and (or as) perversion—embraces a simulcast of competing perspectives and stages which disrupts the phased sequentiality of sexual development.

Owing to the exigencies of master discursivities, new media technologies always succumb to repression before they achieve invention or distribution. Thus Lacan was right: every advent or effect of an apparatus is produced with no other apparatus than a form of language. Hegelian discourse, for example, outlawed the invention of the gramophone by placing an embargo on noise.[12] In the case of television a history of its invention is unavailable precisely because the component parts of its apparatus already existed as ready-made inventions at least by the eighteenth century.[13] Psychoanalysis contributed to this delay of TV's invention which Freud banished from the transferential context. The phenomena of "liveness" and simultaneity were nevertheless addressed by Freud when, on the sidelines of his system, he admitted, in theory, an exceptional status which he assigned to woman and pervert. In practice, this sideline phenomenon belongs to television. Thus if television lies outside the at once funereal and telecommunicative analogues with which Freud conveyed his discovery of transference, it at the same time turns on perversion which was left tuned out of transference. Indeed, perversion was conducted by Freud along the same track of analogy that conveyed transference. But the analogy otherwise reserved for transference, once it was set aside to convey the relationship between neurosis and perversion, could only be reprinted during divergent epochs of Freud's thought like the photographic cliché it addressed—always intact and undisclosed.

In "'Civilized' Sexual Morality and Modern Nervous Illness" Freud once again turned to one of the first analogues he forged out of reference to technical media to illustrate an unconscious relation:

> I have described the neuroses as the 'negative' of the perversions because in the neuroses the perverse impulses, after being repressed, manifest themselves from the unconscious part of the mind—because the neuroses contain the same tendencies, though in a state of 'repression,' as do the positive perversions. . . . The discovery that perversions and neuroses stand in the relation of positive and negative is often unmistakably confirmed by observations made on the members of one generation of a family. Quite frequently a brother is a sexual pervert, while his sister, who, being a woman, possesses a weaker sexual instinct, is a neurotic whose symptoms express the same inclinations as the perversions of her sexually more active brother. (*SE* 9:191–92)

A certain reception of *Totem and Taboo* seems already in place within the span of analogy that opens onto this family album in which the brother's sexual activity corresponds to the symptoms of repression in his sister. But according to this analogy which Freud later applied to the relationship generally obtaining between the conscious, developed thought and the unconscious, perversion becomes media-technologized only within the context of its relation to neurosis. But as the reversed image, shot, or negative it is neurotic thought or symptom formation that remains, within the context it shares with perversion, on the side of media-technicity, the death wish, and mourning. Neurosis or hysteria had indeed alerted Freud to the ancient pedigree of perverse impulses: under the cover of repression, perversion turns on the pinball displacements, orifice by orifice and zone by zone, of hysterical symptom formation. The discovery of the unconscious which Freud received from the discourse of hysterics is at once his discovery of perversion or, in other words, of childhood sexuality. Yet other words uncover the additional link which Herbert Marcuse found otherwise missing or unconscious within psychoanalytic pursuit always only of Oedipus: the link-up of perversion with primary narcissism and thus, according to Marcuse, with the utopian impulse.[14]

This slippage of perversion slides all the way to psychosis. The disavowal Freud addresses in "On Fetishism," for example, installs psychotic double vision inside perversion. The little boy who recognizes neither the mutual fit of his parents' genitals nor that the father comes into this fit owing to his greater maturity, has opted, via this double disavowal of the difference between the sexes and between the generations, for the illusion that his pregenital sexuality is superior to his parents' genital sex. This normal childhood illusion or preference becomes, at the adult end of development, the pervert's creed: like the masturbating child, the pervert cultivates pregenital sexuality by refusing the slide into the inferior position of breeding: a certain kind of development—really the concept of development—remains out of reach for the pervert who does not become or come like his father.[15]

Although the pressure is on to relocate the ego ideal (or the love relation) in the extra-incestuous outer world, this normal activity is no match for the fantasized perfection of the incestuous one-on-one. The sense of perfection the infant experiences on his own account and person—the oceanic feeling Freud called primary narcissism—is transformed into the ego ideal, which provides the institutionalized sense of perfection we carry with us or ahead of us as lifelong pursuit. Freud's analogue and model for this internal institution of censorship—which even broadcasts "public opinion" (*SE* 14:96)—was the radio. But a more direct connection between primary narcissism and the ego ideal belongs to the perversions which Marcuse, writing in California, thus aligned with the utopian impulse which would also circumvent the reality principle and Oedipalization.

Just the same, a close call almost installs radio reception inside the pervert. According to Hanns Sachs, even history-wide it took the same near-miss to delay the invention of the new technologies. Like the Californians Marcuse phantasmatically placed on the horizon of his cultural re-reading, the Greeks could delay their technologization only through the openly narcissistic rapport they reserved for their bodies (which they nevertheless built). Greek culture was accordingly based on an idealized rapport with perversion. The persecution fantasies of psychotics, which always feature media technologies, openly admit an incursion of prosthetization that the Greek or pervert prohibits via inhibition: "the schizophrenic hallucination and the inhibition of the ancients stand in opposition to one another as positive and negative poles."[16]

According to Freud, omnipotence of thoughts fuels the admitted invention of technology; thus the delay of the machine age is overcome in the exchange of body-ego relations (which cannot but become uncanny) for contractual relations turning on identification with some mortal other to whom one is bonded by death wishes. Thus a covert operation of narcissism is required to defend against the inevitable break-up of a merely—mirrorly—corporeal narcissism. The psychotic demonstrates in a flash just how media technologies emerge as the emergency projection of the missing body. "Defense against a narcissism which has become overwhelming causes the schizophrenic to create machines, even if only by hallucination."[17]

Although perversion would appear in its theorization to join psychosis somewhere over the transference, the transferential side or readability of perversion must nevertheless be situated inside psychotic delusions featuring an all-encompassing media-technological sensurround—in the missing place of transference. In a sense, then, perversion is the *negative* of *psychosis*. Also in the sense that the group structures Freud addresses from within his second system are at once psychotic and perverse.

In "'Civilized' Sexual Morality and Modern Nervous Illness" Freud argues that, because perversions are outlawed from the start, even the unambiguously perverse do not submit their passions to regular contact with the sublimating influences which safeguard reproductive sexuality. Within couplification culture the pervert may be on the conscious side of Freud's analogy but he is insatiable—doomed. He has more of a chance, however, within the group. The speed race between sublimation and repression, which Freud first discovered in the case of Leonardo da Vinci, is routed through the couple as (as long as sublimation holds the lead) a reproduction promotional. (Schreber's sublimation breakdown matched his couple's failure to reduce itself to or reproduce one heir.) But the race that repression wins (and the odds are in favor of this outcome) installs instead group psychology or gadget love within the couple. Sublimation both produces media technology (the superego) and subliminally veils every body's inside-out attachment to the outlets of technical media: sublimation's complete withdrawal into repression—in psychosis—unveils the prosthetic extensions.[18] But sublimation's reducibility to melancholic identification (according to *The Ego and the Id*'s redefinition, which reflects and absorbs the system-altering experience of total war) would seem to guarantee this ultimate, unveiled, inside view of our technologization.

While the neurotic is linked and limited, via his commemorative ambivalences, to literature, literacy, and the printing press—and to their visualizable extensions, photography and film—only the psychotic witnesses the media-technological institutions of "liveness." And although perversion may be the developed image of a negative associated with neurosis, its link to psychosis is conveyed via the mass-media analogues specific to group psychology which turn on this "live" transmission and broadcast—and turn around into devices of surveillance. The first TV programs self-reflexively crossed the line of consciousness to find themselves on the other side. But already on one of these primal programs from TV's prehistory, we find George Burns observing on his magic television what Gracie and the Mortons were plotting downstairs or next door so that he could then baffle them with his impossible knowledge. Ask the psychotics studied by Jung, Róheim, or Tausk: the "live" broadcast no longer surprises the person it watches—watch it.

1912/1936

J ung revs up for endopsychic orbit: The force that transforms or converts energy (as in the steam engine) also empowers humanity's analogy-making capacity. "Canalization" or channeling of libido was Jung's fix. He was into the "energy" of myth, machine, and user friendliness. When Freud offered a definition of libido for popular consumption, he called it "our capacity for love" (*SE* 14:306). But the I.D. he gave the public gave away the coming detraction of "libido" from Freud's systematizing takes on the fateful proximity of love and identification. Jung (and Lacan) decided to go for the libido; they applied its currency and energy to mythico-analysis of psychos who were folded out as models of group membership, gadget love, and teen passion. Libido or "love" was thus reserved by the post-Freudians for the machines it fueled.

The living body is a machine for converting the energies it uses into other dynamic manifestations that are their equivalents. We cannot say that physical energy is transformed into life, only that its transformation is the expression of life.[1]

In 1936 Jung plugged the conversion machine into a new medium of the beyond:

> There are two kinds of dictators—the chieftain type and the medicine man type. Hitler is the latter. He is a medium. German policy is not made; it is revealed through Hitler. He is the mouthpiece of the gods as of old.[2]

In 1933, at the technological end of this medium, Jung granted an interview on Radio Berlin.[3] The "special psychic emergency of the young German nation" had been left radically unattended: but Hitler was the "incarnation of the nation's psyche and its mouthpiece." "In times of tremendous movement and change it is only to be expected that youth will seize the helm, because they alone have the daring and drive and sense of adventure." And this adolescent vitality must be defended—against Freud:

> It is, you see, one of the finest privileges of the German mind to let the whole of creation, in all its inexhaustible diversity, work upon it without conception. But with Freud . . . a particular individual standpoint—for instance, sexuality . . . —is set up as a critique against the totality of the phenomenal world. In this way a part of the phenomenon is isolated from the whole and broken down into smaller and smaller fragments, until the sense that dwells only in the whole is distorted into nonsense, and the beauty that is proper only to the whole is reduced to absurdity. I could never take kindly to this hostility to life.

Jung's own adolescent predilection for equal rights, which set up Electra on the side of Oedipus, had led, by 1912, to the deletion of sexuality—that is, sexual difference—from his representation of psychoanalysis. He owed this sex change to "America." On the 1912 trip to America he found (or founded) a master/slave dialectic from which he would later borrow when it came time to analyze the emergence of National Socialism. In an interview that appeared in 1912 in *The New York Times* Jung had already exchanged psychoanalysis for the dialectic of recognition and desire.[4] Thus the self-control, refinement, and prudery of the American only covers for his deep brutality which finds its outside outlet in abstract thought: the Puritan forefathers "chose the greatest abstraction of all, the idea of God, and they sacrificed everything to that idea." The ruthlessness of abstract thought thus broke up families: indeed it drove the Puritans from their homes which is why they landed in America. In the meantime it is the "choice to master its machines or to be devoured by them," which renders America "the country of the nervous disease."

At closer range, however, the underlying brutality of the American is modeled by the black slave. "The slave has the greatest influence of all, because he is kept close to the one who rules him." White Americans treat black Americans "as they would treat their own unconscious mind if they knew what was in it." Thus the black race is "really in control." Jung does not stop short of the other slave who is equally in complete control: the wife. The American man "gives the total direction of his family life over to his wife. This is what you call giving independence to the American woman. It is what I call the laziness of the American man." American men "do not know yet how to love something which is equal to themselves. They do not know what real independence is, so they must kneel down before this slave and change her into the one thing which they instinctively . . . respect: they change the slave idea into the mother idea. And then they marry the mother-woman. . . . In America your women rule their homes because the men have not yet learned to love them." The denial or acting out of the generation gap was thus installed within the couple: whenever an American husband addresses his wife there is "always a little melancholy note in his voice, as though he were not quite free; as though he were a boy talking to an older woman."

The lean machines of adolescence (which model the male body at its most supple and feminine) end up charging woman with reanimation. In the eighteenth century (prior to the machine age and industrialization) machines were playthings and gadgets; they did not yet interfere with body-based narcissism. Once upon a time, then, androids and robots were designed and constructed with equal opportunity for both genders (although—no problem!—every built and displayed body is feminine no matter how you look at it). Once machines of labor are systematically introduced, body-based narcissism runs for the cover of its covert operations (via the superego), and gadget goes to literature which doubles henceforth (until film and psychoanalysis take over) as native habitat of the android and robot. But inside the retreat which the double thus beats to literature, the android grows exclusively female—and uncanny. Has woman been recircuited (inside out)? Was she made over as proof (just like the assimilated Jew in the eighteenth-century Germanic and proto-Californian culture of body-*Bildung*) that the technological is so in control of nature, reproduction, otherness that it's a natural? But she is also a cheerleader, amplifying her body via the group. Not to be confused with her reproductive capacity, woman can also be found on the side of the dead. Her technologization is circuited through her own narcissism. She needs the dead/dad to love her just as she needs a living child to absorb the loss and mourning another child occasioned (which her narcissism could neither admit nor commemorate). Thus made to order, she also models group processes—of psychoticization.

They Got Up on the
Wrong Side of the Dead

The internal track of an orbit Jung automatically repeats between Nazi Germany and America runs
through another 1912 tract—*Destruction as the
Cause of Becoming*—whose author, Sabina Spielrein, withdrew from public published reception with the prohibition
of psychoanalysis in the Soviet Union in 1936. (The invading
armies of the Third Reich finished her off.)

Before she became a Freudian analyst she had been
Jung's patient. It was in 1904 that Jung diagnosed the adolescent who would, in 1912, dictate the discovery of Freud's
second system. Jung was always the one responsible for
introducing endopsychic and psychotic cases into psychoanalytic theory. He turned Freud onto *Gradiva* and Schreber's *Memoirs;* in 1907 he published Spielrein's case as "exemplary," a ready-made designed for reproduction of the
Studies on Hysteria.[1] But Jung's diagnosis also named the
hybridization or gap within a hysterical constitution which

already surrendered the rights to Freud's second system, where her case is in fact on the line: she was classifiable, Jung concluded, as psychotic hysteric. What was also "exemplary," however, was the exchange of transferences that led at both ends of the line to "transference love" or resistance, which Freud was called in to referee. Only at that point was transference established—to the point of parachuting Spielrein into Freudian psychoanalysis. But already at her end of transference-love she dictated to psychoanalysis (in 1912) the concept of a death and destruction drive which was, it turned out—when Freud turned it in almost a decade later—the ticket to the second system.

What she shared with Jung right from the start, and what gave her her start in psychoanalytic speculation, was an occult rapport with psychosis. Via transference-love Jung shared Spielrein's fantasy of reproducing baby Siegfried who would reconcile Aryan and Semitic bloodlines. Her discovery of the death drive, which came in place of this new Christ, corresponded, Jung claimed, to his own—earlier—discovery of the "Terrible Mother," the premier embodiment of death.[2] But by 1909 the father introduced by Freud competed in Jung's thinking for this first place of impact upon the child. In 1949 Jung added that the demonic aspect of father covered every father's connection to the archetype: "The archetype acts as an amplifier, enhancing beyond measure the effects that proceed from the Father." But what he had deleted from this (third) edition to make room for displacement onto the archetype was the Freudian follow-up: "In my experience it is usually the father who is the decisive and dangerous object of the child's fantasy, and if ever it happened to be the mother I was able to discover behind her a grandfather to whom she belonged in her heart."[3]

While doing time inside the Freudian system, Jung kept the "secret" and trauma he had possessed already in early childhood: "My entire youth can be understood in terms of the secret."[4] The son of a reverend, Jung laid the blame on Jesus. Once he learned that certain persons "who had been around previously would suddenly no longer be there," that they would be buried, and that "Lord Jesus had taken them to himself," young Jung "began to distrust the Lord Jesus":

> He lost the aspect of a big, comforting, benevolent bird and became associated with the gloomy black men . . . who busied themselves with the black box. These ruminations of mine led to my first conscious trauma. (24)

While he would reserve this trauma for father figures, Christ was very soon exempt from the charge and chain reaction. The prayers Jung's mother declaimed with her son praised Jesus as the friend who saves one from Satan, who was the devourer featured in Jung's first remembered dream (at age three or four). (His mother recognized and named the phallic alien in the dream as "man-eater.")

> It was of a curious composition: it was made of skin and naked flesh, and on top there was something like a rounded head with no face and no hair. On the very top of the head was a single eye, gazing motionlessly upward. . . . The thing did not move, yet I had the feeling that it might at any moment crawl off the throne like a worm and creep toward me. I was paralyzed with terror. At that moment I heard from outside and above me my mother's voice. (25)

By Christmas 1912 Jung's Christ neurosis was in place: he had saved psychoanalysis—for American consumption—from Freud. A delegate from the 1912 dreams organized around Christ-identifications was a spirit control named Philemon who had sought out Jung as his medium. The resulting work of this ghost-writing team: *The Seven Sermons to the Dead*, which Jung published privately in 1925. Nandor Fodor, who discovered Jung's communication to the dead,[5] found the connection in Jung's *Memories, Dreams and Reflections* where Jung superimposes instruction of the dead onto his personalized rapport with psychoanalysis: "Quite early I had learned that it was necessary for me to instruct the figures of the unconscious, or that other group which is often indistinguishable from them, the 'spirits of the departed'" (74–75). Jung's specters were, like Staudenmaier's personalities, snapshots: since the dead only knew what they had known at the instant of death (of the shoot), they must return to learn from the living. Fodor gives an example:

> A sixty year-old woman-patient of Jung, in a dream two months prior to her death, found herself in the Hereafter before a crowd of friends to whom she was expected to give an account of her life on earth because the dead considered the life experiences of the newly deceased the decisive ones. (75)

But when Jung addressed the evidence of a spiritualist medium's successful communication with the departed in his 1899 doctoral thesis, his early show of interest was still a late arrival of the tele-rapport with ghosts which his maternal line beamed across the generations.[6] According to the diary of her own psychic experiences, Jung's mother Emilie already as a young girl had to protect her father (while he was composing his sermons) from disturbance and visitation by ghosts. Even the fifteen-year-old medium whom Jung studied in his thesis turned out to have been Jung's own cousin. The poltergeist session Jung put on for Freud to demonstrate his maternally charged "psychic-battery" power put Freud out, who fainted twice dead away. Freud identified (with) this occult power surge as proof of Jung's death wish against him. After the Fliess blowout, Jung became the current connection to the two missing persons who already laid the charges that were set to go off within each of Freud's friendships: Freud's brother Julius and his first (and perpetually teen) peer and pal John. The death wish Freud aimed in early childhood at his baby brother he also shared and acted out with his best friend. Jung would always deny the death wish Freud could thus only receive in his back. Jung was being nice when he shared with the popular press his recurring dream which featured Freud as the "ghost" young Jung had already "outmoded" (127).

Bottom Turns

Spielrein drove to the bottom of Jung's perfect face, threw an S-turn, and got totally tubed—inside the Freudian system. She rode out the Emilia effect, which was also a complex. The primal name belonged to her dead sister; it was also already in a haunted place in Jung's family pack. They were the teen team of an autoanalysis that Freud was the first to do (with John, Jung, and Fliess) over the dead body, name, and complex of Julius. What Spielrein rushed in 1912 to address in her thinking and theorizing—but without the mediatic and spectral connections that got her there—was the failure of the couple (forget the individual!) under pressure of the generic and psychotic structures of the group's psychology.

She was Jung's Dora: a teenage girl whose case modeled insights into adolescent psychology and female sexuality. But there is a primal connection that Jung could only cover in passing. As little one, Sabina, the eldest child, had been all-knowing goddess. Her decline began with her increasingly apparent inability to animate the golemesque creations she shaped and left behind: her younger sister Emilia died in early childhood.[1]

Her Emilia complex kept Sabina hungry for the total love or destruction she could receive only from the hands of the father. Libido or destrudo aimed at the outsider always doubled back along the incest track yielding to traffic with reanimation. In other words, she was a psychotic-transference junkie who could only be "born again" through a brother's caring and sharing. But even though Jung thus saved her from psychotic shutdown of all vital signs and support systems, to graduate from Jungian adolescence to the Freudian system she needed a symbolic and symbolizable father (or absence). She had always only known—right down to the psychotic autoanalysis with Jung—imaginary fathers or father *figures*, that is, brothers, who guided, loved, and destroyed her. On the way to becoming one of psychoanalysis's footnotes, the father's incorporation or penetration had to be (as in "'A Child Is Being Beaten'") reconstructed inside Sabina.

To this end she already had, as young child, put her foot not in her mouth but up her anus: in this way, until age seven, she protracted the pleasurable deferral of each bowel movement. Not in her mouth but in her father's hands: when her father beat her buttocks and then played her brother's backside, the dread hands of father took up and held together the strands of her progressive unraveling and reconstruction. As she sat at table she was forced to imagine everyone defecating; one look at her father's hands sent her into ecstasy. Soon she could not look without undergoing fits and seizures. She was doubled over with fear that she would suddenly up and fly away—or that animals or diseases would drag her down, down. The wish and warning that thus get represented on the way to psychotic breakdown: she must flee her parents whose loss, however, would keep her in the dark.

At the end of her transference-love affair with Jung,

Spielrein's father was able to congratulate his daughter on having slapped the man she had mistaken for a god. Her auto-analysis had come full circle within the Emilia complex she shared with Jung. What blocked Jung's own entry into the Freudian system was the double exposure to psychotics and occult phenomena which had empowered him to receive Spielrein's broadcasts. By pursuing a parallelism between psychotic delusion formation and that which myth advertises, Jung provided a context for Spielrein's auto-reconstruction: her wish to give birth to the hero Siegfried (and thus restore relations with the ego ideal) could thus be recognized and theorized.[2]

But she spent the missing nine months with Freud, whereupon she gave birth to the daughter/sister whom she finally got around to replacing and mourning. What helped Spielrein get over herself or her Emilia identification was a structure that with Jung she found herself repeating since it was already in place.

It began on Jung's side with his mother, Emilie, whose "uncanny" aspect (the loudspeaker in the son's earliest remembered dream announcing the phallic blob to be the man-eater) emerged, Jung recalled, "only now and then, but each time it was unexpected and frightening": "She would then speak as if talking to herself, but what she said was aimed at me and usually struck to the core of my being, so that I was stunned into silence." The stun-gun of this maternal self-relation was aimed at the father inside the son. In his memoirs Jung put his father only in silent pictures: "He was lonely and had no friend to talk with" (Wehr: 18, 20).

Before their couplification, which always remained open to friends and groupies, Jung's wife Emma had also been his patient: their transference-love was Emma's chance to write letters to Freud. There was no other father around. The passion that penetrates between Jung and his patients is displaced, via transference, onto a postal trajectory that slides Spielrein into the Freudian system, just as, via the Freud connection, it put Emma Jung through to the paternal position she occupied as defender of the couple (against the adolescent group or "all others" her husband was forever unable to "forsake").

Freud counseled Spielrein to bring her transference-love affair to a close by excluding "the third person": instead of inviting his intercession she should find, on her own, the "endopsychic solution."[3] Here we find in condensed form the difference or limit that Spielrein's discovery sped past while Freud observed it—even following the detour through his own "resistance"—before shifting into death drive. Before following Spielrein into the second system, Freud introduced the theory of phantom transmissions (like the one that gave Spielrein a headstart) which run, ultimately society-wide, on destruction drive. The spookulations of *Totem and Taboo* provide the "endopsychic solution."

Spielrein's *Destruction as the Cause of Becoming* was first published in the year of the endopsychic breakthrough which the appearance of *Totem and Taboo* repeated and rehearsed. On the outside, to give once again the two premier examples, Staudenmaier released his discovery of a science of magic while anthropology discovered the Melanesian Cargo Cult. In the course of inviting and receiving spirit possession, Staudenmaier formulated a "law of reversibility" for psychic processes that telephone, telegraph, gramophone, camera, and cinematograph (to borrow his analogues) regularly demonstrated or modeled; whatever receives impressions can also produce them.

According to mourning's law of reversibility, Melanesians had instantly recognized in the newly arrived white man one of their dead—but not, it turned out, one of their mourned dead. Under these emergency conditions the Cargo Cult was established and promulgated via epidemic hysteria or, interchangeably, states of possession which in turn invite the diagnosis of hysterical psychosis. According to Cargo Cult the white man had brought back from the dead the media-technological sensorium which was the outlet of his undeath. But the mourned dead of Melanesia had built the telecommunications devices which the white phantoms now kept for themselves while continuing to intercept the messages from the dead which the "talk bokis" had as their sole function or program to broadcast. Melanesians thus discovered that by blocking the work of mourning, the vampires controlled a mass-media death cult in which all must await, while waiting around, close encounters with the dearly departed. But since the return of these friendly ghosts would at once play back and erase the work of mourning or idealization to which they owed their internalized broadcast, the media-prosthetized vampire was only the harbinger of a return of death wishes which the technical media harbor and vouchsafe. (Thus in order to make room for the expected Cargo-bearing ancestors, all current possessions and properties must first be wasted.)

In 1912 Freud detected too much ambivalence too soon in Spielrein's personalized rapport with death: "I do not care a whole lot for her destruction drive, since I take it to be personally determined. She seems to carry more ambivalence than is normal" (March 21, 1912). But according to the owner's manual to the psychic apparatus, when it comes to drive power more ambivalence is normal.[4]

The references Freud deposited inside the footnote underworld of *Beyond the Pleasure Principle* have continued to attract recovery attempts aimed ultimately at undermining the foundations of a "Beyond" of—and belonging to— Freud's name. Delegates of the overlooked and underrated have recast psychoanalytic conceptions around primal scenes which hold the place, with each intermission, of yet another banishment into the Freudian system's own "unconscious." These corrective critics are always on the lookout: they see Freud when he's slipping, they know when he's a fake. But Freud gave us the slip.

When Freud for the first time embraces rather than merely combats the concept of primary masochism, he drops down to this concept's footnote and leaks the secret of another's priority: "In a seminal work richly diverse in ideas and content—which unfortunately remains not entirely clear to me—Sabina Spielrein has already anticipated a considerable portion of these speculations" (*SE* 18:55, n. 1). But does Freud accord Spielrein fair play only in name? By the time Freud fully admits the destruction drive or destrudo (in *Civilization and its Discontents*) he appears to have internalized the credits of what now proceeds only as his own projection: "I recall my own resistance at the time the destruction drive first emerged in the psychoanalytic literature, and just how long it took before I became receptive to it" (*SE* 21:120).

By 1920, the era of his own discovery of the death drive, Freud had taken a detour (around Spielrein's fast-forwarding of primal structures) through the primal habitat of ambivalence overload. This detour around Spielrein's anticipation and abbreviation of the death drive became—both historically and metapsychologically—part of the life-and-death theory of drives.[5]

The subject of Spielrein's trigger-happiness is an adolescent one (conjugated, that is, with the feminine and with the group): this subject affirms life in spite of (and via) the annihilation phantasms which, as in fast food, represent the satisfaction instantly to be got. The Freudian subject, who even within the second system is Oedipalized, can say no (to life) and thus withstand and sustain deferral of instant gratification. This one's the lifeguard; the other one is a total cheerleader.

Freud was the first always to arrive late: *Nachträglichkeit* in turn secured a past or context for psychoanalytic structures of thought endopsychically recorded and stored at every stage of a coterminous genealogy featuring the nuclear family and media technology. The missing feminine place of interminable mourning and, in group format, of adolescence turns on and conceals the connections.

Freud first addressed the Oedipus and Hamlet couple to determine, against the backdrop of primal man, the tragic dimension or blind date of modern neurotic thought: the couplification with an other who keeps always to another time zone. The work of mourning—the work of analogy— thus came to dominate the onset of Freud's recasting of the human subject; in turn, the death wish forged every pact or contract with the always ghostly other. But another Everyman, emergent within another coupling (of drives), would take shape or effect within Freud's speculations only upon time-release action. This other figure of thought, which Spielrein first introduced, was not of neurotic provenance, but was based upon her study of schizophrenics. Freud would in turn realize that the Hamletian schedule of hysteria did not cover the psychoticized society-wide track of Dostoevksy's neurosis. The post-modern or post-Hamletian man Freud profiled in "Dostoevsky and Patricide" is the side-effect of mass-cultural and group-psychological constitutions.

The Casting Couch

*T*here is no difference whatsoever between transference
onto the analyst and every other transference: insofar
as you give your personality you take in the personality
of the one you love.
—Spielrein to Jung, January 27/28, 1918

The grouping of concepts which Spielrein's destruction drive
proposes and presupposes follows the vampiric course
which transference can take. On transferential wavelengths,
as Spielrein admits in a letter to Jung dated January 6, 1918,
the thoroughgoing analysis of the unconscious either robs
the analyzed material of its energy or leaves it "drenched with
blood." This second option, the drenching or drinking offered a vampire, describes the way an analyst might, by
showing too much interest in his patient, encourage him "to
brood on his interiority and 'drench with blood' his wishes."

Now the demon, accordingly disguised, penetrates into the subconscious, where it enters into a compromise formation with 'higher tendencies'; this 'compromise formation' is the subliminal symbol which becomes ever more archaic, the contents of the individual consciousness metamorphose into those of the generic consciousness, the individual problems into ancient problems etc.

While Jung gets the prize for always following out the transference beyond the immediate context of treatment, Spielrein's description of the inward course of transference taking a wrong turn lights up all the props and counters of her pinball match-up of Freud's and Jung's systems. Her ongoing attempt to plug back into Freudian thought structures the psychotic-occult complex she and Jung had cohabited reinvents, at the convergence of sublimation and subliminal consciousness, the links and limits of the culture industry ("psychoanalysis in reverse").

Spielrein started out a follower of Jung's different way: the effects of sexual repression and its symptom formation could be viewed as simulacra symptomatic of another failure at the cultural level. Since libido was already so domesticated or acculturated that conflicts arose directly within cultural values, the suppression of a cultural aim or life goal would already be sufficient explanation for the development of a neurosis. Only when one of these higher goals cannot be achieved—the danger zone—does the Jungian advance drop back down into the Freudian system that such backfire alone fuels. The libido apportioned for the failed goal presses back into infantile or (same difference) phylogenetic regions and, at the same time, forms matching wishes which (since repression has set in) depend for their format on the unconscious. But, Spielrein interrupts the broadcast, Jung's subconscious and suppression do not replace or improve upon Freudian structures; instead Spielrein discovers in the options Jung proposes a supplemental zone of consciousness that would not be superimposable onto what Freud calls the unconscious.

"Since the symbolic lies in the character of the subconscious (subliminal) thought process," symbols do not pop up via repression or censorship (December 20, 1917). The phantasmic visualizations or "hypnagogic figures" one is prone to witness in states of exhaustion bring into focus the subliminal thought processes which convey conscious thinking once again, but this time around synchronized or advertised in symbols which are more general and archaic than their counterparts in conscious thought. The subconscious is the place of sublimations, which cannot be confused with the horrific remainders and false combinations that emerge from the unconscious.

In the afterglow of transference love the two missed each other—but Spielrein knew that next time they would take better aim. Thus she hangs out on Freud's side when Jung attempts to distinguish between the suppression of thoughts and that of feelings; Freud, Spielrein counters, excludes "feeling" from repression's target area: "there can be unconscious 'tendencies' 'wishes' (with the proviso 'as if'—the unconscious acts 'as if') actions etc. but no *unconscious feelings*" (December 15, 1917). For Jung, however, this restriction proves that Freud's "unconscious," if it is thus coextensive with the repressed, simply disappears upon being analyzed. But Spielrein asks, "can the repressed ever be analyzed," that is, completely analyzed—to the point of no return or remainder (January 6, 1918).

It is the subconscious which succumbs to the repression of infantile sexuality: "The tracks, however, which infantile instinctual life stamps within us, have not disappeared; there is constantly a back flow of energy onto these old tracks, and in this way sensations of sexual excitement are produced, the cause of which cannot penetrate into consciousness" (December 20, 1917). The surmounted infantile sexual wishes, since they have, owing to censorship, no access to conscious language, must also make use of the subliminal symbolic language. "But they would have access to subliminal language even without censorship since consciousness is only a fixed perspective which takes in relatively little. Censorship simply guarantees that these infantile wishes remain *unconscious.*" The unconscious remains "much more alien" than the symbolizing sublimations gliding beneath but ahead of conscious thought.

In Spielrein's own case, the subconscious gives comfort by answering as though future wish-fulfillment were posed (in dreams) in the form of questions: "probably yes" or "completely possible." As she confides to Jung, she always listens to these subconscious advertisements for delay while contemplating, often in dreams, her new-found rapport with music. Whereas in her psychoanalytic work she must always overcome (even her own) resistance, her rapport with music is instant and direct. When it comes to music Spielrein joins Jung and cops a special "feeling" of unambivalence. But direct connections to music put through resistance—to psychoanalysis.

But how to talk to your teen, who wonders (between earphones) just when after the rush toward and of completion is one free to like or dislike one's own musical compositions? The subliminal answer: first wait (January 6, 1918). "Decidedly we find in our subconscious warnings, hints and directional pointers for our future life" (December 15, 1917). In what she renames "sideline consciousness," now that she has dialed it within the Freudian system, the thoughts suppressed through the one-way conceptions of the "gaze consciousness" *(Blickbewusstsein)* are gathered together in proximity to the knowledge and symbolicity of the ancestors.

Is That All There Is?

The Freudian "demon" cheerleading the transference which has taken a vampiric turn is the projective aspect of the "enemy inside" who first dictates Spielrein's discovery, inside sexuality, of a destruction drive. It was woman's anxious rapport with the realization of her desires which revealed to Spielrein that every transference—and every couplification—must also give the destruction drive a turn:

> It is moreover a quite specific form of anxiety: one senses the enemy inside oneself, it is one's own passion which imposes upon one as constraint of necessity what one does not want: one senses the end, the transience from which one in vain would wish to flee into some unknown distance. Is that all? one would like to ask. Is that the highpoint, the climax, and nothing more beyond that?[1]

Is that all there is, Spielrein gags. Sex resembles nothing so much as organ transplantation—right down to the consequent doubling of antibodies onto foreign bodies. One sleeps with the other's death: destruction and reconstruction, which are always alternating alterations in an organism, turn over in the sex act on fastforward (10–11). Disgust is thus not a side effect of the proximity of sexual orifices and excremental outlets, nor does it develop the *Negativ* which abandonment of sexual activity signifies: it is a feeling that corresponds to the destructive component of the sexual instinct (11).

The interchangeability of pleasure and pain (or disgust), which master-mixes sexuality with destruction, is always a question or effect of timing. "According to Freud the unconscious is timeless to the extent that it consists only of wishes which it represents for the present as realized" (59, n. 3). Spielrein synchronizes the Oedipus complex by dating the timelessness of wish fulfillment "for the present" diachronically in terms of a notion of generation that goes beyond the two sides of just one gap. First, Spielrein argues, there is, psychically, no present experience: an event or experience becomes emotively charged—immediate—only to the extent that it has triggered feeling-laden contents experienced earlier and now stored in the unconscious. All that is transitory is thus only metaphor for some unknown primal event which is on the look out for analogues in the present. Spielrein lip-synchs the awesome closing lines of Goethe's *Faust* in which life totally tubes death. But doing some lines that gave Goethe this intense conclusion, she goes back to "the mothers" "to determine the primal terminal through which all communication must pass" (12). Spielrein wears leather when doing and downing the allegorical character of the present moment inside Faustian desire—the pleasure to be had at the moment from which it slips away:

> Pleasure is just the affirmational response of the ego
> to these demands springing from the depths and we
> can take direct pleasure in unpleasure and in

pain. . . . So there is something deep inside us which, as paradoxical as it a priori appears, wants this self-hurting, since the ego responds to it with pleasure. (16f)

Spielrein slashes the wavelengths beyond "the life of the ego which seeks only pleasure." In the normal crowd an ego develops when one "complex" displaces the others in competition for priority. But the schizophrenic is ruled, on all sides, by the complete collection of non-superimposable complexes: in one corner the generic psyche, in the other the ego psyche. The terms of the contest: the generic psyche would render ego conceptions impersonal or typecast; the ego psyche defends itself against such dissolution through the inadequate affects of the patient who, on the verge of psychotic breakdown, anxiously affixes the ego to some peripheral association onto which he has displaced the "feeling tone" *(Gefühlston)* of the retreating complex. Even the afflicted sees that the feeling tone does not correspond to the thought structure onto which it has been transposed. Depression thus gives way to uncanny role modeling: his every thought is made for the patient. The down side, from which such thoughts are the release, already replaced "I" with "we" or "they." Psychotic patients, on the other side of breakdown, "no longer take anything personally" (21).

The turn-over of shifters swings typical or primal generic representations into the place of ego-differentiated representations. Such affectless representations (which shape whole nations) pull up contents that are always along for the drives (21). But the generic psyche also brings us, through denial, the discarded ego psyche's comeback: the sunken ego particle reemerges—more glorious than ever—decked out in new representations (a rebound readily observable in artistic production) (22).

Since regression within the ego always leads back to infantile experiences: why, Spielrein asks, should we not automatically only become what we are, why do we not always repeat the same experience. But alongside the wish to remain there is also a wish to improve or transform oneself. Thus an individual representation is dissolved within one that resembles it, one that moreover dates from some ancient past. In place of the individual wish, a typical or generic wish emerges which is projected outward by the individual—for example as work of art. One searches for that which one resembles (one's parents or ancestors) in which one's own ego particle can be dissolved gradually, controlledly, and by imperceptible degrees. What else can this dissolution signify—but death (22).

Everything that moves us presses to be communicated to an other whose understanding and participation is desired. While every representation is the product of differentiation of primal experiences which constitute our psyche, it remains conscious and individual—as long as the other does not receive it. But once the other has tuned in, the consciously advertised and produced impression, which belonged to one individual, is processed unconsciously and sent to "the mothers," where it is dissolved. The unconscious provides the mythic props for restaging the individual present impression. This remake on unconscious channels is sponsored by words—the symbols which render generic the personalized labels of individual experience (23). Thus the personalized is undone by language: communication submits the personal to unconscious generalization or mythification which replaces it, makes it replaceable (23). Thus myth is love, the ultimate object of love (291). In love one has survived oneself and now turns back toward life—toward the witness, neighbor, or friend one likes to be like.

Every representation seeks out not identical material but that which is similar; similar material provides the basis for the other's understanding and reception of the individual's representations. We like our friends because they (are) like us. The feeling of sympathy which understanding always produces leads, in those so inclined, to sex or, in other words, to the point of surrendering ego to other. For the ego this is the most dangerous phase of the procreative drive; but it is accompanied by ecstasy since the dissolution takes place via the lover who looks like you. And since you love in a lover the parents whom you resemble, you really want to experience the "destiny of the ancestors, specifically the parents" (24). One is thus destined to experience in love one's genealogy, with one's parents at the front of the line. Sexual experience is therefore a program predestined for reruns; these experiences—internalized and projected outward through the look-alike contests with ancestors—can by chance achieve activation and thus get the complex satisfaction. Otherwise, and more frequently, they remain in the psyche as coming attractions and releases which, barring the outside chance of release, induce tension. This tension can only "release itself by unceasingly releasing the always once again supplemental analogous contents of mental representation" (24).

Endless release makes complete satisfaction completely negative: in the moment of merger with a predestined love object one is left psychically impotent. Every mental representation achieves its vital maximum the more and more intensively it must wait around for its transformation into reality: "with realization the mental representation is at once annihilated" (25).

But even realization of a mighty complex cannot make psychic life stand still; any complex is only one in a crowd of differentiations of primal experiences which continue to inspire ever more and new differentiation projects; these in turn are transformed now as acting out and audience participation, now as art. These transformed efforts of sublimation are, in terms of content, unopposed to the procreation wishes which have been adapted to reality. They seem opposed only because they are less adapted to the present and less differentiated. Such typical conceptions (Spielrein gives the example of love of Christ) are not annihilated through activation—it's not that kind of turn-on—but "persist in the psyche as the highly tensed yearning for return to the origin, specifically for dissolution in the engenderers" (25).

Likes or dislikes shift the balance between passionate love and desperate, sadistic hatred. This passion must destroy by exceeding the boundaries of self-preservation; each boundary or impediment further excites the passion which in turn seeks out more limits to transgress: it finds satisfaction only in death (only, that is, in the parents). Death fantasies join incest wishes not to punish, to represent interdiction, but serve to realize or represent the incestuous merger that is also—nothing is hotter or better—murder (39). The reruns of the Oedipalized program can be watched in sublimated phantasmatization in the form of nature worship or in religious symptoms.

Girl Talk

S pielrein allows that the exceptional place to which Jung would reduce and restrict—as untenable—the Freudian discovery of the unconscious is in fact attained by the pervert who alone could, conceivably, achieve "a relatively complete lack of repression": such a type would be capable of inflicting "the most awful things upon his parents etc. without the least resistance. And even in this case there could still be found in all likelihood a certain inherited contribution of the 'unconscious,' perhaps less as a result of 'moral' inhibitions, than simply on account of the instinct for self-preservation, which must, out of necessity, posit somewhere a boundary" (January 6, 1918).

Thus even the pervert must *become* what he is and like his objects to (be) like him. Even the "procreation drive" couplifies not two individuals but two antagonistic component parts; it is at once a drive of becoming and of destruction. Thus Spielrein destroys the bipolarity of the drives that

Freud on his scanner could also only bring into focus as already mixed. The blender that Spielrein switches on turns in the two directions modeled after the out-of-phasedness of couplified libido. In *Destruction as Cause of Becoming* she repeats what she first found rehearsed as her souvenir of her own parents: "He loves her, she is loved by him." "With the first tendency one remains subject and loves the outwardly projected object, with the second, one is transformed into the beloved and loves oneself as his object."[1] The second case, that of the coquette, is femininity's address where homosexuality and autoeroticism are cohabitants: "transformed into her lover the woman must to a certain degree experience herself in a masculine way, as the object of a man she can love herself or some other girl who embodies her fantasy personality" (32).

But the distribution of femininity among positions assigned by autoerotic fantasmatization also belongs to every child who, vis à vis the parents, must play a passive role: the child "must imagine how he is loved and must put himself accordingly in the place of the parents." Hostility can be discharged only by being turned against oneself. The enraged child pulling at his own hair is the logo at the start of everyone's development (33).

The range—rage—of the destruction conceptions and phantasms, which Spielrein covers, is held together by the masturbating hand. Autoeroticism fantasmatizes by turning around even (and especially) aggression. On one's own person misfired aggression triggers a reverse series of mental representations which has as target the cynical subject who abuses himself. By opening up the primal scene to multiple identifications and positionings, bisexuality (the counterpart in the couple to autoeroticism) guarantees that heterosexual coupling will be turned on, on both sides, by sadomasochism. When merger with a beloved other turns up the intensity of object representations, unalleviated self-love can lead to self-destruction or self-flagellation (33–34). Thus Nietzsche, who remained his life long solo recipient of his libido, orchestrated as dividuus what the couplification of sexual difference tends to obscure or close off between two individuals (29–30). Nietzsche's phantasm of becoming—his own mother—and giving birth to the Eternal Return shares a mass appeal of at once sadomasochistic and melancholic provenance (even "baby" Zarathustra is a dead person who must be born again) with traumatized soldiers and adolescent girls (who, in Stekel's precursor analysis, which Spielrein cites, dream of annihilation in order to affirm life).

In the first case Spielrein anticipates the post–World-War-I rereadings of wartime traumatic neurosis which would accompany the death drive into the Freudian system; she observes a chain reaction set off by the destruction of warfare which activates in everyone conceptions of destructive components even inside procreation. But if the neurotic in particular is thus incapacitated, he has also been waiting around for these external representations of his own destruction fantasies.

In the second case Spielrein follows Stekel's establishment of murder in the dreamed or waking imaginings of his girl patients as "a sex act strongly colored by sadism." A dream in which young girls witness themselves being knifed features not so much the "death of virginity" or the "life of the woman" as (once again) the sadistically shadowed sex act sticking it to the dream girls (26).

The teen girl dream of lying in coffins is a fantasy Freud decoded as return to the womb. Stekel sticks into this return the etymological resonance of the grave that includes, as the reversal of burial, the thrust of penetration. Up in the above (of displacement upward) the grave is a portal opening onto the after life. Spielrein observes her patient put through this connection to Christ, who represents the grave that gives life. In the patient's glass womb lie the bones of her stillborn baby; these bones must be among the ingredients used, in powdered form, for the making of another child (28). The dead child encrypted within Snow White's coffin thus shares the undeath or unbirth of Christ—the first child to exist (but only to exit). For Spielrein's patient the normal course of reproduction must be circumvented via the Christian crypt or crucible. Everyone has plugged into this terminal because the pressure is on—everyone—to bypass the unmournable death of a child. Sublimation's origin in melancholic identification must be absorbed (libidinized) within the couple: "for the normal girl" the double notion of burial (which Christ vouchsafes) gives great pleasure once she conceives of her dissolution with regard to, and inside, her lover (28).

Perversion is not so much the exception to the likeability principle as its ground (which it shares with femininity, traumatic neurosis, adolescence, music, and conversion). That which ticks off aggression and the mortality timer Spielrein discovered already inside desire and reproduction; in her own case it already doubled hysteria onto psychosis. Within Freud's second system, the group derives its (sexual) identity, psychology, and metahistory from a communion of identifications which the out-of-phasedness of the attractions constituting the couple (according to Spielrein's account of her own origin) attracts. The couple gets invaded by the group.

According to Spielrein, psychoticization follows out the genealogical track of group psychology: from mass-media culture to Christian mass identification all the way back again to the primal constitution of peer groups, the unconscious withdraws and asserts itself in the psychotic breakdown of the ego that must go generic. Spielrein's analysis skips around the Freudian distinctions which are still, however, implicitly superimposable onto her dialectic of psyches. The generic psyche coincides with the superego—but only within psychotic or group contexts. This superego of the group (which beams back ancestral identifications) was the only Freudian concept Jung could later acknowledge (in his work on flying saucers) since it could be readily replaced by the collective unconscious. Spielrein's ego psyche would belong to the couple, sexual love, or relations of difference with the ego ideal and superego—if the couple were not for her always crucified by undifferentiating identifications across the generations and sexes. In every couple only the drives get couplified—as sadomasochism. Where sexual love has been replaced by likeability and self-destruction, the superego and ego ideal, which no longer safeguard relations that make a difference, are merged with the ego through the maternal bonding of the group. The generic psyche is thus also the ego—as group member.

Giving Grief

Their God is Expression, and their spiritual counsellors are the Freudian psycho-analysts. . . . their exultant ecstasy—their mystic experience—consequently finds its only channels of expression in the processes of getting things, of social domination, and of sexual diffusion.". . . And there can be no doubt that the errors of the Freudian psychology (together with various popular misinterpretations of it, especially the popular identification of all self-control and restraint with repression) have vastly promoted this emergence of the waster mind to dominance.
—William McDougall, *Psycho-Analysis and Social Psychology,* 1936

Stanley Hall, who understood very little about neurosis, got me to investigate a man of his acquaintance whose agoraphobia was so severe as to make it impossible for him to earn a living. It turned out that he could not overcome a longing to be

supported by his father, who, incidentally, was a stern pa-
triarch. When Stanley Hall then asked me what he could do for
the poor man I jestingly replied "kill his father." Hall was so
alarmed that I had to assure him I had not made the same
remark to the patient.

—Freud to Hitschmann, November 6, 1935

A Freudian reception of the French Revolution is readily available through intellectual history: the authors Freud turned to in *Group Psychology and the Analysis of the Ego*— Trotter and McDougall, Le Bon and Tarde—had developed their sociopsychological advance previews of Freud's second system by interpreting structures of thought released in the name of the French Revolution. As Freud notes with regard to his select roster of precursors: "The characteristics of revolutionary groups, and especially those of the great French Revolution, have unmistakably influenced their descriptions" (*SE* 18:83). But because of the detours Freud had followed out before joining the lineup of earlier crowd theorists, group psychology came to him, ultimately, without model or manual. For while such cultural rereaders as Trotter and McDougall were on a direct line to crowd phenomena, Freud was putting through connections to primal time zones which would ring up a group psychology that Freud by then considered a challenge even to the Marxist interpretation and advertisement of revolution.

When Trotter in 1915 reviewed the contribution of psychoanalysis to the discovery of the "herd instinct," he made passing reference to Freud's notion of endopsychic perception.[1] But (like Spielrein) he thus named the difference or limit that his—or Le Bon's or Tarde's—discovery shot past while Freud stopped for it before shifting into death drive: the theories of haunting and mourning, of the death wish and media-technicity, determined Freud's delay on the way to his second system. The endopsychic analogies Freud borrowed from archaeology and media-technology—and, thus, both from his hysterical and his psychotic patients—accessed the unconscious structures of thought he discovered and the-

orized. The endopsychic connection between psychic apparatus and technical media sent Freud to the Coast and thus,
finally, to adolescent or group psychology. Psychoanalysis
"was there" when user-friendliness pulled up the Nazi past
on the (sun)screen of the future. The technological and the
cryptological are the parallel fast tracks along which the tech-
no-future unrolls. Germany (in the twenties and thirties)
and California (to this day) are the two fronts of total (suicidal) war installed within the group between self and other.

Blocking Trotter's view of an irreducible herd instinct
which thus did not follow the leader, Freud cast the leader as
primal and the individual as a group of one. According to
Trotter, every child's fear of solitude proved his notion of a
herd instinct that was as basic as the sex and self-preservation drives. But Freud viewed Trotter's interpretation of
fear as readily reducible to the unilateral relation to the
other. "The fear relates to the child's mother . . . and it is the
expression of an unfulfilled desire, which the child does not
yet know how to deal with in any way except by turning it
into anxiety" (*SE* 18:119). Something like herd instinct does
develop, says Freud, but only within the young child's relationship to siblings or rivals which skips the beat of mother-
and-father via a Big Brotherhood of friends.[2] But the contemporary or adolescent example of group psychology
which Freud inserts at this turn addresses only groupies:

> We have only to think of the troop of women and
> girls, all of them in love in an enthusiastically senti-
> mental way, who crowd round a singer or pianist
> after his performance. It would certainly be easy for
> them to be jealous of the rest; but, in the face of their
> numbers and the consequent impossibility of their
> reaching the aim of their love, they renounce it. Origi-
> nally rivals, they have succeeded in identifying them-
> selves with one another by means of a similar love for
> the same object. (*SE* 18:120)

Freud's multi-pronged reception of the crowd psychologies
that brought us the French Revolution proceeds from the

multiple outlet and significance, within psychoanalytic re-reading, of conversion hysteria. On the way, Freud tours the American outcome of revolution or conversion. Everyone's real nice and friendly but emptied out, like Schreber's "cursory contraptions," by unmourning. In "Timely Thoughts on War and Death" Freud diagnosed the modern tendency to retain loss in the form of irreplaceable relations as finding its symptomatic expression, at the devalued end of life, in "American flirtation." Society-wide distribution of melancholia is an American achievement; history-wide, therefore, American mass-media culture is the late arrival of Christian group identifications. "Very much later," Freud concludes his countdown of the monotheisms and the historical regressions they advance within the child's or youth's relation to father; "Very much later, pious America laid claim to being 'God's own country'"(*SE* 21:19). American piety, born again in the trail of intoxication's withdrawal, demonstrated the interchange between narcissism and narcosis which mass-media society must administer and contain. "That the effect of religious consolation may be likened to that of a narcotic is well illustrated by what is happening in America. There they are now trying—obviously under the influence of the rule of women—to deprive people of all stimulants, intoxicating and other pleasure-producing substances, and instead, by way of compensation, are surfeiting them with piety" (*SE* 21:49).

As reported to Joseph Wortis, who was Freud's didactic analysand for four months in 1934, the aside regarding the rule of women slides to the inside of Freud's ongoing critique of America. The out-of-phasedness of heterosexual desire—whereby the man's Oedipal love is attracted to the woman's pre-Oedipal bond with the phallic mother—achieves institutionalization through American college coeducation. The result: the extension of group or adolescent friendliness to marriages which should be bound by love to resist group bonding. Freud advises Wortis:

> There you see all the complex results. . . . The young
> men fall in love with the young girls and often marry

them, and in America the girls are usually much more mature than the men at that age, . . . and that is why you get your *Frauenherrschaft,* your rule of women in America. That is one main reason why you have the sort of culture you have in America, and so many other things. . . . Though the American woman is an anticultural phenomenon, she has her good points too that one must admire: she hasn't the European woman's constant fear of seduction, for example— but she has plenty of other faults. She is discontented, too.[3]

On the way to *Civilization and its Discontents* (on the way, that is, to Freud's second system) there has emerged an American rule of women in place of hysteria, which (at the group-psychological end of psychoanalytic investigation) can only be found missing. American women are not hysterical, they do not dread seduction, but they share a discontent which, within Freud's lexicon, covers the psychotic structures of mass psychology.

Beginning in the 1920s Freud charted a genealogy of these group structures—from mass to mass to mass—which pushed only the relations of identification. From Christianity to America all the way back to primal-time programming, the only pleasure to be had belongs to the phantom projection which takes pleasure—but only in the group membership's lack of enjoyment. But this legacy of religion cannot be readily neutralized since its broadcasts of belief or public opinion have already been installed as part of the psychic apparatus. Freud must therefore ventriloquate some opponent to his proposed disposal of religion in *The Future of an Illusion;* the dummy continues: look at the French Revolution's attempt to substitute reason for religion. Freud counters through reversal of charges: consider in turn the American Prohibition. "This is another experiment," Freud concludes, "as to whose outcome we need not feel curious" (*SE* 21:46).

In 1927, in response to an American journalist's interview with Freud, which had also explored Freud's views on the afterlife, American readers, who had their own opinions, sought an exchange. "Struck" by the interviewee's declared lack of interest in questions of survival after death, one American physician wanted to share with Freud the experience or fantasy of his own religious conversion. As recorded also by Freud in "A Religious Experience," the physician long ago glimpsed, while passing through a dissecting room, the sweet face of an old woman who had passed away. His thought upon seeing her: "There is no God." But when he returned home the thought was outblasted by another voice that tuned in from deep within: He had better consider (the inner voice was reported as saying) the step he was about to take. God having thus revealed Himself to him by infallible proofs, the American physician in turn felt compelled to urge Freud as his "brother physician" to remain open to the possibility of conversion.

But Freud had his Freudian ears on: the appeal to brotherhood doubly alerted him to the significance of the sweet-faced corpse awaiting dissection. Freud mentions in passing, in the Wolfman case, that whenever we call someone sweet we have already dropped down to the cannibalistic stage of development; and dissection, as Karl Abraham demonstrated in his interpretation of a melancholic's dream of his deceased wife, can represent bodily resurrection through incorporation: the cut-up parts are spliced together and reanimated through filmlike projections.[4] But dissection also demonstrates every physician's proximity, as Géza Róheim argued, to murder; healing repeats the primal crime of patricide, only stopping short of the final outcome which is exchanged for its cure.[5] In the case of the American physician, Freud attributes the sweet face to recollection of mother—whose death by proxy and imminent dissection, under another's control, replayed that primal scene in which father always has sole access to mother, who can only be brutalized in exchange. This indignation against the father—inside him—turned up the volume of protest that God did not exist. But since he was only repeating steps he took on the way to finding himself cornered and covered by the Oedipus complex, he soon encountered and succumbed to what Freud calls "a powerful opposing current." The current of conversion shortcircuits the impulse of protest and turns on reborn conviction—in the form, Freud concludes, of hallucinatory psychosis.

This incident doubles as contribution to a psychology of conversion on two counts: first, it showed how a determining event (of identification) caused "the subject's skepticism to flare up for a last time before being finally extinguished." Second, the hallucinatory psychosis which brought the born again impulse full circuit resulted from the transposition of an internalized complex to another sphere, that of the complex's projection. Insofar as projection conveys the body within what Freud called the "outer world"—to the extent, for example, that the ego, too, is ultimately a "projection of the body"—the psychotic disposition underlying the psychology of conversion repeats in marvelous condensation a mechanism that one year before the note on "A Religious Experience" was published Freud had abandoned once and for all (in *Inhibitions, Symptoms and Anxiety*) as too "obscure" (*SE* 20:112).

Within the first system, whenever it came time to link and separate the various disorders comprising the discovery of the unconscious, Freud always only touched down on conversion to pursue, along its boundaries, the more structural or grammatical aberrations of obsessional neurosis, anxiety neurosis, or even—even in the early days—paranoia. But this place of stop-over was also the main terminal of work in progress: only around the enigmatic mechanism of conversion could Freud first formulate, for paranoia, the unique mechanism of projection. "Paranoia must," Freud wagers in "Further Remarks on the Neuropsychoses of Defense," "have a special method or mechanism of repression which is peculiar to it, in the same way as hysteria effects repression by the method of conversion into somatic innervation." And indeed, Freud concludes: "In paranoia, the self-reproach is repressed in a manner which may be described as projection" (*SE* 3:174–75). This shift—around hysterical conversion—all the way to projection was already in place in *Studies on Hysteria* inside the notion of conversion that Breuer accredited within their joint account to Freud. Whereas on his own Freud despaired that "the formation of symptoms in conversion hysteria" would remain forever "a peculiarly obscure thing" (*SE* 20:112) or that its "leap from a mental process to a somatic innervation" would "never be fully comprehensible to us" (*SE* 10:157), for Breuer conversion posed no problem, owing to the metaphoricity that Freud's encounter with American religious conversion could also only plug into. But while in *Studies on Hysteria* Breuer attempted to limit the "comparison with an electrical system" (*SE* 2:203), he nevertheless found himself addressing only breakdowns or breakthroughs at points of resistance which, since they corresponded to wear and tear around matching points of "insulation of electrical conducting lines" (204), could be accommodated only within the system that had thus exceeded analogy to occupy interchangeable places with the psychic apparatus. This double apparatus is thus constructed around its breakdown: the primal scene of mental breakdown always opens onto a machine—that breaks down. "If the tension in such a system becomes excessively high," Breuer warns, "there is danger of a break occurring at weak points in the insulation. Electrical phenomena then appear at abnormal points; or, if two wires lie close beside each other, there is a short circuit" (203).

Hysterical reactions, by contrast, "are based on recollections which revive the original affect—or rather, which would revive it if those reactions did not, in fact, occur instead" (205). An original souvenir or image is thus relocated as decontextualized affect, corporeal image, or symptom. But with this insertion of the image the electrical system doubles on contact into a photographic or cinematographic apparatus. Indeed, it turns out, the system has all along been simultaneously recording every sense impression; that was why association was always burdened with the prospect of breaking through resistance. As

Breuer puts it: "Every sense-perception calls back into consciousness any other sense-perception that appeared originally at the same time. . . . If the original affect was accompanied by a vivid sense-impression, the latter is called up once more when the affect is repeated; and since it is a question of discharging excessively great excitation, the sense-impression emerges, not as a recollection, but as a hallucination" (208). Thus, in this premier account, trauma or its souvenir releases an original affect which, via conversion, finds—in place of the missing affect—transformation into a somatic phenomenon. Outside, on the somatic screen, we find right from the start among the many typical symptoms or signs brought to us by conversion: hallucination (which beginning in the 1920s would become the only remaining legacy of conversion's symptom formation, but by then largely available only within the psychotic's native habitat). What turns on conversion—and even installs in conversion the video program of conversion's own ultimate missingness—is the irreconcilability of equal ideas which alone can inhibit a course of association to the point of rendering psychical excitation pathogenic. "Such are the torments of religious doubt," Breuer concludes: "What are mostly in question are ideas and processes connected with sexual life: masturbation in an adolescent with moral sensibilities; or, in a strictly conscientious married woman, becoming aware of an attraction to a man who is not her husband" (210). Indeed this zone of the "first emergence of sexual feelings and ideas" which Breuer discovered and claimed for the unconscious—the period, in a word, of adolescence—is the first turn-on of a double conversion, which also gives woman a charge.

Teen Passion

I *t appears to be far more difficult to create a fresh conver-*
sion than to form paths of association between a new
thought which is in need of discharge and the old one
which is no longer in need of it. The current flows along these
paths from the new source of excitation to the old point of
discharge—pouring into the symptom, in the words of the
Gospel, like new wine into an old bottle.

> —Freud, "Fragment of an Analysis of a Case of
> Hysteria"

Freud's first invitation to America doubled as reading assignment: his host Stanley Hall was the author of the two-
volume study *Adolescence*, which already included reference to Freud. Within the range of Freud's reading—and
writing—Hall postulated an "adolescent psychology of conversion" based on the "modern idea of a re-birth as essential
to the salvation of the soul." Hall continues:

the origin of the idea that there must be a change so radical and transforming that it can be definitely recognized, and yet wrought chiefly on and not by the subject of it, and that may profoundly reconstruct character and conduct, can be fully traced in the history of what might be called a culture epoch, beginning about 1735, which is of profound interest and significance for the psychologist.[1]

William James, who was within the same range as Freud of Hall's discoveries, devoted extensive coverage to conversion in his 1901-1902 *The Varieties of Religious Experience*.[2] His celebrated source was Californian:

> In his recent work on the Psychology of Religion, Professor Starbuck of California has shown by a statistical inquiry how closely parallel in its manifestations the ordinary 'conversion' which occurs in young people brought up in evangelical circles is to that growth into a larger spiritual life which is a normal phase of adolescence in every class of human beings. (195)

Edwin Diller Starbuck, who was Hall's student, broke James's resistance to statistics. This resistance has a special context within the study of social groups. Gabriel Tarde, whose work Freud consulted in the course of developing a psychoanalytic group psychology, saw statistics as the current counterpart to archaeology (both sciences observe a dialectic of invention and imitation) and at the same time hooked up statistics to such inventions of desire as telephones. Thus James's resistance could be relocated within the endopsychic sensurround. Tarde places the point of his dialectic (namely, that only if minds are not only open but even absolutely alike can a new invention of imitation spread instantaneously) between media technology and America: "The rapid diffusion of telephones in America from the moment of their first appearance there is one proof in point."[3]

In the precincts Starbuck excavated via statistical inquiry conducted exclusively in California ("A few records were gathered at a Methodist conference at Santa Barbara, Cal.")[4] conversion asserts itself as norm (which also reflects James's standard reception). While there are, according to Starbuck, two types of conversion, one deliberate, the other unconscious, this division has not been installed to protect against a projected pathology. Every normal development, James summarizes, participates in both conversion types. "Our education in any practical accomplishment proceeds apparently by jerks and starts, just as the growth of our physical bodies does"—indeed just as the recollection of a forgotten name "jams" until, after one has given up trying, the name completely returns on its own. (This will double as the frame of reference for James's reception of the 1906 San Francisco quake, which exerts its force as that of a name which would return and be recognized.)

The inside view of adolescent "development" (as a recycling or recircuiting project), which Starbuck shares with James, originates with a Californian music teacher who always tells her charges: "'Stop trying and it will do itself'" (202). Since jerking and jamming are generic trends of thought, James must accept "man's liability to sudden and complete conversion as one of his most curious peculiarities" (225). Conversion's born-again sensation, James concludes, recovers the outside with the sweet cast of newness which ecstatic comparisons of Before and After pictures advertise. Inside-out conversion partakes "directly of Christ's substance" while, in the other direction, the power of conversion enters "through the subliminal door."

Starbuck, who groups support for his conversion study only around Californian cases, builds in his research, from the footnotes on up, the Californian body.[5]

> The most rapid growth of the individual is at puberty, and . . . the greatest increase and readjustment is in the nervous system. (SC 303)
>
> Nervous growth seems to consist largely in the formation of new nerve connections. The rapid growth at puberty probably means that at that time there is a great increase in nervous branching. . . . The rapid

formation of new nerve connections in early adolescence may be the cause of the physiological unrest and mental distress that intensifies into what we have called the sense of incompleteness which precedes conversion. The mind becomes a ferment of half-formed ideas. (SC 303)

This reorganization of the nervous tissue furnishes the basis of new insight, the means of appreciation of the larger spiritual world. (SC 303)

Starbuck announces the constitutive out-of-phasedness of this bio-destinal work-out he calls adolescence: *"Insight during adolescence is in advance of the power to execute"* (97). Already in infancy, sight comes complete with mechanisms of identification and projection which belong in the movies. Just as the infant must auto-technologize and turn the place that lack of motor coordination assigns little one into a kind of projection booth, so insight, the advance preview of a rich interiority, rewires the adolescent, who must turn to or into the dream screen: acting out, make believe, imposture advertise the only means of embodying the radically premature insight. The body-ego, circuited during infancy through the mirror senses of identification and projection, is rewired in adolescence for TV on which, via the "live" transmission of nontransference, the converted group member henceforth must watch himself maintain and re-attain his conformity. "Conversion seems to be a feeling of ease, harmony and free activity after the last step of assimilation and readjustment has been made" (SC 295).

According to the feedback Starbuck's questionnaires invited, on the Coast conversion tunes in as norm and standard reception simulcast both as conscious "volitional type" and as unconscious "type of self-surrender." Because he introduces into the conversion complex a series of maxi-protection separations and segregations, Starbuck points only symptomatically to the convergence of religious conversion and conversion hysteria and only via a near-miss: adolescent females who, more so than males, tend to develop hysteria and other nervous disorders, exhibit (when in these states) symptoms which are the same as those shown *before* conversion. The connection that is thus kept out of sync (since Starbuck assumes, for example, that the Christian mass and the adolescent pack together embody the norm and the way to go) introduces, in its place, the preconversion phase of depression called conviction. With conviction one receives the news of the former self's death; the good news, conversion, brought to us by adolescence, advertises a new expanded and generic self with a free gift of group membership—but it's hard at first to follow or believe.

> "Before conversion I had not a single happy day, because of dread of the future." (70) "Everything seemed dead." (70) "I stayed away from revivals and prayer meetings for fear of giving way to my convictions." (62) "I strictly avoided any conversation tending in any way toward moral or religious topics; conviction became torture, yet I could not yield." (62)

Starbuck summarizes: "The person is pulled in two directions. This conflict between the old habitual self and a possible better one results in those conviction phenomena described as the sense of sin and the feeling of incompleteness" (SC 305). The sense of sin and incompleteness (which was the outcome of nervous-system reconnections growing in the gap between insight and ability or license to produce and reproduce) presses for acceptance of conviction which must thus seek the relief and release of conversion.

> "Conviction came so strong at 14 that I thought I would die that very summer if I did not get relief." (83)

Out of a double sense of heaviness or separation from friends the convicted turns to Christ his brother.

> "I prayed earnestly for pardon; I was willing to do anything for Christ." (83) "I didn't care whether I lived or died." (83)

Another ex-con had his own opinion or bumper sticker:

"One day I made up my mind I would be for Christ always." (91)

As the convictions rise to the top of the charts, the attractions of conversion are announced as coming soon:

"Everything depended on 'Him that cometh unto me,' etc.; 'cometh' was the pivotal word; one evening while walking along the road it came to me that it was all right now." (92)

Starbuck comments: "The feelings are reduced to the last degree of tension, and then recoil; are pent up, and suddenly burst" (SC 288). In other words conversion comes "like a flash" (91):

"It was simply a jump for the better." (77) "My conversion was just a jump for the better in the direction of the gradual growth which had preceded." (SC 293) "I perceived a load go off." (83) "Somehow I lost my load." (SC 296)

Following its jump start the new body-ego is recircuited through the cult of the friendly, nice, and cute:

"Felt everybody to be my friend." "God was not afar off; He was my Father, and Christ my elder Brother." "Fear of God was gone; I saw He was the greatest friend one can have." (SC 297)

Ever since the advent and turn-on of mass conversion, the body, the perfect body, one's own body complete with the rights to it, in other words, the mother's body, is always only simulcast as the greater body—that of the adolescent group of friends.

But Starbuck shows that when it comes to the Californian body or group, while its age is adolescent, it shares its gender with groupies. Resistance to conviction, Starbuck announces, is less among the revival females. While this resistance, which predominates among males, reflects, Starbuck argues, the very nature of conversion (62), females are declared throughout the study to be, owing to those periods of depression and solitude which even their cheer-leading cannot shout out, more readily convertible (86). While Starbuck thus sets up the male as nonperiodizable standard of rates of conversion, he has little to go on: "The males did not make as full a record of motives as the females" (57). So-called male resistance is pre-mediatic and pre-adolescent. Female receptivity finds and founds the happy medium; religious conversion and conversion hysteria, otherwise kept out of phase through Starbuck's notion of resistance, plug into a single outlet. The female featured in Starbuck's statistical invention of California tunes in and turns into the adolescent group member. "Resistance to conviction we saw to be less among the revival females," Starbuck reports; "the strength of sermons, the rhythm of music, the encouragement of friends, the force of example, and all the impetus that comes from a religious service, often furnish the last stimulus needed to carry the restless, struggling life through its uncertainty and perplexity." Starbuck interviews the star of this support-group psychology, the adolescent next door, whose teen talk is at its most typical—wired, suggestible, and sharing—when it is, at the same time, "female":

> "As the choir began to sing I felt a queer feeling about my heart, which might be called a nervous tremor. There was a choking sensation in my throat, and every muscle in my body seemed to have received an electric shock. While in this state, hardly knowing what I did, I went forward. On the second night I was converted, and felt that God was pleased with me." (79)

In the fifties, American psychoanalysis came full circuit within this orbit or teen age: the unacknowledged model of its post-Freudian borderline cases and disorders (the impostor, depersonalization, acting out, the dream screen) was TV. In the era of TV, gadget goes to psychoanalysis, which sets nontransferential structures of "liveness" or "onness" on its interchangeable cases of perversion, psychosis, or perpetual adolescence. American psychoanalysis, from the fifties on, provides the TV guide to the adolescent—the one who likes to be different like everyone he likes to be like. As patient, the perpetual teenager (or impostor) imitates all the positions from his analysis which he has divested of transference or turned into something like a TV set before which he "acts out."

The Californian learns from the pack, frat, or group of friends how to get a charge out of socialization—how to feel good about himself and party and have fun. (College in California has no higher purpose than to sponsor and promote this native pedagogy.)

TV is a new-testament technology based on conversion.[6] Even the university (which has for centuries been in denial) is locked onto this nontransferential beam. Beginning in the eighteenth century the modern university and college provided crisis centers and support groups for the new invention of adolescence. The modern educational institution, which TV has increasingly monitored and replaced, was originally the channel of a controlled release of teen passion—the impulse and problem of our epoch. The placeholder of these institutionalizations was mass conversion, in which the releases of a dangerous adolescent interiority were redistributed—new and improved—via the group.

In Freud's *Three Contributions to a Theory of Sexuality* adolescence need only be implicit: the young child's body is already covered with family tracks of every sexual impulse to come. The extensive inner/outer pinball circuit of sexual charges (which unconscious incest programs) builds the body of the child. Adolescence enters this circuit as the threat and crisis of its overload. If the child's body is overcharged in the teenager, the other body which must be built, the group, pack, or frat of friends, must share the overload. Conversion, the primal circuit breaker, and its equally primal institutionalizations, the university and college, slide out of sync with an adolescence that has grown as perpetual, "on," or timeless as MTV or TV Evangelism. In other words, conversion now flips through all the channels—out of phase and on remote control.

Circle Jerk

all's historicizing reading of conversion focuses on an era of its invention—as American fad—which also lends its era to current TV Evangelism. According to Hall's cultural rereading, adolescence was only recently invented—in the eighteenth century—around the society-wide interchangeability (intercharge-ability) of religious conversion and its model or analogue, pubescent sexuality. This invention of adolescence doubled as origin of the crowd psychologies which attained their premier application in the French Revolution. This covers the historical side; on the hysterical side adolescent conversion doubles as invention of the unconscious.

Hall's internal scan thus begins on the outside by probing the mid-eighteenth-century American craze of conversion. During what was called the great awakening, group meetings that released alternations of distress and joy, melancholia and mania, also in the form of "bodily manifestations," led in one instance, at Harvard, to the conversion of up to fifty thousand persons. Hall cites an eyewitness report: "The floor was covered with the slain. Some found forgiveness, but others went away spiritually wounded, suffering uncontrollable agony of soul" (286). This rage, as it was called, was broken down into genres of convulsion ranging from the falling exercise to the holy laugh to the barking exercise to the jerking: "The jerks began with the head, which was thrown violently from side to side so rapidly that the features were blurred and the hair almost seemed to snap, and when the sufferer struck an obstacle and fell he would bounce about like a ball" (286–287). Hall concludes: "it is thus no accidental synchronism of unrelated events that the age of religion and that of sexual maturity coincide" (292). In 1802, to give another example, adolescent jerking came full circle at Yale; but only one third of the student body achieved conversion. Princeton followed; the early history of these institutions consisted chiefly of efforts to secure the conversion of students. At closer range, the pivotal point of adolescence, recast as conversion, is discernible where the ego submits to the other (and becomes a group of one). "Christianity marks the same pivotal point in ethnic adolescence where self-love merges in resignation and renunciation into love of man" (304). Jesus Christ, "the death killer" (336), brought us with his resurrection "perhaps the greatest of all revolutions" (335). With each adolescence we ride out its upsurge of racialism. Just as Christ conquered death, so the adolescent may rise to the higher life of the race of the self (334). On the way to being reborn as representative of the species—for love of man—the adolescent engages in self-punitive exercises that betray a fascination with death which gives a sharp rise to the suicide curve. But via a more controlled release of conversion, the adolescent counters or contains the suicide pact with phantoms through the writing of love letters and the keeping of journals (his own forum or medium of confession, opinion, self-punishment, and soft porn). This then is the primal—adolescent—origin of journal-ism.[1] At its center according to Hall: the self-reproach.

Underlying this journalism we find the melancholic course the self-reproach can also take before reaching the outside as violent outburst. When the self-reproach turns inward into melancholia, Hall argues, the regime of self-abasement only ends up enlarging the target ego which ultimately turns around—Stockton-style—to persecute or murder innocent bystanders.

What Hall thus already assigned to melancholia—the self-reproach—was that which had grounded, Freud discovered upon discovering the mechanism of projection, the conjunction of orbits shared by conversion hysteria and paranoia. Hall's constitution of adolescent psychology around the melancholic self-reproach supplies a connection that Freud skipped over on the way to picking up Gustave Le Bon's work on crowds, but which rebounds nevertheless from yet another skip, in Freud's record of Le Bon, which completes the intertextual complex covering Freud's theory of mass psychology.

According to Le Bon the crowd is ruled by unconscious remote control: just as the ideas or beliefs of the French Revolution—notably belief in equality—could only propagate "themselves by suggestion and contagion," so "conversion," the revolutionary belief or impulse of the Reformation and the placeholder thus of the idea of equality, "was effected almost exclusively by mental contagion and suggestion." This contagious belief in equality always builds an "automaton who has ceased to be guided by his will." There are two prongs to this connection, only one of which finds an outlet in Freud's *Group Psychology*. The automaton or group-member is comparable to the so-called primitive, Freud repeats, thus including Le Bon's crowd in the projective sensurround in which death wishes are crowded out by ghosts. But that which Freud left out at this place he was nevertheless broadcasting at the same time but on another station: alongside the political front that Freud reached with his discovery of group psychology another front or affront was opened: the speculations that comprise the late essays on female sexuality. Thus the phrase from Le Bon that Freud overlooked or rather included via a displacement that invites the double analogy with conversion: "Crowds are everywhere distinguished by feminine characteristics."[2]

This feminine connection, which conversion conducts, runs deep—within what Freud called the "underworld of psychoanalysis"—before emerging on the outside as the equal rights of group membership. What always rendered the mechanism of conversion so obscure to Freud had already been incorporated by the analogy he first chose for its symptom formation and which he could thus only recycle for its final appearance in his theorizing: the memory of psychic trauma that produces the symptoms of conversion hysteria—that souvenir which turned the electrical system into a projector—"acts like a foreign body which long after its entry must continue to be regarded as an agent that is still at work" (*SE* 2:6). This foreign body, which, like its counterpart and correlate "the talking cure," invites cryptonymic rereading,[3] holds the place of the missing connection between Freud's two systems which conversion, by plugging right away into projection, had embraced, indeed leapt to, but without connection. But it is melancholic identification, although emerging spectacularly only on the other side of hysteria as the initiation rite of all socialization, that had all along put through the connections. What Freud called in his own case a melancholic "germ of self-reproach" is always a maternal legacy. Thus in "Female Sexuality," Freud scheduled the aetiology of hysteria in sync with the "phase of attachment to the mother," "which is not surprising when we reflect that both the phase and the neurosis are characteristically feminine, and further, that in this dependence on the mother we have the germ of later paranoia in women" (*SE* 21:227).

Tubular

One of the gravest dangers is the persistent ignoring by feminists of the prime importance of establishing normal periodicity in girls, to the needs of which everything else should for a few years be secondary.
  —Stanley Hall, *Adolescence*

Thus young men are taboo at their initiation ceremonies, women are taboo during menstruation and immediately after giving birth; so too new-born babies, sick persons and, above all, the dead are taboo.
  —Freud, *Totem and Taboo*

Many of my patients actually complained of having someone else inside. "My husband says I'm two completely different people, especially before my period" was a frequent comment. Equally frequent was "that's just not me!" Others confided that "somebody" inside them undermined their resolve to diet, or to

stop smoking or drinking, etc. "Somebody says to me, 'You're
not going to stick to the diet. By noon you'll be eating again.'"
These patients spoke of their conflicts very openly, because
they assumed they were talking about two different parts of
their personalities—that they were at war within themselves.
But I began hearing and interpreting these remarks as possible
clues of possession.

> —Edith Fiore, *The Unquiet Dead: A Psychologist Treats*
> *Spirit Possession*

Ever since Hall declared America the place where "young
people leap rather than grow into maturity," the analysis of
this "unhistoric land" which is "so precociously old for its
years" has leapt beyond sexual difference to the group,[1]
which under the cover of a neutral unisex borrows its sex
and ego ideal (as does every child who lacks paternal guidance in an antigenerational crowd of pals) from mother.
The temporality of the (adolescent) group is one of periodicity. As Michael Bálint argued in 1937:[2] "I am of the opinion
that menstruation, in the same way as erection, may be
interpreted as a conversion symptom, and consequently
that it unites in itself different opposing wishes and instinctual impulses" (346). When menstruation skips around or
slows down in its scheduling, the brotherhood of adolescent
friends has been disturbed (often to the point of the bros
developing period symptoms). "The usual male wish is that
the woman shall wait until her turn comes; she may be excited and exciting only then, and only to that degree which
is agreeable to the man. It is a rare exception if a man finds a
menstruating woman sexually desirable" (351).

In the *New-York Daily Tribune* on Sunday, February 9,
1902, Hall was reported as coming down hard on the other
curse: "Rum Is One of the Greatest Curses of This Land."
But Hall's first move, according to the interview and report,
was to distance himself from that which he, even though
himself a teetotaler, cannot abide: "the temperance physiol-
ogy." Indeed he concedes that on the short term "taking a
drink is somehow like taking a vacation," while on long

term it is inconceivable "what the race would have been without narcotics or stimulants." Inebriation guarantees what everyone has periodically required: "religious ecstasy." Indeed most initiations or celebrations of "adolescence and marriage are simply drinking bouts." Religious intoxication promotes ongoing adolescence: "the craving for youth and life." "Youth is the best part of life, everything that makes us feel young is valuable." In short: "The drunkard is strikingly susceptible to sudden conversions." His schedule is borrowed from the other curse: "The drink habit seems to have a rhythmic period, monthly periodicity of drunkenness being sometimes seen."

Young woman requires and introduces "regulated conditions" at the same time as she embodies, also on account of her own periodicity, the concept of initiation or adolescence. The rule of women, then, is what in French and German is simply "the rule": menstruation. Hall devotes one chapter of *Adolescence* (vol. 1) to periodicity. Because woman seems to be or to react in sync with "moon, tides, reproduction, race, climate, and all the environment in its every item" she has been received, Hall confirms, with "superstitious awe" (503). The scientific version of this veneration, however, charges menstruating woman with susceptibility to hysteria, psychosis, and criminal violence. "Abnormal brain conditions, then, must be regarded as concurrent symptoms of anomalous menstruation, and not as the cause of it" (495). On the normal side, the changes and variations of menstruation cause women to "differ from each other more than they differ from man" (493). The rule of menstruation governs and develops sexual difference as a female exclusive; sexual differentiation, as differentiated from identification, operates, according to the rule, only among females. For the male, sex is the same difference. The female body-builds the Freudian system she models with her own person and projection. The male readers of this body talk (with Freud at the front of the line) have accessed the system auto-analytically through mediatic or maternal identification.

The female body (of symptoms) models peer group formation and the family pack. The rule that promotes female bonding also (according to Hall) periodically unbinds female adolescence from pack psychology by forcing young women into seclusion. If a woman dissimulates group membership during her period, not only are her honesty and character at stake but she risks, in fact, toxic shock. Because it turns every groupie into a secluded goddess or demon, menstruation ultimately delivers a dowry of retemporalization whereby male libido, which on its own is consistent only by hours or days, is bound to one woman on a monthly (and hence year-round) basis. Woman becomes through menstruation many different objects to the same man and thus reroutes his "polygamous instincts" by "appealing by turns to his pity, his passion, and ruling him now by sympathy, now by service, now by admiration, while her repertory of changes gives her an added charm and ever-stimulating interest" (1:503). Thanks to menstruation she is a match for the group.

From the distance that makes menstruating women "actually though unconsciously, if entirely healthful, . . . more attractive to man" we glimpse woman's narcissistic empowerment: "She feels her womanhood and glories in it like a goddess." Indeed up to this point of her encounter with adolescence "she has first dreamed of some ideal of manhood and is altruistic, and only later comes the conception of selfhood" (493). Thus conceiving her self in time for the onset of periodicity "she exults in her womanhood as something superior" (493). Her narcissism will be the match for the other detour on the way to or away from the couple—male to male transmissions.

The curse that creates Sleeping Beauty—and adds Prince Charming as reward—must be registered differently, on the down side, with regard to PMS, which gives the newscast on one's own person that the present was not pregnant with a future. This character (and calendar) of periodicity can be observed as a rule in men: "spells of discomfort, distraction, irascibility, and depression in males thought to be of this character are probably much more common than is generally supposed" (501). But if you are woman, PMS at the same time rides the anticipatory resoluteness that unifies three time zones and two systems: "Time stops when you're in the tube."[3] On this united front of differentiation, menstruation will nevertheless seep into a fundamental sense of being left empty or simply left that pushes women, in the first place, into the zone of tension between the couple and the group.

According to Sándor Radó,[4] individuals of depressive (and, hence, aggressive) disposition are "feminine in their narcissism": "With this type the mere 'danger of loss of love' is sufficient to compel formation of the superego" (434), which is, however, constitutively malformed, forever in need, on the outside, of a libidinally saturated environment of mutual admiration or identification so as to absorb the roller coaster ride of crushes and crashes. Popularity with friends, in short, provides narcissistic supplies for the one unable to love. Dodging on the inside the rebound of good and bad objects—one's best friends and worst enemies—, the depressive or "feminine" disposition, which must act out the ambivalence it must forever deny, is too busy to be (although it sure can fall) in love. The "feminine" or depressive disposition slips out of the child's doubling and division of the parents into good and bad objects of identification. The child learns to separate from himself on the spot: the bad child, he agrees after the tantrum subsides, is "gone"; the good one is back again. The superego in this case is one-sidedly based on the good-object side of the parents (and on the child's love of that side). But there's a punchline: the superego also receives from the bad-object side of the parents the license or "content" which permits punishment of the ego. The ego, which absorbs the bad object's target status, loves the melancholic superego since it guarantees that, internally speaking, the parents will always be on their good side—even or especially when it hurts so good. Melancholia, in Radó's reading, reacts to the loss of a love object because its constitutive disposition (in the ready position) had already covered over loss (or fear of loss) of love (including of libido, one's own capacity for love). The melancholic superego lines up with sadomasochism and adolescence; it plugs into menstruation on account of a radical ambivalence which is "born again" on the person of the bleeding woman.

Her enforced capacity for solitude, her being off-limits to group participation also gives her sexual control over the group member, her husband. Bálint explored the duality of menstruation that makes it (or redeems it as) a conversion symptom: "Such a dual wish would be genital-sexual excitation and defense against this; or, described from the standpoint of object-relationship, the *tendency* to excite the partner, to seduce him, and the opposing tendency to refuse the excited and seduced parner" (346). It is well-known, Bálint reminds us, that the bride's periodicity sets the wedding date, which falls between periods. And yet, symptomatically, as though to mark the forsaking of all others (that is, of the group), the newlywed will often start menstruating on the night that's the night. Now that's not just a defense, Bálint points out; it's also profoundly ambivalent (346): at the same time as it prohibits sex, bleeding (much like the group's consumption of alcohol or spirits) is also openly sexual. Menstruation comes as a surprise but just in time to preserve virginity—the hymen or the marriage bond—and reserve its penetration for another. As Freud notes: "Menstruation, especially its first appearance, is interpreted as the bite of some spirit-animal, perhaps as a sign of sexual intercourse with this spirit. Occasionally some report gives grounds for recognizing the spirit as that of an ancestor and then, supported by other findings, we understand that the menstruating girl is taboo because she is the property of this ancestral spirit" (*SE* 11:197). Through this relay of ancestral figures she gets FAXed—by the father function—to the paternal place of couple protection. Freud shows how the taboo on menstruation bleeds into the one on virginity: the virgin bride so desirable in our culture, Freud admits, was originally or primally off-limits. Instead, some delegate of father first ritually penetrated the virgin before she could be given over to her husband. Thus the first time, date, or period (on which she goes all the way) remains forever dedicated to the father function. That's why the wife can get laid—to rest. She's one of the mournables.

Alongside the installation of smiley faces in the face of danger of loss of love, the mega-vicious *and* nerdy-depressive trends which menstruation can set guarantee and correspond to, according to George Gero,[5] a sadomasochistic fantasy life:

> In some women pain becomes a danger signal activating the fear of genital injury, the female counterpart of castration anxiety. With the onset of the menses, pain connected with the female sexual functions of ovulation and menstruation causes a regression to the exaggerated sado-masochistic fantasies of the phallic phase. Depending on individual factors, these regressively reactivated conflicts lead to frigidity, intense penis envy, and masculine protest. (34–35)

The counterpart in men to a phallic defense against genital-masochistic anxiety is a desire for femininity to which Poul Faergeman even attributes, above and beyond assumption of certain character traits, all doodling—another origin of caricature.[6] At the origin of caricature (in menstrual bleeding), adolescent initiation rites always belong to the desire for femininity: the model for these blood-letting rituals, including circumcision (which was originally practiced on pubescent males), is the pubescent female's automatic ability to menstruate.[7]

According to Faergeman, Freud's 1937 observation (that it was difficult to influence or analyze a strong bisexual disposition) also holds for the masculine adolescent wish for periodic bleeding (16). Man's (wishful) reception of menstruation can depend upon feelings of guilt (demands of the superego for punishment or self-destruction), castration anxiety, and phallic masochism. In men menstruation fantasies wipe out on the blood bond of identification: drinking and delinquency, sleeping around and acting out—go with the flow. Menstruation and aggression were first conjoined in the "angry mother"—the "mad woman" and "bloody hysteric"; "identification with this bleeding, potential aggressor" is the only available defense "against the threat from the terrifying witch, vampire, and goddess" (17). The mummy's curse always afflicts male explorers who get the bad vibes of identification. When the bonding or timing of menstruation thus goes under (and unconscious) it can install within the couple a group plan featuring the mother-wife, who makes fewer demands on her husband's libido than do his outside investments in work—or at the bar where the bros barrel a manic-melancholic orbit.

Menstrual blood is the primal ingredient in the witch's brew. Thus it is kept remote from the activities or rituals of sowing, watering young shoots, preserving fruit, handling cut flowers. The menstruating woman would thus be forced into seclusion, even, that is, if her condition did not already demand this of her, because of the radical ambivalence of her position. Bálint: "ambivalence of environment is very dangerous for all young life" (352).

Before scrambling (for) libidinal connections, the vampire or mummy must represent or hold the place of the couple via her withdrawal from the group into a solitude that is (like the solitude of diary writing) at the same time the franchise of the group. Little sister is on her own person the (PM) tension between the group and the couple, between the body and the future. Here's some advice she must follow as she cheerleads the way through the stressed-out conditions of teenagerization:

> Take note of the days when you feel changes occurring. You may see a pattern develop that correlates with your menstrual cycle. On these days, be extra good to yourself. Plan activities that are fun and keep you busy. . . . Schedule some quiet time to take stock of your feelings. One great way to record your feelings? Keep a daily journal that's meant for your eyes

only. Use this special journal to jot down your feelings about everything and anything. It can be a great help in beating any monthly blahs before they meddle with your happy days![8]

Menstruation, as in the keeping of diaries (written with the blood of the father function), introduces "dating" structures into the group and the group-of-one. Like the loss of virginity, the date must be unique, must fall once and for all. But the date must, like menstruation, be periodically repeatable if it is to be at all recognizable. The catalyst of the moment that is constitutively a switchboard of tele-relations (both with one's ancestors and with one's heirs), menstruation initiates the body into adolescence—and technologizes it. Look at the description of conversion experiences (look at Brian DePalma's *Carrie*): the first onset of menses goes down as the technologization of the woman's body.

Bitch Bunnies

Already in Freud's 1908 essay "Hysterical Phantasies and their Relation to Bisexuality" a direct connection between hysteria and paranoia was openly admitted—into the system. "A common source and normal prototype of all these creations of phantasy," Freud argued, "is to be found in what are called the day-dreams of youth" (*SE* 9:159). The phantasy that gave the adolescent sexual satisfaction during a period of masturbation remains the source of pathological symptoms shared by hysteria and paranoia. "At that time the masturbatory act . . . was compounded of two parts. One was the evocation of a phantasy and the other some active behavior for obtaining self-gratification at the height of the phantasy. This compound . . . was itself merely soldered together. . . . When . . . the subject renounces this type of satisfaction, composed of masturbation and phantasy, the action is given up, while the phantasy, from being conscious, becomes unconscious" (*SE* 9:161).

When daydream fantasy, which always ultimately lends a hand to adolescent masturbation, goes unconscious, the masturbating hand installs the projector: the adolescent fantasy henceforth reaches the outside only via conversion or projection—for example under the pressure of religious conversion. Only from within the deepest deposit of the primal schedule—the posthumously published *Survey of the Transference Neuroses*[1]—can Freud give simultaneous broadcast to the neuroses across the different standard times. Just as any daydream hovers between three periods of time and ideation—between the current impression that sets off the fantasizing, the memory of an experience in early childhood, and some situation in the future in which wish fulfillment achieves representation—so psychic disturbance is always scheduled three times over in three separate time zones: primal time, the time of the disorder's fixation, and the time of its outbreak. For example: schizophrenia breaks out in adolescence but is already in place at the early age to which schizophrenic autoeroticism regresses (72).

In the genealogy Freud reschedules, following Ferenczi, in sync with the impact of the ice age, civilization or, interchangeably, neurosis commences once the pleasure of procreation contradicts the instinct for self-preservation. The immediate result: infanticide, which was thus at the beginning the first law; it encountered "resistance in the love of the narcissistic mothers" (75). In the long run, conversion hysteria arises from the primal condition of narcissistic grieving. The symptomatology conversion produces in the flesh proves, Freud argues, that humanity was at this earliest time of contraception still *infans*, nonspeaking.

In the next phase, following the conversion that kept women turning in a holding pattern over the fateful proximity of love and identification, men alone became the carriers of development or spiritualization: redirection of sexuality released omnipotence of thoughts which was matched on the outside by the invention of language, magic, and technology. At this point then (and out-of-phase with nar-cissistic grieving for unmournable loss) the reception of the death wish—its cult of broadcasting—was first installed or, via projection and haunting, retrieved. By the close of this era of spiritualization (during which the narcissistic baby bonds were redistributed via power relations with the spirit or phantom realm), the primal father and his horde had orga-nized the group or race—between repression and identifica-tion. The conditions for primal consumerism were set.

So far Freud has conveyed a history of the transference neuroses; across the gap between generations a history of the narcissistic neuroses or psychoses leads civilization into the second phase. The primal father drives out or castrates his adolescent sons. Thus in the extra-linguistic place of infanticide, castration emerges as law-giving phantasm spanning the time zones. What commenced primally as threat to or crime against adolescents is otherwise installed (in the course of any individual's development) in early childhood. But childhood is also time for the brotherhood bonds of adolescent or group psychology to slide into place via the identification that must resolve sibling rivalry. Just as infantile autoeroticism becomes the only remaining op-tion for the adolescent sons castrated by the primal father, so the psychotic who breaks out with schizophrenia in ado-lescence must inhabit autoerotic prehistory.

Adolescent or modern group psychology was mounted through the logic of succession which kept primal fathers coming: through the mother's intercession and because the father was at last too old to care, the youngest son ultimately claimed the primal position at the head of the horde (78). Thus the murdered children the narcissistic mothers could not mourn ultimately achieved resurrection. Adolescence only fully emerges with the murderous insurrection against the father. But by the time the primal father was murdered and mourned—the official onset (according to the phy-logenetic timetable) of the disorders of melancholia and mania—unmournably dead children already haunted the primal precincts of consumerism: henceforth the father should be eaten and mourned—identified with—to abort the unmournables. What commences as invention of the modern brotherhood provides the fixation phases of the psychoses. But in the prehistory of this invention, during the period that ultimately turns on conversion hysteria, melancholic (that is, nonpaternal) identification had, via "the mothers," already gone down. According to Freud, the formation of fraternity as the group format or phantasm that would henceforth command absolutely also enclosed "the germ of the institution of matriarchy, described by Bachofen, which was in turn replaced by the patriarchal organization of the family" (*SE* 13:144).

Bachofen's contribution to the psychoanalytic reception of matriarchal structures has been restricted to the difference between the blood bonds between mother and child and the adoptive relation between father and child. The paternal rapport requires "a far higher degree of moral development than mother love."[2] But Bachofen also prepares and performs the superimpositions which psychohistory has applied in the course of rereading American mass culture: "woman guides the wild, lawless existence of the earliest period toward a milder friendlier culture, in whose center she sits enthroned as the embodiment of the higher principle" (86). The family, which matriarchy introduced and invented, continues to serve woman's "need for regulated conditions" (94). But the original matriarchal family was more universal than the "family based on father right," which "is a closed individual organism" (80).

> The idea of motherhood produces a sense of universal fraternity among all men, which dies with the development of paternity. . . . Every woman's womb, the mortal image of the earth mother Demeter, will give brothers and sisters to the children of every other woman; the homeland will know only brothers and sisters until the day when the development of the paternal system dissolves the undifferentiated unity of the mass and introduces a principle of articulation. (80)

Matriarchy's own history-wide "articulation" was warfare. Bachofen joins Aristotle in remarking that the virtues of warfare—danger, beauty, and adventure—were ever in the service of woman; they "betoken the fullness of a nation's youth" (84). Matriarchy is accordingly far more diversified in its holdings than possession only of blood bonds would suggest. Its warlike articulation and extension are the result of "artificial forms" through which mother right must be bolstered. The "weakness" of matriarchy was transformed into political viability via religion, warfare, and thus also through the invention of telecommunications devices which, inside the double invention of adolescence and the unconscious, continue to exercise "matriarchal" remote control. Thus the origin of letter and diary writing has been attributed "to Asiatic queens confined to the interior of their palaces."

Honkies for Jesus

In a culture pressing toward nihilism, members or bros of the group and horde press for equal rights that turn out to be those of the unborn (or undead). According to the personalized brand of psychic organization which the second system delivers in *The Ego and the Id*, melancholic or mass identification installs itself (much as cannibalism or human sacrifice inside bread and wine) as internal model and half-life of the primal socialization processes (sublimation and superego formation), which, owing to the nature of their head start systemwide, cannot but be faulty, indeed doomed. Thus although, according to Freud, the leader is primally inseparable from the herd, modern group formation, from the Christian church to American mass culture, has been relieved of following the leader: group members only identify among themselves; there remains no relation to the ego ideal that would make or tolerate a difference.

Thus in *Group Psychology and the Analysis of the Ego*

Freud warns that sexual love is threatened by extinction. It is now more than ever the inner/outer program of Christianity that, having gone unconscious and thus slipped into the position of teleguidance which secularization only covered over, increasingly realizes itself as the replacement of love and war by friendship and suicide (or total war).[1]

At this stage hysterical symptom formation can be reduced by Freud "completely" (as he stresses) to identification. Thus Freud must retreat to his first pre-Oedipal rehearsal of the Oedipus complex's formulation. In a letter to Fliess (May 31, 1897) Freud had assigned mourning disorders to the ambivalent two tracks along which hysterical identification gives the stereo broadcast: a survivor could suddenly develop the symptoms of the ailment that disposed of the parent who, before departing, had been featured "live" as moving target within range of the child's death wishes. By the time of crowd psychology, then, the cryptological and sexological sides of psychoanalysis, which until then had been granted equal but separate coverage, achieve uncanny cohabitation. The desire or hysteria that was to figure as the legacy of Oedipus was now always and already displaced by identification.

Only sadomasochism realizes the pleasure principle which, with Christianity, became the rule—not only because suffering came to be celebrated around a doubly charged Passion but also because Christian eschatology keeps everyone in suspense; in turn waiting around is the essence and holding pattern of mass masochism.[2] Freud anchors the orbit of this revaluation in the third person, who is by definition the one sexual love excludes: the third person ("the one") is at best granted the strain of waiting in line among the other substitute parts of desire. But the group turns around this relation of exclusion according to the logic of sadomasochism: only the third person, who comes to occupy the place of projection, gets off at the prospect of everyone in the group being on standby.

A ghost thus holds the place of the ego ideal and the beloved has been replaced with the sweet-face or happy-face of the friend maternalized through identification. Group instinct is more ancient than love or ego ideal: but what comes even before the group in terms of primal rescheduling is the egoism of the primal father, which every young child shares. Thus group bonds are forged according to a split-level design: first, the reaction of envy and rivalry with which the older child spontaneously welcomes every new sibling must retreat from the open and assume the undercover identity (through identification) of sense of community. This shift is covered over again by the relationship to parents which gives the outer form of the formation of the first group bond. But this external aspect—in fact, says Freud, the unbearable gaze of father—also beams back from a primal date, that of the invention of the unconscious, which shares the grounding of an adolescent. When the primal father imposed abstinence upon his sons, the unconscious was created—as group or adolescent psychology. From that broken date onward only father *figures* rule the family unit bonded to the group—just as Christ, Freud points out, relates to the members of his group as older brother. Before the adolescent brotherhood thus assumed— only by transforming—the place of the primal father, an obscure episode asserted and inserted itself within group psychology's make-up. The rule of women, the immediate follow-up to the murder of the primal father, first had to be shunted to the side, to the inside, of the new psychology. According to Freud this merely overthrown rule of women, which in exchange achieved on the outside the invention and worship of mother goddesses, established the maternal appeal ultimately of Christian mass culture.[3] But the more recently developed alternatives to group psychology—ego ideal and love—reach beyond the brotherhood of father figures or friends by individualizing and parceling out the murder of the primal father as personalized works of mourning. The ego ideal was originally created by the first poet to fashion the fiction of the hero, a proper heir to the primal father. Not unlike Freud himself in *Totem and Taboo*, the poet thus forged a primal anecdote—and antidote—

that secured as ego ideal a safety zone for love in the midst of identificatory brotherhood. Because sexual love demands the one-on-one correspondence of couplification—or, as Gertrude Stein put it, being alone together—it cannot but resist, often through jealousy, every group bond.

By contrast, the sexuality of groups, or group sex, which places every body at everybody else's disposal, is devoid of shame or jealousy. This sexual stage of the group was created—and could henceforward always be regressed to— by the primal brotherhood's introduction of totemic exogamy: thus love and sex became separable. By declaring the maternal body—and thus, in a word, the body—off limits, the brotherhood imposed this double body as an inner/outer limit: in the group, pleasure is linked and limited only to corporeal analogues or projections of bodies. What has been sacrificed (or sacrificed to) is the infinitude of pleasure which the coupling of the imagination and language vouchsafes—and which the ego ideal guards but cannot guarantee. Thus when the ego ideal is away, the egos, which are ultimately only projections of bodies, can feel good about themselves; everyone's *friends* can party and have fun.

The unconscious side of crowd behavior always included what it presupposed, the adolescent psychology Freud had otherwise pushed back—onto America. But what Hall, Le Bon, and Freud diagnosed under the double heading of adolescence and Christianity, recent cultural rereading has pursued as a relation between female sexuality and psychoanalysis which allows one to inhere in the other as the other's unconscious. Access to the missing or unconscious link is provided, as Cavell has advised, through mourning. Since mourning always passes through the relay and delay of representation, the connection Cavell would put through must be synchronized with a genealogy of the work of representation in mourning. Modern literature commences by coinciding in the mid-eighteenth century with the era of adolescent conversions and closes, around 1900, with psychoanalysis's discovery of hysterical conversion. This also covers a history of women writing and of writing designed for female consumers. The mid-eighteenth-century upsurge of love-letter and journal writing was also the first medium in which women—often via a ghost writer's or brother's censorship and revision—nevertheless achieved publication.[4] These first women writers were the grandmothers of the women patients who dictated the discovery of the unconscious. Their legacy: conversion.

Psychoanalysis's discovery of hysterical conversion coincides with its disappearance: hysterical blindness, catalepsy, paralysis, and false pregnancy have largely withdrawn into extinction. Which is to say that conversion, via yet another conversion, relocated, as was always part of the program, within psychosis and group psychology. Just as the case studies of hysterics starred only women so most cases of psychosis are vehicles for women. Schreber of course embodied the spectacular exception, as he himself realized in his rush to attain group membership in womanhood via automaton-building abnegations and supplementations.

But these convergences also fall into place according to another genealogical timetable. It has been argued that the era of hysterical symptom formation spans the era of a literature designed to be read—consumed to the point of identification—by women. From *Pamela* onward, hysteria was dictated to women by literature, which thus doubled as semiological reserve of female sexuality's representation (or repression). Hysterical conversion accomplished, at the blocked or consumerist end of writing and desire, what Christianity had only talked about: the word became flesh. Soon this flesh would be cut up, spliced together, and reanimated via projection. For what had already commenced by the time psychoanalysis discovered what was thus also a literary phenomenon: the visual media would replace literature as primal habitat for representation of the feminine. Even while Freud was observing Charcot commence lending an ear to hysterics, a loan that would ultimately write psychoanalysis, asylum photographers were actively recording—and thus erasing—all signs or symptoms of hysterical conversion. As Manfred Schneider concludes, psychoanalysis shifted from allegiance to a science of literature to the alliances it holds to this day—as science of technical media.[5]

Just as the electrical system that Breuer and Freud built to convey psychic disturbance turned into a mechanism of projection once conversion had been turned on, so hysterical conversion always found itself doubled on the psychotic side of the psychic apparatus. On that side Tausk's psychotic patient Natalija A. is persecuted by a projection of her body that, all agree, is indeed a cinematograph.[6] But on both sides (as Prado de Oliveira argues) it can be observed that inside Freud's oeuvre a certain early case study of conversion hysteria could be recast as interchangeable, point by point, with that case of female paranoia running counter to psychoanalytic expectations.[7] Thus these interchangeable cases include, on the psychotic side, as commemorative token and hinge of hysteria's disappearance, a camera that externalizes as thud or click—and as visual record and evidence in the other's possession—the sensations of her sexuality.

But Don't Forget to
Breathe

Starbuck of California saw the teen psychology of conversion emerge from "the rapid formation of new nerve connections in early adolescence"; the "great increase in nervous branching" builds tension that requires the release—of support group activities (SC 303). That conversion thus belongs to a generic structure of adolescence is the conclusion Starbuck's own branching out comes to. The specific gender of conversion or adolescence withdraws into group structures that tower above, lifeguard style, the vital sign and self-help function—of breathing.

The thrill of renouncing an addiction by submitting totally to one's "unselfing" bonds conversion to the breaking of habits within groups. The group effort is required for the complete surrender which habit-breaking demands (since partial surrender admits the force of displacement which always comes around to restoring the dependency).

The conversion experience of one of Starbuck's Californians, another hypnotized/transitorized group of one, is a primal breakthrough to the beyond (which continues to this day to penetrate a certain Californian dread of dependency as in vigilant nonsmoking or, on the other side of dread, the channeler's submission to the voices of Ramtha or Mafu):

> "When I was about 40, I tried to quit smoking, but the desire was on me, and had me in its power. I cried and prayed and promised God to quit, but could not. I had smoked for 15 years. When I was 53, as I sat by the fire one day smoking, a voice came to me. I did not hear it with my ears, but more as a dream or sort of double think. It said, 'Louisa, lay down smoking.' At once I replied, 'Will you take the desire away?' But it only kept saying, 'Louisa, lay down smoking.' Then I got up, laid my pipe on the mantle shelf, and never smoked again, or had any desire to." (SC 302)

What is thus born again—only a breath away—is an aggressive impulse which American psychoanalysts, beginning in the fifties, sought to isolate. What Samuel Atkin investigates under the concept of "war readiness," for example, situates the unconscious relation to the recently evolved institutions of war and state both within modern group psychology and back in prehistory.[1] When the primal horde—or peer group—triumphed over father, whose corpse was then devoured and thus maternalized, made friendly, the mutual admiration society of teen group identification was primally founded. These primal group structures continue to reinforce narcissism in the prefab form of aversion to strangers so as to rise above the ambivalence situated within one's hostility to loved ones. But group membership is thus far removed from those libidinal processes or "immunities" (560) which you can only get in family packs. Thus, in the group, long distance covers for relations of aggressivity and ambivalence, which are intensified rather than bound: pent-up aggression breaks down reality-testing and releases projection onto the outsider. The converter called adolescence must thus be set up between friends and parents, the group and the couple.

Perpetual adolescence or war-readiness, which is pre-superego in origin, is a mode of preparedness that protects against the earliest narcissistic state, situated beyond pleasure or unpleasure, the state of indifference. Freud rates every rerun of this indifference later in life "a special case of hate or dislike." Indifference requires reinforced shock-or-quake-proof narcissism which only the friendly and (un)-stressed-out relations of adolescence can mix and pour. I'm bored: let's party.

Since adolescent or group narcissism is always ready to wipe out—the other—the state must monopolize and safeguard against teen violence by programming its acting out: on the domestic front every adolescent must be made to consent voluntarily to the projected demands of the state. The mere potential for illegal action—such as smoking currently represents in California—must be suppressed by near-vigilante and, hence, internal efforts. Smokers are rebels without a cause; since they are in the ready position to break the law, they must be persecuted prophylactically, that is, internally and, hence, eternally.

American psychoanalysis, at once California's ideology, its consumer projection, and, at the same time, the native habitat of its critique and excavation, addresses suicide, aggression, and indifference in one breath. Atkin lets Leo Stone do a set building up and toning the argument groups he sought to define.[2] Stone works out on the problem of aggression starting with the literal meaning of "aggress," to approach, go forward or go for it, and concluding his reps with aggression's ultimate aim: the total destruction of objects. Atkin laid the group trip on the defensive function of projection of aggression. Stone adds or advertises that aggression already comes complete with this function:

> In becoming functional aggression must have a target, whether it be the subject's own ego or an external object, or the ego's projection. The phenomenon of narcissism, the lever for externalization of aggres-

sion, contributes decisively to the sense of differentiation of the self from the outer world and later . . . to the modes . . . of externally directed aggression. (210)

According to Stone, suicide, the fact of life confined to the human species, represents "the coexistence in one organism of the impulses 'to kill' and 'to die' in an apparent unitary drive" (221). Stone Californiaizes the verb and impulse "to die" to articulate the double pull, in suicide, of aggression on one side and identification and projection on the other. The impulse to die or to die someone else is more popular than the urge to kill: "'dying' someone is a killing of oneself in effigy employing the strange human capacity to merge or interchange or even confuse oneself and the object" (229). In other words, aggression gets around more than sex does. Since unlike sex it has no specific physiological apparatus or constant urge requiring specific physiologic satisfaction, it obtains—it must obtain—vicarious satisfaction via identification and projection (222). Thus always and already interconnected we find the three accomplishments that in fact separate man from animal: the lack of motor coordination in infancy, the protracted transition into maturity (redoubled as perpetual adolescence), and suicide or, put differently, the highly developed capacity for introjection and identification (220–21).

The forms of human aggression are also unique (or adolescent). The American psychoanalysts consulted here stress in their separate takes on stress management a most crucial or excruciating form of aggression which is conjugated not with beating but with cutting—in the sense of failure to greet a neighbor or friend. Failure to utter the apotropaic "Have a nice day!" puts one under suspicion of being a potential law breaker and smoker.[3]

Right away, at birth, aggression emerges in the effort to master (via identification and projection) the traumatic state of helplessness which birth introduces. Two functions, breathing and sucking, are instantly animated and charged with two chores or drives: either live under terrestrial conditions or restore the features of intrauterine life. The "rejection of the instinctual obligations of extra-uterine life can become, in effect, an inclination to die. This latent inclination may reassert itself in the future; for example in the severe psychotic stupors" (238). Thus little one may right away "refuse the instinctual challenge without psychic representation of such refusal"—total narcissistic blow-out: "not breathe, not suck, and thus, in effect, die" (235).

With both breathing and sucking, libidinal gratification remains corollary to the fulfillment of a life function aggressively attained. But while not to eat or suck remains a refusal within relations with the other, the refusal to breathe rides out a narcissistic and, thus, group-bound current. Hence Freud's conviction that indifference toward objects antedates any libidinal orientation. Here in the space of breathing and not breathing—or whatever—lies the first dim representation of an urge to die, later a wish to die, to die someone else.

While feeding time is the time of the other, we breathe on our own. Breathing can even require separation from the nursing breast to avert suffocation: the separation, thus, between breathing and nurture, drives a split between aggression and sex. The proximity to the object which can impede respiration, as when, to give Stone's Fleissian example, the nose gets "buried" in the breast, produces a second split and trauma that resonate with the Californian teen demand: don't violate my personal space.

> In a sense, then, the vital function of respiration has in it the seeds of a dynamic narcissism and demonstrable aggression, and is conspicuously independent of the first object. . . . [Breathing] is the earliest prototype of aggressive riddance of the object . . . of the interest in "open space," of "room to breathe," of "elbow room" (perhaps also one aspect of *Lebensraum?*). (213)

The innate capacity for forgetting to breathe (for example, as one works out with the machines or gives natural childbirth) was taken by Freud, in the case of Dostoevsky's epileptic attacks, as sadomasochistic origin of postmodern Pacman. At this breath-holding origin we discern, in the articulations of support-group psychology, a state of preparedness, denial and acting out, which Jim Jones called White Nights but which we must call, working, working out, on location, California.

Stoked!

*Y*ou will laugh—and rightly—but I confess to new
anxieties, which come and go but last for half a day at
a time. Fear of a railway accident . . .
—Freud to Fliess, August 18, 1897

In the 1912 and 1913 papers on techniques of transference, the telephonic model Freud provided the analyst for wiretapping a patient's "free associations"—"He must adjust himself to the patient as a telephone receiver is adjusted to the transmitting microphone" (*SE* 12:115–16)—alternated with the analogue with a train, which gave the patient his set of instructions. At the patient's end of transfer and training there is only a train of association: "Act as though, for instance, you were a traveler sitting next to the window of a railway carriage and describing to someone inside the carriage the changing views which you see outside" (*SE* 12:135).

Freud scheduled this audio and video spectacle of

transference and association in sync with the release of his theory of ghosts in *Totem and Taboo*. But the zones of theorizing in which techno-magic, haunting, and improper mourning received equal but separate coverage were not superimposed by Freud. Since train and phone remained, according to Freud, mere detachable analogues, these early connections were not put through or caught. But over time Freud would grant only the analogies with techno-media and archaeological excavation endopsychic status, thus moving their range, after the fact, beyond analogy or squarely within the psychic apparatus. By the second system, train wreck or traumatic neurosis and the telephone had installed a shift in range which exchanged the death wish for its society-wide manifestation—death drive—and mourning or haunting for another group equivalent— sadomasochism. In *Civilization and its Discontents*, the train slides into the lineup for a speed race between means of transport and technical media. With every emergency measure taken to overcome or traverse distance and death, the insured bond or tele-touch with the nearest and dearest only retrieves in their absence the death wishes (and ghosts) jamming the circuits. "If there had been no railway to conquer distances, my child would never have left his native town and I should need no telephone to hear his voice" (*SE* 21:88).

Bertram Lewin recognized behind Freud's 1913 training analogue the maternal breast at station identification.[1] On a train journey from Leipzig to Vienna at around age two, little Freud was indeed the roused spectator of his mother's nude body. This he confided to Fliess on October 3, 1897, just prior to a visit with his friend in Berlin. Following the return trip, Freud switched tracks via analogy to his discovery of the unconscious:

> I am living only for "inner" work. It gets hold of me and hauls me through the past in rapid association of ideas; and my mood changes like the landscape seen by a traveller from a train; and, as the great poet,

using his privilege to ennoble (sublimate) things, puts it:—"And the shades of loved ones appear, and with them, like an old, half-forgotten myth, first love and friendship"—as well as first terror and strife. . . . I am now experiencing myself all the things that as a third party I have witnessed going on in my patients. . . . An idea about resistance has enabled me to put back on the rails all the cases of mine which looked like they were breaking down, with the result that they are now going on satisfactorily again. Resistance . . . is nothing but the child's character. (October 27, 1897)

Lewin's coverage of Freud's train phobia and its theoretical sublimation (through the work of analogy Freud described in the funereal lines borrowed from Goethe) refers only in passing to the other early train trip which Ernest Jones thought could be superimposed onto the one featuring mother. Thus another reference to an other's passing has been missed. It was in anticipation of their next meeting and upcoming round trips that Freud conveyed to Fliess (on December 3, 1897) the missing scene from his train phobia's prehistory.

Every now and then ideas whirl through my head which promise to explain everything, and to connect the normal and the pathological, the sexual and psychological, and then they disappear again, and I make no effort to retain them, because I know that both their appearance in consciousness and their disappearance are not the real indication of their fate. . . . All this is only introductory to the subject of our meeting—in Breslau, . . . if the train connections suit you. . . . Breslau plays a part in my childhood memories. At the age of three I passed through the station when we moved from Freiberg to Leipzig, and the gas jets, which were the first I had seen, reminded me of souls burning in hell. . . . The anxiety about travel which I have had to overcome is also bound up with it.

After two years had passed within the correspondence with Fliess (a time period always modeled on the proper duration of mourning) Freud returned on the anniversary of their "congress-times" (which had of course intersected with round trips), to the other side of analogy, the side archaeology always excavated, to reschedule his own dread rapport with train travel in terms of a patient's break-through recollection.

> Buried deep beneath all his phantasies we found a scene from his primal period (before twenty-two months) which meets all requirements and into which all the surviving puzzles flow. . . . It is as if Schliemann had dug up another Troy which had hitherto been believed to be mythical. . . . He has demonstrated the truth of my theories in my own person, for with a surprising turn in his analysis he provided me with the solution of my own railway phobia (which I had overlooked). . . . My phobia . . . was a poverty, or rather a hunger phobia, arising out of my infantile gluttony and called up by the circumstance that my wife had no dowry. (December 21, 1899)

Schliemann's rapport with archaeological excavation was purely phantasmatic: he was pulled to the site of Troy by his close reading of *The Iliad*, which he tested with a stop watch. And once he uncovered what he took to be Trojans, he watched their perfectly, prophylactically preserved remains vanish on contact with air and light. This is the full range of Freud's coupling of the psychoanalytic intervention with excavation. But it was not, in Schliemann's case, repression alone which locked the researcher onto the beam of mummification. Rather it was a trajectory of identification that sent Schliemann all the way to the final frontier of the archaeological phantasm—to California—to search for a missing brother.

What falls within the period which the two train trips frame and the view of mother screens is the death of Freud's little brother Julius (information Freud does pass on to

Fliess immediately following the revelation he also forwards that he had tripped out on his mother's body): "his
death left in me the germ of reproaches." The reproach
lodged within relations with the dead—the melancholic
self-reproach—was indeed the germ of Freud's endopsychic
discovery of the society-wide effects of unmournable death.

Near Miss

Freud's railway phobia runs the circuit from his wife's
missing dowry back to the funereal and primal occasion for his own infantile gluttony. The wife's dowry or
Mitgift—doubly paranoid reference to the mother's milk—
aroused, in its withdrawal, the infant Freud's withdrawal
reaction. The haunted journey with the mother (in which a
dead child was concealed and preserved) is put back on the
rails of analogy by Freud's women patients. Indeed, the direct
precursor of the technical analogue Freud employed in 1913
to illustrate the patient's proper attitude was modeled by one
of those early hysterics and "mourners" who dictated connections Freud later repeated (within the correspondence
with Fliess) on his own person. The installation of the train is
at this point complete: the mechanism of a literal kind of
(cinematic) projection preserves the train connection by
reversing the sides of the train's projector-effect. "It was as
though she were reading a lengthy book of pictures, whose

pages were being turned over before her eyes" (*SE* 2:153).

Freud discovered the enigmatic force of transference in his first psychoanalytic case study, which happens to be of an adolescent girl, where transference revealed itself in its near missingness. Although Freud postulated the possibility of a mother transference which might have succeeded where his had not been received, he was left addressing bonds of identification circuited through a series of collapsed couples, which, undermined by the group structures into which they had withdrawn, remained inaccessible to his person-to-person call of transference. The Dora case already belonged, in a sense, to the second system.

But the first place of transferential encounter—within the correspondence with Fliess—took the form of haunting. On these transference tracks, Freud's primal train view was animated by projection: outside little Freud glimpsed a ghostly terrain advertising—externalizing—"the germ of reproaches." But even though this first run of transference would appear to belong to the first system, the switch which Freud pulled in the flashback forwarded to Fliess from his earliest misdeeds to a teenage souvenir ("when I was fourteen") gives yet another preview of the second system. Lewin situates the "sublimation" process which Freud has Goethe sponsor—and which Freud's own 1913 analogue accomplished—within the journalistic institution of adolescence.

> For it seems really as if Freud had started with a rough draft of the train-ride metaphor (not available to us) based on unconscious note-taking in a childhood diary, which was later mislaid and only much later retrieved when the metaphor came to mind "somehow." (83)

The correspondence with Fliess was thus the supplement to preexisting adolescent journalism—just as Fliess was the ghost not so much of Julius (who was too far gone to figure except as the "construction of psychoanalysis" he never underwent) as of John, Freud's childhood colleague in aggressive misdeeds and teenage friend forever. According to Freud's flashback, John returned on a visit to Vienna when Freud was fourteen; they promptly improvised for an audience of children a Julius Caesar pageant in which Freud played Brutus to John's Julius. The death wish that Julius had attracted in early childhood was openly admitted on this stage of adolescent acting out, the mode of return or replay which circumvents remembering and transference. The train of association which the correspondence with Fliess conveyed thus passed through the adolescent terminal where transference does not stop.

Shanky Spaz

According to William Bullitt and Freud's analysis of Woodrow Wilson,[1] the switches of Wilson's "one track mind" are operated from within an adolescent conversion experience which first brought him into "direct communication with God" (74). Conversion fixed in place the future president's lifelong identifications:

> There are many bits of evidence which indicate that Wilson's identification of himself with Christ first became the accumulator of a great charge of libido at the time of his "conversion." (76)
>
> He seems to have identified his father with God at a very early age and to have established this Father-God as his Super-Ego and thus condemned himself to expect of himself the impossible. He probably identified himself with the Only Begotten Son of God shortly after identifying his father with God, but it seems likely that he did not begin to employ this identification

with Christ as a major outlet for his libido until his adolescence, when his increased activity needed to be reconciled with his passivity to his father. (78)

The identifications that determined the case of Wilson—and thus the course of modern European history—aimed at psychotic disconnection from "reality":

Therefore, through his identification with Christ he convinces himself that he does not need to fight, that by submitting he will achieve his aims. And, if he has not a firm grip on reality, he is apt to convince himself after he has submitted that he has in fact won a victory, although in reality he has suffered complete defeat. Thus, however desirable identification with Christ may be as a means to reconcile an inner conflict, it is disadvantageous in so far as it produces an inclination to submit when facing battle, and a tendency to turn away from the facts of reality. (78–79)

But Wilson got as far as he did—aiming, paternally, for the ministry and choosing, as compromise between active and passive relations with father, a political career instead—in a public context which did not cover for him as, for example, Dostoevsky's art did. How did Wilson go psychotic out in the open and in charge of world events? Surprise! He was American.

The Lollard tradition of the British non-conformist middle class transferred to America, in which he was brought up, produced an atmosphere in which it was difficult for a man whose masculinity exceeded his femininity to flourish, except economically; but one well suited to women and to men whose femininity exceeded their masculinity. The "Thou shalt not!" of Lollardry is intolerable to a masculine man but congenial to women. . . . The problems of Wilson's life arose not from conflicts with his environment but from conflicts within his own nature. He would have had to face those conflicts if he had been brought up in the comparative freedom of European civilization. The screen of rationalizations which allowed him to live all his life without facing his passivity to his father would have fallen early on the continent of Europe. He was fortunate to have been born in a nation which was protected from reality during the nineteenth century by inherited devotion to the ideals of Wyclif, Calvin and Wesley. (71)

Toxic Shock

Traumatic neurosis tracks back to the primal scene of cinematic projection afforded by the window seat in the moving train, which, framed and spliced on the outside by the telegraph poles lining the tracks, ultimately conveyed the train-wreck trauma to the point of advancing out, via frontal footage of a train's arrival, into the audience. Moviegoers first reacted by fleeing panic-struck. But over time audiences became accustomed to swallowing the mass shock of techno-crash. Identification with one's own technologization thus kept in line the projection of one's body as mechanical aggressor; both lines of defense alternated in bringing about a reversal of charges; the shock was internalized, inverted, phantasmatized. Roller coasters are a crude memorial to this training for disaster's thrill. According to Benjamin, the culture industry processed or developed shock through the work of mourning into inoculative doses against it which Disney films also administered. Via shock inoculation everyone's assimilation to the techno-media and the masses proceeds by controlled release—and not by fastforward into mass psychosis.

For Freud, too, it was "a severe shock or a sudden bereavement" that could exert radical impact on pathological conditions—often inducing complete remission—just as it might shorten the life of one not pathologically conditioned (*SE* 7:287). Freud accordingly rejected stress as cause of neurosis. In the etiology of one case of hysteria, the recollection of an actual train crash serves only as analogue conveyed by the patient's associations. Even the more primal recollection of a corpse is not, in this case, a candidate for pathogenesis. Only the earliest disturbances within the sexological register were programmed for rerun as symptoms (*SE* 3:196, 206).

By the time of *Beyond the Pleasure Principle*, however, Freud shifted from the sexological to the cryptological and technological. It is at this turning point that Benjamin admits Freud into his own rereading of relations of identification with the apparatus. According to Freud, shock value lies beyond or outside the inner apparatus and its prehistory only by being constitutively prior to this interiority's service to wish-fulfillment. This prior or primal phase can only be known via the playback which the dreams of the shell-shocked afford.[1] Thus it is by no means extraneous or incidental to Ernst Simmel's work on wartime traumatic neurosis that the organizing metaphor both for the illness and its cure covers the forward and reverse projections of film.[2]

According to Benjamin, *Gedächtnis*, the German term for memory which is commemorative in makeup, is that which consciousness, in order to shield the apparatus from shock attack, must not receive. Instead, *Erinnerung*, the internalizing German word for remembering, must record in place and thus erase: consciousness contains shock by "incorporating" it within the register of *Erinnerung*.[3] But the poets, who, Benjamin stresses, reject the inoculation-effect as foreign to inspiration, nevertheless register this effect's side-effect (against which they specifically seek protection through outright rejection) of "sterility." Shock defense quarantines the traumatizing event by assigning it an exact time and place *(Zeitstelle)* in consciousness. A diary or a journal—or a journalism—must be kept to protect not so much against the shock of events (which are already, in any event, produced or processed as singular and interchangeable headlines) but against the constant pressure exerted both by technocontact and contact with the masses. Shock absorption has produced the immune system of the group always prepared for catastrophe. But to preserve this group protection plan, the group member must libidinize or participate in (via diary writing and gadget love) his own teen-agerization, technologization, or massification.

Group rapport with a terror that originally went on the warpath in the "American wilderness" turns each mob member into a detective or informant in a society-wide work of detection which the disappearance of individual traces within the crowd first inaugurated. With gadgets, each moment comes equipped with a trigger, which (everyone's share in) *Erinnerung* pulls: the invention of the match was matched both by the lifting of the telephone receiver, which no longer required windup, and the snap or shot of the photo image. "The apparatus," Benjamin concludes, "awards the moment in a sense a posthumous shock" (630). Once the techno-devices of unmourning get the moment where we, killing time, wanted it, they leave it there. On top of this pile-up of dead moments we find the immunized body—of the group.

On the other side of the tracks (but still within the endopsychic sensurround), Wagner-Jauregg began to investigate and champion the value of shock as therapy.[4] By 1917 he concluded that the most successful mode of fever shock could be obtained through injection of active malaria (which could be checked with quinine). But a more direct connection between the curative power of fever shock and mental disturbance—that is, on the same side of analogy or etiology—was uncovered by Meduna. The belief that the schizophrenic process had a curative effect in epilepsy obscured the important connection through its reverse application: the ongoing attempts to transfuse the blood of schizophrenics to treat epileptics were unsuccessful. "Meduna sought to achieve the reverse, to use the epileptic process to treat schizophrenia." But while Meduna searched for the convulsant drug that would turn on the natural antagonism between the two processes, Cerletti, working in Rome in the thirties, discovered an effective method still current to this day: electroshock. Electricity, it seems, allowed Cerletti to keep his method distinct from the primal purpose: "I have always maintained that in the therapeutic mechanism of electroshock the electricity itself is of little importance: it is only an epileptogenic stimulus, while the important and fundamental factor is the epileptic-like seizure, no matter how it is obtained. Therefore, maintaining that only the convulsive attack induced with the minimum stimulus is the essential therapeutic factor, I have never paid much attention to the different variations of the electric machine proposed."

In 1939 Cerletti treated his first patient, a thirty-nine-year-old man who had been found wandering the streets of Rome. His mood was indifferent to the environment while he advertised in neologisms that he was under telepathic influence. Cerletti gave this standard set of withdrawals from society a fine tuning: eleven electroconvulsive therapy sessions later, the patient recovered and was soon back at his job. The series was back on the air. By the fifties (the first era of TV) ECT was the dominant treatment of psychotic states.

Double Date

What gets synchronized in the instantaneity of shock absorption is our deaths. One's singular death was inconceivable. The plural that accomplishes the singular is the form of suicide. Even when at least three internal positions negotiate one self-destruction, the impulses to kill and to die (or die someone else) have been merged into one unitary drive. As one of the adolescent suicides analyzed by Barrie Biven put it (ultimately to the mother), "If I go, you go too."[1]

According to William Spring's calculations, if suicide were not the easier way out than murder, then, on the way out, suicides would have by now done everyone in.[2] Sadism tends to turn inward, thereby releasing suicidal impulses and delusions of impending death and world destruction (53). "In these patients there appears to exist an identification of the whole world with their own bodies" (55). Thus emerges the idea that the world is coming to an end (or has already been totaled), which is so common among schizo-phrenics, adolescents, and saviors.

> In its details this idea varies tremendously. Earth-quakes . . . may be held responsible, or specific descriptive details may be entirely lacking. . . . These ideas have in common that large masses of people are wiped out, usually the whole human race. (48)

The inward turn that sadism tends to take has also been undertaken in these fantasies: "To face a murder wish against an actual person is far more difficult than to face a wish to injure a whole community or the whole world. To destroy the world is therefore an act of self-injury" (52).

> It appears to be more pleasant to think of the end of the whole world than of one's own death alone. Mis-ery loves company, and the idea that the world is coming to an end involves the simultaneous gratifica-tion of sadistic and of masochistic impulses. (56)

When *Mitsein* ("being with") gets extended to what is sup-posed to be *Dasein's* loneliest hour: it's Jonestown. "The *Da-sein* of Mickey Mouse is such a dream of contemporary man" Benjamin writes in "Experience and Poverty." But Benjamin is still trying to sell shock's rapport with the anti-body, Mickey Mouse, "whose *Dasein* is full of a wonder which not only surpasses technical marvels but also makes fun of them":

> For its most marvelous aspect is that it all comes im-provised, without machinery, out of the body of Mickey Mouse, out of his partisans and persecutors, out of quotidian furniture, just as it comes out of trees, clouds, or the sea. Nature and technicity, primi-tivism and comfort have become completely one. And before the very eyes of a populace exhausted by the endless complication of the everyday and for whom life's purpose appears only as the most distant point in an endless perspective of means, there appears redemption, a *Dasein* which at every turn is self-

sufficient in the most simple and at the same time comfortable manner, in which a car weighs no more than a straw hat and the fruit on the tree grows round as quickly as the nacelle of a balloon.[3]

Laugh Track

Martin Grotjahn confirmed in his essay on *Ferdinand the Bull* Benjamin's view that Disney humor is so successful and popular because it is uniquely (and infantilizingly) grounded in shock appeal:

> The contrast of laughter is the shock. In psychoanalytic literature it is never pointed out that the harmless shock is the only form of comic about which the child in pre-Oedipal age is able to laugh. Children are comical only from the viewpoint of the adults, they have very little sense for humor or wit. The pleasure in the phenomenon is originated later; the small child laughs only if it is shocked by the kidding adult. The child is all set to react with fear or even with panic, then suddenly realizes that there is no true reason to be afraid and finally discharges the activated energy in the form of laughter.[1]

But as Adorno and Horkheimer put it, laughter's group effort (which is child's play) invents anew, with each renewed outburst, caricatures—of and in place of harmony and conciliation:

> In the false society laughter is a disease which has attacked happiness and is draining it into its worthless totality. . . . Such a laughing audience is a parody of humanity. Its members are monads, all dedicated to the pleasure of being ready for anything at the expense of everyone else. Their harmony is a caricature of solidarity.

Conciliatory laughter, which is what false laughter "parodies," resonates with escape from those forces and constraints to which the false or terrible kind succumbs in order to overcome fear: "There is laughter because there is nothing to laugh at. Laughter, whether conciliatory or terrible, always occurs when some fear passes."[2]

The genealogy of the group formation of laughter (in the face of fear and shock) was originally trapped inside that of laughing gas. Invented in the eighteenth century by revolutionaries who were America-bound, laughing gas became in the early nineteenth century a sideshow attraction (together with hypnosis, telepathy, and other occult placeholders of the new media technologies). One member of the audience, who happened to be a dentist, witnessed the anesthetic side effect of the gas: henceforth the gas was another sublimation of medical healing's primal proximity to murder and torture. Otherwise the gas came to be reserved for philosophical speculation. Under the guise of gas (as later again in conjunction with the group) laughter recast every issue of dialectical or individualist provenance. Under cover of laughing gas, philosophy first admitted mass culture's alternation (it was the same difference) of affirmational or suicidal relations with "nothing."

Because Benjamin Paul Blood had celebrated it in 1874 as "anesthetic revelation and the gist of philosophy," William James experimented with the philosophical gas within the context (he helped establish) of all the other modes of religiosity (conversion, for instance) that comprised American shock preparedness.[3] James's gas experiments proved to him that "our normal, waking consciousness, rational consciousness as we call it, is but one special type of consciousness, whilst all about it, parted from it by the flimsiest of screens, there lie potential forms of consciousness entirely different." This "delirium of theoretic rapture" taught him the rush—and hangover—of Hegel's philosophy: "all opinions are thus synonyms, are synonymous, are the same. But the same phrase by difference of emphasis is two, and here again difference and no-difference merge in one" (78). On laughing gas the mind sees the "identification of opposites": "vomiting and swallowing" and countless other contrasts figured on the pages James filled up while under the influence. "The mind saw how each term belonged to its contrast through a knife-edge moment of transition" (78). But James "faded" and was let down precisely at the point Blood reserved for revelation of "the genius of being"—the point of coming to. Whereas Blood went on to "enter into the sadness and majesty of Jesus," James concluded otherwise:

> The identification of contradictions, so far from being the self-developing process which Hegel supposes, is really a self-consuming process, terminating either in a laugh at the ultimate nothingness, or in a mood of vertiginous amazement at a meaningless infinity. (81)

The Other Reich

I n *The Mass Psychology of Fascism*, Wilhelm Reich warned that if man did not distinguish himself from the machine that had, by 1946, become part of him, he would be destroyed by it. But while gagging on the machine, Reich slipped us a Mickey.

> The advance of civilization which was determined by the development of the machine went hand in hand with a *catastrophic misinterpretation* of *the human biologic organization*. In the construction of the machine man followed the laws of mechanics and lifeless energy. This technology was already highly developed long before man began to ask how *he himself* was constructed and organized. When, finally, he dared very gradually, cautiously and very often under the mortal threat of his fellow man to discover his own organs, he interpreted their functions in the way he had learned to construct machines many centuries

before. Trapped in a mechanistic picture of the world, man was incapable of grasping the specifically living, non-mechanistic functioning. Man dreams about one day producing a homunculus a la Frankenstein or at least an artificial heart or artificial protein. The notions of homunculus, which man has developed in his fantasy, project a picture of a brutal monster, man-like, but mechanically stupid, angular, and possessing powerful forces, which, if they are set loose, will be beyond control and will automatically cause havoc. In his film *Fantasia* Walt Disney brilliantly captured this fact.[1]

Did Reich, like the ideologues of electroshock, assume a separation between the machine and the charge he sought to give his patients when, beginning in 1939 in America, he introduced the "orgone accumulators?" But already in 1921, in his essay "The Concept of the Libido from Freud to Jung," Reich compared libido to an electric current; from 1935 on, sexual energy was for him bioelectricity. The topography of what had gone wrong in our creation by machines had also gone down, gone unconscious. At some level, then, Reich realized—like Staudenmaier or Schreber or Schreiber—that to attain revitalization he had to rev up within the analogical life-line connections to machines, the placeholders of the body. Reich's diagnosis:

> *Thus, the machine has had a mechanical, mechanistic, "dulling," and "rigidifying" effect on man's conception of his own organization.* This is how man conceives of himself: The brain is the "most consummate product of development." His brain is a "control center," which gives the individual organs commands and impulses just as the "ruler" of a state orders his "subjects" about. The organs of the body are connected with the master, the "brain," by telegraph wires, the nerves.[2]

On the outside, Reich aimed at attaining revitalization (or reanimation) through the machines of his own devising (primal, animistic contraptions that with little modification could also serve as "cloudbusters"), which countered equally projective technologies—in particular the UFOs he claimed had a hold on the globe.[3] But out of this combat zone an immortal life was to emerge that would not, like Homunculus, remain in rigorous pursuit only of the spiritual side of pleasure. Immortal monsters have the body (the mother's body) and exceed it too—via their phantom share in spiritualization. They inhabit the alliance between language and the imagination. (And that's where it's at, when it comes to pleasure.) But Reich sided with the body and not with pleasure. The death drive, which Reich had spent his career debunking as mere internalization of extraneous constraints—from which the "complete" orgasm like some cure-all could release us—had reversed direction: it was the on ramp to his own affirmation of life force.

Since nonneurotic man would always only want to feel good about himself, the body (or body-ego) would be the only constant measure or model of the pleasure obtainable by a self which was already having fun. Through the reinvention of technology (as a science of magic), Reich hoped to reclaim that nice side of man which had been wasted on animals: "it is striking that man invests the animals he portrays precisely with those traits he misses in himself and does not give to his homunculus figures. This, too, is excellently brought out in Disney's animal films."[4]

Outside the Freudian system, Reich joined Jung in addressing a vaster symptom of Californiaization—the UFO phantasm, dream, or rumor. According to Jung, the flying saucer either conveys the dead or emerges (literally hysterically) as uterus wandering across the skies "from the so-called unconscious which still precedes consciousness in every new human life, as the mother precedes the child." But because the alien encounter is also with the dead, projection guides the flight of unidentified objects (of identification).

The following dream comes from California, the classic Saucer country, so to speak. "I was standing outside. All of a sudden I saw something round and fluorescent coming towards us from way in the distance. I realized it was a Flying Saucer. I thought someone was playing a trick, then I thought it was real—I looked up behind me and saw someone with a movie projector."[5]

The primal Californian, who carries his body with him or in front of him (as a compact and dispensable projection), also bears, a la Frankenstein's control knobs screwed into the monster's neck, the support systems comprising his serious and inward rapport with the other, that is, with the group. For Reich's own Californian relationship to the non-neurotic self or body (a turn-on that turned inward or outward; in a word, psychotic), the foundation of a utopian community was indispensable. The adolescent support group was dedicated to cleansing the earth of the parasitic and deadly orgone (DOR). The rainmaking devices were now called DOR busters; they also served as space guns aimed at invading saucers.

Of course the support group was countersigned at first by a third party or *pater:* The Ministry of Wartime Production promoted the manufacture of Orgone Energy Accumulators. There was a time when Reich resisted not only the machine connection but also its ideology called mysticism (that is, hysteria). Now he built superman booths in which the body could be recharged with the orgone energy he considered, simply, "cosmic."

The animistic or homeopathic logic that got Reich this far also governed the ORANUR experiment in which the nuclear threat was exorcised through administration or controlled release of actual radioactivity. But this was the wrong kind of capsule: the participants fell ill. It was at this point that Reich began to believe—in UFOs. On the other side of this turning point Reich already entitled his next opus *The Murder of Christ.* Alien spacecraft ran on the orgone energy he had discovered (and he should know, since he was son of spaceman). While spacemen attacked, Reich reread the New Testament. Next he excised sexological considerations from his theorizing, just as he refused to plug homosexuals into his treatment apparatus. At one end the group (or Reich) banished sexology, childhood sexuality, and homosexuality; at the same end Reich awaited invasion or penetration (all the way from outer space) of every system of defense.

In the fifties, however, during the first era of television, the era, that is, of television's banishment from the endopsychic sensurround, opposition to Reich emerged. Not only did the government pull out; Reich's rapport with the other shifted out of the couple. His marriage suddenly turned into a rapid turnover of marriages in which new wives were compelled to write confessions and recant. His other became the group or groupie.

Threatened by FDA intervention, Reich, who now signed all correspondence EPPO (Emotional Plague Prevention Office), regularly decked out Organon for the official visit he expected his protector, President Eisenhower, to make. Then he armed the town in preparation for the FDA attack. It was Jonestown. Reich's program or orbit of psychoticization and arrest was contained in the only model of anthropomorphizing grounding of the subject Reich admitted within the accumulation of machine analogies: the world of Disney.

Bringing Up *Beben*

*After the earthquake there was a strange mixture of
elation and despair. . . . We united as friends.*
—*Time*, November 20, 1989

In *Faust* II, Homunculus, the preserved brain cryonically in
search of corporeal life, merges suicidally with the sea in
literal enactment of Nautilus. On the way to his anticipated
rebirth as mega-hunk, Homunculus has flipped through the
two channels of creation: surf and quake. An earthquake
instantly raises up a valpeak of life—which a fastforwarding
of human history once again withdraws into annihilation.
Out of the sea more gradually a life with staying power
emerges. Goethe's notion of "repeated puberty," which already fits his evolution theory, that is, his doctrine of metamorphosis (which features his brand of neoteny), fits right
in here. Goethe sides with the ritual repetitions of surfing.
The quake temporality of adolescent genius and genus (like

the sheer interiority of Homunculus) must reconnect—as "repeated puberty," surfing, or working out on the beach— with the place of its eternal or internal disconnection from the maternal body. There can be no theory of evolution without the invention (and repetition) of adolescence.

Goethe's *Faust* II already registered on its Richter scale a fault which is no longer father's. In the 1989 quake the body of mother nature was on projective rebound. The aftershock of cinematic projection featured the 1990 movie *Tremors,* in which the return of the earthquake as a gigantic worm is greeted with "mother humper" or, elliptically and more to the point, with "mother."

The shock that the psychic defense system was designed to withstand—down to the internalized aftershock protection that sadomasochism stages—was first contained in a philosopheme which "California" soon came to supersede: the earthquake. A reading of the culture industry or mass media society—or California—could begin with Emerson's diagnosis in "Culture" that those who lived in dread of earthquakes could not read tropes—or happy faces.[1]

Friendliness is a more efficient emergency-state disposition (preparation or proofing) than efficiency itself. Friendliness holds California together—in the face of the quake. It admits and libidinally binds the live participation of all in one sensurround of total (hallucinatory and projective) destruction. San Francisco earthquake 1989: earthquakes are hooked up to the unconscious as catastrophic inside/out turns of events or as conveyer belts of *Nachträglichkeit* (the preserve of its traumatizing effects and after shocks). While it is happening, the building almost crumbles or collapses—but doesn't. Did it happen? Was I having a dizzy spell? A hallucination? The quake is thus immediately an internal experience: you can't locate where it's taking place. The internal bridges are forever reserved for col-lapses.[2]

In the movie *San Francisco,* the cinematic projection of quake preparedness and shock absorption surrounding the first Big One was grounded in a production of Faust. The San Francisco earthquake of 1989 erected a wall in the place of a double bridge—to Germany, where another wall, the one separating unification of East and West, collapsed in the wake of the quake. The wall binding the bicoastal constitution of Germany/California falls only in stereo or not at all.[3]

William James traveled to the Coast in 1906, arriving at Stanford in time to share the experience of the Big One, which even then was a personalized label or license plate, the apotheosis, in short, of the first name basis. By 1906 even the ground or basis of California—the earthquake—was Californian. "To me," as James concludes his analysis of his own response to the 1906 earthquake, "it wanted simply to manifest the full meaning of its *name*."[4] James analyzes the responses he shared with other innocent bystanders as the model for all group bonding in defense against shock. The first way in which his own consciousness had taken in the quake was via the catastrophe's animation or personification "as a permanent individual entity": "It came, moreover, directly to *me*. It stole in behind my back, and once inside the room, had me all to itself, and could manifest itself convincingly. Animus and intent were never more present in any human action, nor did any human activity ever more definitely point back to a living agent as its source and origin." Indeed, all those around James at the time agreed: "'it expressed intention'" (211–12).

While the "experience was too overwhelming for anything but passive surrender to it," the inner state of the group was one of interested seriousness (215, 219).

> The terms "awful," "dreadful" fell often enough from people's lips, but always with a sort of abstract meaning, and with a face that seemed to admire the vastness of the catastrophe. . . . When talk was not directly practical, I might almost say that it expressed . . . a tendency more toward nervous excitement than toward grief. (224)

Indeed it is grief or mourning which the serious interiority of Californian quake preparedness overcomes. On the other side of the instant immortalization that new techno-media administer we find the synchronization of "equal" suffering or instant death of all at once, which replaces the "cutting edge of all our usual misfortunes": the aloneness of suffering and death.

> Children die, our house burns down, or our money is made way with, and the world goes on rejoicing, leaving us on one side and counting us out from all its business. In California every one, to some degree, was suffering. . . . The cheerfulness . . . was universal. Not a single whine or plaintive word did I hear from the hundred losers whom I spoke to. (224)

In the course of rejecting Benjamin's implicit claim that a notion of collective consciousness or of collective unconscious would improve upon "the individual" as subject of dreams, Adorno admitted one exception Benjamin could claim for his side: "It is open to criticism from the vantage point of psychology in that a mass ego exists only in earthquakes and catastrophes" (August 2, 1935). Thus on the eve of beaming across the unacknowledged connection between Germany and California, Adorno allowed that only one genuine collectivity would emerge along the fault in relations to father. In *Poetry and Truth* Goethe recalled the Lisbon quake as dislodging his faith in paternal support systems. Within Kleist's "The Earthquake in Chile," Adorno's forecast comes true: a massive, synchronized death remains interchangeable with the murder of an individual. And this confusion or quaking of representation and thought served as propaganda for the all-out warfare against Napoleon which Kleist's military-literary complex demanded.[5]

Kierkegaard's journals recorded the news from the other front:

> Then it happened that the great earthquake occurred, the frightful revolution which suddenly thrust upon

me a new, infallible law of explanation for all phenomena. Then I surmised that the great age of my father was not a divine blessing, but rather a curse; . . .
then I felt the stillness of death grow around me,
when I saw in my father an unhappy creature who
was to outlive us all, a cross on the grave of all his
own hopes. A guilt must rest upon the whole family, a
punishment of God be upon it; it was to disappear, to
be struck out by God's almighty Hand, wiped out like
an experiment that failed.[6]

The wipe-out of the experiment that failed was, in the twentieth century, the dual phantasm or legacy of two coasts:
Germany and California.

The quake question, which can be measured within
Germanicity on a scale from Goethe to Kleist, from Kierkegaard to Adorno, was introduced into the intertextual circuit of Hall, James, and Starbuck writing on adolescence or
conversion by Jung, who presented his 1909 lecture "Psychic Conflicts in a Child" as third in a series of talks he
delivered at Clark University on "The Association Method."[7]
James, by the way—and in this way gave license to its
deconstruction—saw conversion as possessing a regularly
effective psychic counterpart in association. In Jung's analysis, the quake question a little girl poses sounds in German
too much like another big one: "Where do *Beben* come
from?" Quaking will synchronize her withdrawal from the
paternal support system that cannot withstand the question. What emerges as safety zone from the quake slides her
case to the inside of the case of California. According to
Jung's analysis, the only way out for the little girl patient as
she withdraws her love from her parents who lie to her—
about *Beben*—would be sublimation if she weren't too
young for sublimation to render her "more than symptomatic service" (132). But the Messina earthquake helps her
out: "That was the beginning of her nocturnal fears; she
could not be left alone, her mother had to go to her and stay
with her, otherwise she was afraid that the earthquake
would come and the house fall in and kill her" (132).

Her next (society-wide) step toward self-help is the invention of the "stereotyped fantasy of a 'big brother' who knew everything, could do everything, and had everything": "The next day at lunch, Anna announced, apparently out of the blue, 'My brother is in Italy and has a house made of cloth and glass and it doesn't fall down'" (136). Her wish that the earthquake no longer be dangerous is thus fulfilled. Although the model for the fantasy brother was the father ("who seems to be rather like a brother to Mama"), a "childish fear of the father" persists amidst the aftershock effects. Between the drifting plates of her libido "there was some obstacle preventing the transference of love to the parents and that therefore a large part of it was converted into fear" (142). While Anna imagines that Papa and the gardener wish to kill her, Jung projects around this blockage and conversion the endopsychic and psychotic expansion or application of her case: "(This childish fear of the father is to be seen particularly clearly in adults in cases of dementia praecox, which takes the lid off many unconscious processes as though it were acting on psychoanalytical principles.)" (142). If she were to flip her lid we could observe, in principle, the converter that was in fact turned on in the '89 earthquake. The earthquake packs the teenage charge: it runs, beginning in the eighteenth century, down the modernist channels of adolescence. Group formation, preparedness, denial are some of the society-wide aftershocks. If one peels away from its simultaneity a genealogy of the quake, one discerns, at first, a random catastrophe that escapes a fault in relations with father. But in the wake of the primal quake (already in Kant's reflections on the Lisbon disaster, for example), preparedness, denial, and group bonding survive to schedule catastrophe, certainly in California, as always and already happening. Group preparedness absorbs shocks and tremors against which paternal support systems were not proof—and could not be quake-proofed. And yet one cannot be sure, even when it happens, that it is happening.

Serfs Up

I *had to squeeze the serf out of myself, drop by drop.*
    —Chekhov

In 1939 and 1940 Wittels linked phantom formation to the epileptic origin of postmodern Pacman (in other words, as we will see, to the case of D.). But if the loss of awareness or spell of absentmindedness which heralds epileptic attack can be relocated as the enabling condition for phantom formation, then it is on account of the same-sex constituency of a bisexual constitution which, having gone under, has come up for phantom rebound.[1] In the normal or neurotic course of socialization/sublimation, which, however, the psychotic and even the pervert must also, in some part, pass through, every narcissistic identification reserves a place for phantom possession.[2] By thus insisting on "the obvious difference between the mechanism of identification, and its effect: a figure, a phantom existing in one as a result of identification" (141), Wittels develops the haunting effect as primal group psychology. The first crowd the ego (in the family pack) faces is that of its phantoms:

> Narcissistic wish fulfillment crowds our psychic space with a number of phantoms, all of them results of identifications (141). The crowd the ego must find its way in is, primarily, comprised of these phantoms. (142)

As the intertextual complex of conversion already advertised, the reversal or control of the ghostly effects of the inward and solo course of melancholia requires a grief management which only the support groups of quake preparedness, sadomasochism, or adolescent friendship are designed to provide. The earthquake shares its shock absorption with the epileptic attack, which Freud analyzed in "Dostoevsky and Patricide." The seizure joins the grimace as primal apotropaic modeled upon what it enacts: the body's identification with another body. In D.'s case, epileptic attack had been preceded or anticipated by childhood twilight states of depression which gave way to epilepsy (conceived as the displaced expression of sexual union) only after his father had been murdered by rebellious serfs.

On the down side of his earliest mood swings, young D. feared imminent death. He would leave about the house little notes requesting that, should he die in his sleep, a delay of five days be observed before burial. This primal rehearsal of his writing project already repeated an identification with a dead person or with someone, still alive, whom he wanted dead. In either case the fear of death covered for fear of retribution by the superego, which helped D. out: "You wanted a dead father—go ahead and *be* the dead father!"

The only release Freud can conceive would have been the cessation of symptoms brought to D. by Siberian exile, the externalization of the otherwise inner, symptom-producing need to be punished. Reactionary politics supply (society-wide) the requisite alternation between externalization and symptom formation. D. thus doubles as the Everyman of group psychology—the Oedipus or post-Oedipus of Freud's second system. In the case of D., then, Freud develops the post-modern heir to the primal couple that gave us the tragic dimension of neurotic or modern thought.[3] Oedipus and Hamlet, the unconscious and the neurotic, were, like the heterosexual couple, linked out of sync with their respective (time) zones of desiring. Arrival always at the "hour of the other" required Hamlet to unfulfill the desire Oedipus had inimitably satisfied. Once the Oedipus story is in place, the Hamletian neurotic or modern can only restage, play within play, mirror on mirror, a primal scene in which he recognizes every position but the one he in fact occupies. Thus rather than enter (or split) the scene at the triadic point that admits substitution, Hamlet reproduces his own scene by killing Polonius and forwarding Laertes into his place. But he creates the double relation with Laertes by double disavowal of his patricidal position. If Hamlet is thus dropped onto the track of psychoticization—whereby he ends up face to face with Laertes, the double from whom he receives his death— then at this personalized end Hamlet has anticipated the fallout of the failure of couplification, namely, the group membership in psychotic and perverse structures which D. embodies as group of one.

In the case of Dostoevskian man, Freud discovers that relations with father, which must issue in identification, are the most difficult or imperiled because the bisexual constitution has overlibidinized the paternal bond. The castration threat deflects the son in the direction of mother with whom he identifies as recipient of father's punitive penetrations. But again castration is also at this end the requirement for being loved by father. Thus two impulses undergo repression: hatred of father and being in love with father. The first impulse—hatred of father—turns on the "normal" scenario of repression. But it receives pathogenic intensification when a strong bisexual constitution requires that love of father or fear of the feminine also go the route of repression. Freud argues that this cornerstone of his second system arouses "the most universal repugnance" or resistance as something "unsavory" and "incredible." But that's not all: the repressed passivity is reestablished through the introduction of *the* sadomasochistic couple: the superego and ego. One can defend against dependence on a severe father only by internalizing the relation of dependence; identification is always the only alternative to joining what one can't lick.

The ego develops a need which could not be fulfilled on the outside but only repressed. The need for punishment (some call it "fate") supplies both punitive penetration and, as punishment, castration. This is what the epileptic seizure and death symptom enacted. "For the ego the death symptom is a satisfaction in fantasy of the masculine wish and at the same time a masochistic satisfaction; for the superego it is a punishment satisfaction, that is, a sadistic satisfaction. Both of them, the ego and the superego, carry on the role of father." This is the repress release which covers death wishes the father introduces and attracts. The news of the father's death is the headline announcing the liberation or liquidation of his charges. Comic or manic responses correspond to the moment of bliss which also inhabits the epileptic attack. But the punchline instantly follows: cruel, tortuous punishment enacts the father's destruction upon the person of the son. That's why D. turned reactionary the moment he was persecuted by the authorities. Relieved of having to punish himself, he got outsiders deputized by father to exact punishment. Now at least (—at last!—) the police were fucking with him.

On the evening news: a Santa Barbara High School basketball player, who is in the first place a reformed juvenile delinquent, tells all. And how does he size up the extent or cause of his past problems? He lost his father at age three thereby foregoing having his "butt whipped."

Queen for a Day: the compulsion to confess already fulfills the need for punishment which, under the cover of an external threat, courts "internal instinctual danger." According to Theodor Reik, confessions "represent a kind of verbal masochistic exhibition, of self-punishment in words. When a person makes a confession of this kind . . . it can only correspond to an overpowering of the ego by the super-ego. Moral masochism"—which results from the resexualization or reanimation of that which, at the close of the Oedipus complex, had been laid to rest as idealizing identification—"has become overwhelming."[4]

Punishment was what D. needed to lube his relation to that which guilt, without his recognition of its just cause, otherwise impeded and paralyzed: the writing which he first took up to address the outside chance of his being buried alive in exchange for the death wishes against the dead or dad. Soon the bisexual contract, which group membership puts out on relations with father, reintroduced as sadomasochism and epileptic attack (or, in bicoastal contexts, as quake) what continued to be libidinized ("abused") in the course of its protracted disappearance—the father and child relation.

Radical Ambivalence

The melancholic's confession of guilt, Freud realized, would make no sense but for the existence of another psychic process at work which, parallel with melancholic atonement, has its origin, as Radó established, in the sadistic trend of hostility to the object.[1] This hostility trend flies high (in a bitchen ambivalence sesh) when the rebellious ego is convinced (definitely) that the object alone is to blame. But the rebel is without a cause and the ego adopts instead a masochistic attitude of remorse toward the superego. Having withdrawn in narcissistic fashion, the melancholic ego attempts not to procure pardon and love from his object but to secure the superego's double blessing (423–24). To this end the ego offers itself up as object to the superego—which demands sacrifice. The ego's rage against the object is thus visited upon the ego by the superego. As mania demonstrates, the process of melancholia is designed "to do away with . . . the ambivalence of the ego and that of the object" (435). In mania nothing stands in the way, for a spell, of the purified ego's merging "in reciprocal love" with the object purged of offence. The task of undoing ambivalence enlists the same childish efforts which ended up building-blocking the superego.

The processing of unpleasure is out of phase with the pleasure principle, which comes first. The integration of good and bad—in the (first) person of the mother—becomes the impossible task that installs as its legacy stressed-out relations between ego and superego. Ambivalence must be established through education: the still weak ego of the young child does an S-turn around ambivalence by splitting mother into isolated good and bad objects. But education can teach the child only repression of the most flagrant application of his aggressive tendencies: "His aggression, warded off by the ego, then remains in the unconscious fastened upon the isolated representation 'bad mother.'. . . The isolated image of the 'good' mother now persists in his mind as a strongly-cathected *wish-idea*" (432).

If the child's longing for parents who would always be good motivates the formation of the superego (which is the repository of the good object) then the melancholic self-reproach—the ego's demand, as bad object, for punishment—represents a longing for love (425). The ego's own sadism (which also made a move against ambivalence) brings to grief its narcissistic craving for love. The inside job of seeking narcissistic gratification causes the ego to submit to the overpowering force of the aggression drive (429). First, because the ego cannot but fall "victim to the indestructible infantile illusion that only by yielding and making atonement can it be delivered from its *narcissistic* distress" (430). But second, aggression is irrepressible: whereas sexuality and genitality remain within range of repression, aggression can be defended against only through reaction: "Evidently the ego is incapable of erecting a barrier against the manifestation of aggression as it does against those of gross sensuality" (426).

A melancholic's incapacity for love grooves on the primal depression which a double disappointment at the end of the Oedipal engagement can install. The melancholic is a love addict whose incapacity for feeling—for affirming life—is always on the line. Alice Miller argues that the child who has (invariably) been denied the right to express feelings of anger will perpetually assert a right to feel which, not bonded to or bound by free speech, turns on the nonstop audio portion of a loveless existence.[2]

Every missing object, following this schedule of disappointments, will henceforward undergo "two different processes of incorporation, being absorbed not only by the superego but by the ego" (431). Doubled between good and bad incorporations, the departed object releases the rerun of an "unrestrained tyranny of the sadistic superego" which, as Freud observed in *The Ego and the Id*, arrogates to itself the consciousness of the melancholic subject.

Why WE THE PEOPLE
Don't Get Off

O   *nly the living can suffer. This is related to the frequent
         sadistic "tying fantasies" and impulses; the dead per-
         son does not require to be tied. Thus there is some-
thing in sadism and masochism as perversions that tends to
avoid death.*
      —Leo Stone, "Reflections on the Psychoanalytic
      Concept of Aggression"

Sexual liberation or freedom serves an ideology of spontaneous individuality (the internal, journal-keeping counterpart, in adolescent psychology, to group membership).
But this last stand of the individual is stood up, already, by
the other individual: only the interlocking machinery of
interchangeable parts (or "friends") works like the sum of
rifle parts to empower the group member with the solo status of the one holding the warm gun. The group member
stays together by preying, together with the other members,
on any outsider or individual who threatens couplification.

(Thus boredom in the couple always amounts to the symptom of a repression that finds support groups.)

The groupification of sexual coupling is what the Sadian session admits in place of belief in spontaneous creation (the output Benjamin refers to, in contrast to Mickey Mouse's energy, as the naive or Faustian constructive relation to technology). Conventionally eros has been aimed against technologization, mechanization, or conventionalization. But eros or drive (de Sade recognized) is the least personal or individual attribute a person possesses. The drive is thus the medium best suited for the bringing to consciousness of the sexual body which, to this end, can be fragmented, functionalized, and recombined across sexual configurations that recharge and splice together the parts. Discipline permits liberation from a body that can in turn be turned (around) into a medium of consciousness.

Building, in the eighteenth century, Oedipus's primal antibody, de Sade introduces the Californian native whose cult of body ego and "the friend" follows the Sadian directive but, caught up bicoastally in the *dialectic* of Enlightenment, also continues to grow, guiltily, supplements of interiority, which are not yet on the side of "intelligent life." The Californian has not yet brought to consciousness the charge of abuse: only the living are fit to be tied.

For de Sade, sexuality is only completely pleasurable when consciousness separates from the body and, projected back onto the body as a kind of condensed energy, takes charge of that bodily rapport which is entirely body building. Thus fantasy (and not "reason") is put in the place of control—in order to free thought or speech. In the Sadian session, the force of fantasy makes it all come from the head: immediate conversion of fantasy into sexual energy is what gets accomplished. The imagination, the Romantic detour and postal route back to one's self, is recircuited by de Sade as a direct or instant connection.

But an elaborately planned-out context of positionings and discursive interventions serves the endlessness of language which alone corresponds to the endless resources of the imagination—especially when it comes to sex. Here again the Sadian directive brings to consciousness what is, in any case, the case: one comes to conventional signs or images for which the other body only serves as screen, prop, or copy. The seemingly endless discharge of Sadian libertines, like the almost endless *Verkehr* ("traffic" or "intercourse") at the close of Kafka's "The Judgment," remains but a weak reflection of the endless flow bridging language and the imagination.

We know the target of Sadian praxis and critique: the family, which was on the rise, in the eighteenth century, to the top of institutionalization. Enlightenment propaganda protecting this dominant institution crowded literature and philosophy just as it crowded out of the family unit madness, crime, or, in short, the other side of the drive.

"Our family is the family of Oedipus," as one of de Sade's libertines puts it in *The New Justine* before transgressing in one sex act three incest limits on the body he has bred and positioned over the years precisely for this detonation: the object of his aimed emissions and penetrations is his daughter, niece, and granddaughter in one. The family of Oedipus is more commonly ruled by unconsciously committed incest: the Sadian support group makes incest the law and not the desire (that is, the Oedipal desire) to which subjects are otherwise constitutively subject.

Circumvention of the body as limit (as off-limits) would free pleasure from Oedipal bondage to corporeal analogues. But when the womb attracts in de Sade a violent shutdown (in *Philosophy in the Bedroom*) the ultimate law has, at the same time, been reenforced: the mother's body (the body) is kept radically off-limits. In de Sade only language gets off: there are only libidinizable words and graffiti to which material or maternal objects have already been sacrificed. We face a law or principle of pleasure which guarantees that only the Other will get off at the prospect of the unpleasure we derive from our limitedness, our waiting or sleeping around. In other words: the superego is sadistic; the body-ego is masochistic. And that's the law—of pleasure.

Eating Bambi

H itler's proclaimed abstinence from meat, coffee, alcohol, and sex . . . proved his moral right to free the Germans from their postwar masochism and to convince them that they, in turn, had a right to hate, to torture, to kill.

　　　—Erikson, *Childhood and Society*

Castle construction became in the twentieth century the specialty of haunted Californians and (as in Kafka's *The Castle* or Ludwig's Bavaria) of their correspondents on the other side of the same unconscious. In San Jose, for example, the haunted heiress of automatic weapons money feverishly rebuilt and expanded the Winchester fortress estate according to a layout conceived in the ongoing attempt to misguide the approach and reproach of phantoms. (Similar avoidance mechanisms were built in Fresno and Death Valley.) At San Simeon, Hearst projected the souvenir, ultimately, of his two-year European trip alone (in early adolescence) with his mother. Thus the two-year period of mourning had already been overbooked. After mother's death Hearst manically consumed and fragmented Europe and, at the end of the doubled trip and departure, threw up inside the quake-proof concrete crypt the residues and facticity of "European Civilization."

The bicoastal orbit of California increasingly comes full circuit as Disneyland replicas are placed ever closer to Neuschwanstein, the model of the Disney castle and crypt (paintings in the Singer's Hall are previews of Bambi). King Ludwig II, himself the advance preview of the case of D., combined gadget love with background music. The grotto at Linderhof was an experimental electrification project which Siemens provided (when the red light shone it was Venusberg; blue light on meant Capri). It was the primal amusement-park float or ride: its mix of late Romanticism and turbine-powered media technology promised the small world after all. While the hidden band played in the grotto, Ludwig drifted in the swan-shaped boat to the backup tunes of the generators making waves and Wagner. This continental drift coupled the king with Sacher-Masoch (and his mistress). But since those were still "individuals," it remained a blind date without consummation or consequence. Once the couplification of drives was admitted by mass culture, Ludwig would become, in the trail of his withdrawal into suicide, one of the ghost writers of Disney culture.

By 1966 one-third of U.S. citizens were under fourteen: From 1940 to this point of doubling—of the number of children between the ages of five and fourteen—and D.'s death (in 1966), everyone had shared the same formative dreams with which "Disney's machine" replaced the secrets and silences of childhood it had shredded.[1] Richard Schickel borrows Eric Hoffer's evocations of the American as perpetual adolescent or "go-getter" to characterize D., another teenager at heart. Technologization, Hoffer argues, creates a "juvenile, primitive and plastic" type; this "archetypal man in transition" is the adolescent.

The present trend toward juvenile behavior has been gathering force for over a century. . . . the American go-getter, though he has no quarrel with the status quo, is as much a perpetual juvenile as any revolutionary. (65) History is made by men who have the restlessness, . . . credulity, . . . ruthlessness and self-righteousness of children. It is made by men who set their hearts on toys. (68)

The history thus made—in the service of "nostalgia for a carefully falsified past"—is that of parents and ancestors. Preoccupation with the father's past is the only pastime available to one whose own childhood was reduced to abuse, just as it is also the only means left for the survivor to declare the father "history."

D. told his daughter that in his youth he had regularly submitted to basement whipping by his father "to humor him and keep him happy" (44). A track was thus beaten all the way to D.'s right-wing politics in his later years. But before externalization there is the inward turn: When D.'s big brother Roy performed a job washing the town hearse—in Marceline, the place of D.'s most cherished childhood memories—he allowed little brother to share in the profits after letting him play dead inside the hearse (36).

Odd jobs D. performed around 1923 give the preview of his art: he covered natural disasters for newsreel companies (62), while, free-lance, he made little movies of babies for parents to project in their living rooms. At the time of his father's death, the additions that comprised D.'s projection of (onto) Salten's *Bambi* were, one, the scene of father and son bonding over the mother's dead body and, two, the sequence devoted to natural catastrophe.

The modern group or mass that emerges in the move that turns mass murder into catastrophe was pre-programmed, Freud argues in *Civilization and Its Discontents*, when the Christian mass placed love and identification, sex and violence, in primal proximity. The "danger of a state of things which might be termed 'the psychological poverty of groups,'" as Freud unpacks it, " is most threatening where the bonds of a society are chiefly constituted by the identification of its members with one another, while individuals of the leader type do not acquire the importance that should fall to them in the formation of a group. The present cultural state of America would give us a good opportunity for studying the damage to civilization which is thus to be feared" (*SE* 21: 115-116).

In Freud's first system the phantomized other enjoyed personalizable relations with the one haunted by unmourning. This Frankensteinian couple leads in Freud's second system a group existence. Another way to get from a couplified haunting that still follows the leader to the mutual identification of catastrophe preparedness—from the vampire to the zombie—is to follow Freud on Rudolf Kleinpaul's research-and-destroy missions. Freud introduces the vampire in Kleinpaul's name in the midst of *Totem and Taboo*'s discussion of unmourning: "originally, says Kleinpaul, *all* the dead were vampires" (*SE* 13: 59). Driving home the point of the at once psychic and cinematic projection that is at stake, Freud refers here to Kleinpaul's *The Living and the Dead in Folklore, Religion, and Legend*.

In another tract,[2] also within range of Freud's reading, Kleinpaul lodged the trajectory of the death wish inside every act of consumerism—which, according to Kleinpaul, must be consummated always with regard to some sacrifice. As in the animism or animation already underway in Salten's *Bambi*, even (or especially) vegetal life drops off smacking of meat and murder.

Responding to turn-of-the-century charges against Jews of child sacrifice, Kleinpaul opens *Human Sacrifice and Ritual Murder* by first dedemonizing this singular accusation and relocating it within a history-wide projection. Beginning thus with prehistory, Kleinpaul situates cannibalism as prior to the rituals of human sacrifice it enabled: we would not have sacrificed humans to the gods if we ourselves were not already accustomed to enjoying their meat. A taste for tots and teens was shared with the fire gods who received choice specimens. Following certain reforms, these gods were transformed into demons and devils (hence Satanic cults are assumed to this day to sacrifice infants).

Kleinpaul desublimates the uplifting take on our already upbeat history of identification. The band, which played in primal precincts of consumerism in order to cover the cries or last words of victims of torture and sacrifice, continued to play as sacrifice was refined through selection and substitution. To a background beat only widows were burned in India. They turned up the volume while circumcision was enacted upon the screaming baby's body as contractual agreement (which replaced actual sacrificial murder). Eventually the sacrifice of lambs would substitute for human sacrifice, at which point certain double features— such as Dionysus being not only god of wine but also eater of raw human flesh or Oedipus being in the first place a sacrificed (or abused) child (11, 15)—could be forgotten.

But once lamb was served up to the gods, sublimation reversed itself: a certain vegetarian regression and revaluation of orality reinstated the primal repast. So far there has been no way out that wasn't a way into carnologocentrism.[3] Jesus Christ went beyond the Passover-lamb sacrifice by drenching bread and wine—our vegetarian fare or fear— with this primal repast; for the last supper show he put himself up, in place of the animal, for sacrifice. Christ was billed as reverting to this position so that, repeating it once and for all, sacrifice would henceforward be strictly symbolical or not at all (20–21). But the sacrifice to end all sacrifice (the war to end all war) backfired. Within this context vegetarianism appears as double aberration featuring such agents or actors out of radical denial of dependency on sacrifice (or identification) as Wagner and Hitler. The refusal to eat meat—to identify with the father—leaves the corpse unmourned, unburied, and, hence, no longer killed but murdered. (The refusal to eat the dead could indeed be seen to mark the onset of a certain history of vampirism.) But this refusal also denies—while participating in the phantasm—that all nourishment, at least since Christ's sacrifice bled into bread and wine, will have been of meat, will have swallowed sacrifice.

The sacrifice of animals was replaced by Christian communion, which was itself, however, more than image or symbol. Kindness to animals accompanies the establishment (in the midst of all food) of a direct line to the (super)-human sacrifice which preserves Christ's body and blood forever as reservoir for fulfillment of and irrigation of every object of consumption (or consumerism) (22). The first pagan eyewitnesses of Christianity's emergence got the message: they stepped back horrified at a cult that clearly sacrificed not lamb or steer but only human beings (24). They were convinced that in Christian circles sacrifice of infants accompanied orgies in which the sacred union was reenacted or acted out as incestuous coupling. Soon each early Christian sect accused the other of the same transgressions.

To update the Christian legacy of mass murder, Kleinpaul takes his readers on a tour of a turn-of-the-century Catholic mass as though the readers were complete outsiders, tourists—like the witnesses Nietzsche invites (in *On the Future of our Educational Institutions*) to visit the university. First, the guide intones, note the priest with tonsure, decked out circumcision-style as one already sacrificed in part to God. We watch the bloodless sacrifice undergo through consecration "live" transformation into blood sacrifice. By the close of the ceremony everything has been carefully consumed to underscore that no part of this valuable nourishment may be lost (29–35). On another field trip Kleinpaul tours Oberammergau, where the passion, performed as the repeatable show of crucifiction, is clearly a human sacrifice (55). The passion play, like every mass, is at once original and copy (77). Thus the Oberammergau passion play began as a sacrifice, one of many franchises installed in towns throughout Germany in the course of exchanging the plague's epidemic of mass death for the catastrophe that mass identification absorbs and prepares for. The more contemporary franchise, says Kleinpaul, is located in Bayreuth.

Between the early reception of Christianity as a cult of human sacrifice and the chain operations of passion plays, Christianity lets roll mass murder on its own projective sensurround. To divert the cross fire of internal accusations of murder, Christianity openly (and then under the cover of secularization) charged the Jews with human sacrifice. A double trajectory of projection was thus permanently installed within Christianity to protect against the mass-murder side effects of mass identification. This defense was established at the same time (in 1215) as the Church's declaration that transsubstantiation was an accomplished and repeatable fact (up until then its status was uncertain, mysterious, and debatable). Instantly the Jews were found everywhere stealing the host which they in secret dunked in Christian blood (27).

Prior to their turn to lamb sacrifice, the Jews had protected themselves from destructive effects of human sacrifice by developing the scapegoat concept, a ritual of doubling in which one animal was consecrated and sacrificed to Jehovah, while the other was reviled, tortured, charged with all guilt, and then sent into exile. Upon the return (with Christianity) of human sacrifice, the Jews were sent on this ancient but now always fatally shortcut trail of expulsion: "It seems that now the Christians, who have the true body and the true blood on their altars, search at Easter for a scapegoat, and that is the Jewish people" (80). But while the Jews end up doubly charged with sacrifice, Christianity regularly makes a demand which (not only in Kleinpaul's estimation) surpasses every sacrifice in history: the injunction of Christian love both to love Jesus absolutely, body and soul, and to love one's neighbor as oneself (78).

This love shows Freud the way the discrete and personalizable identification or sacrifice which goes down in cases of melancholia again goes down—and out—as sado*mass*-ochism, psychosis, group psychology. The inward bleeding that Freud put on the map of melancholia (already in his letter to Fliess dated January 7, 1895) flows outward in the Christian mass, the last supper of the first system (the second system specializes in mass identification). The alternation of identification and projection builds the masses that go with the blood flow. That's why mass murder's so popular; the burned-down site of Ed Gein's murders, for example, has been consumed relic-style by groups on a pilgrimage.

Mass murder was acknowledged by George Romero and John Russo to be the prefab dread, which *Night of the Living Dead* had successfully realized and tapped. One of the main backers of this film was a meat packer who supplied the props for the movie's main taboo-bust: the open, uncut-away view of what monsters have always eaten. "The 'guts' used for the scene affectionately known as 'The Last Supper,' in which the zombies feast on the remains of Tom and Judy, were graciously provided by an investor who owned a chain of meat markets. '. . . They were all goodies belonging to lambs, which are supposedly somewhat similar to human organs.'"[4]

As the zombie trilogy develops or spreads (in *Dawn of the Dead* and *Day of the Dead*), the epidemic of undeath returns, "just when you thought it was safe to be dead," to replace the one-on-one close encounter with the person-alizably dead or undead with the global threat of desubli-mated cannibalism (or vegetarianism). Zombies do not completely devour their objects but always only in part, leaving the rest to reanimate along the lines they model of undeath and unmourning.

Like vegetarians, they don't kill, since they don't con-sume the always available mortal remainder, but only leave what remains lying about murdered and unmourned. No leftovers for the zombie. Like Christian love, the vegetarian or zombie appetite is sustained from a source of violence which lies in noncontamination. Every Last Supper must be pure; but the advertisement of its purity cannot be deliv-ered in all its purity. As Derrida has argued, not even or especially inside humanist instances of nonsacrifice or pure sacrifice, sacrifice itself (or the violent proximity of identi-fication and sexual love) has never been sacrificed but has only always—as dependency—been denied.[5]

Zombies, who like vampires cannot feed on their own kind, find that with every bite they take the food they must eat is already turning into the food they may never eat. One of the radio broadcasts overheard in *Night of the Living Dead* puts it to the point: "In all cases the killers are eating the flesh of the people they murder." In the zombie sequels, human kind, in order to survive, must first control the zombies by feeding them completely consumable meals of dead flesh, a rudimentary process of sublimating primal cannibalism that gets the zombies to the point of consuming background music, which of course is not at all far off from the primal starting point. But once we have the zombies where we want them, we leave them there. According to Romero: "The zombies are us."[6]

Memoirs of a Viennese Whore

Bambi opens onto the melancholic preserve which sadomasochism must sexualize or couplify. Salten's description of winter's arrival as it finishes off the animated leaves is a leave-taking synchronized with its desperately familiar precedent. The mortality timer is everywhere set in the animistically charged (or "caricatured") natural habitat. The "life in the woods" appended to *Bambi* as subtitle belongs to organisms shaped and shattered from within by destrudo.

> In the multicellular living organism the libido meets the death or destruction drive which holds sway there, and which tries to disintegrate this cellular being and bring each elemental primary organism into a condition of inorganic stability. (*SE* 19:163)

Libido must undo this "return-to-nature" drive by reintroducing the couplification of sadomasochism. The death drive dominant in the organism (in "life in the woods") was, as primal sadism, already "identical" with masochism (*SE* 19:164). But this state or scene of being "identical" is a primal; it is at all recognizable only in a mixed and separable state of identification. The death drive cannot but take a spin around the reflexive and internalizing orbit of masochism's invention of itself and its enemy or appetizer, which is sadism. Thus, "even the subject's destruction of himself cannot take place without libidinal satisfaction" (*SE* 19:170).

The interaction of S & M went native with the "Russian character-type"—Dostoevskian man. In *Bambi*, already via his uncanny P.R. job, generic man (the He, the strange smell, the terrible tele-caster of bullet-teeth, and bearer of the "third limb") reroutes destrudo out from and around its native habitat. In the resulting S/M confrontation he holds the place of fate, imaginary father or big brother. John Galsworthy could write without irony but right on the mark, in the forward and blurb advertising the 1928 English language edition, that *Bambi* could be "particularly" recommended "to sportsmen." Man's carnivorous externality introduces order or survival into the vegetarian life in the woods, in which animation of all life turns on endless destruction and pointless (unwitnessed) suffering. At gun point, and under the aiming gaze of man the father of the animal, animated existence shares its projected pleasure with the Other—who alone gets off at the prospect of the share thus denied the cute little critters.

In an (anonymously published) work, Salten again libidinizes Bambi's melancholic preserve in order to help the ego out: *The Life of Josephine Mutzenbacher: The Memoirs of a Viennese Whore.*[1] According to *The Ego and the Id*, the superego always turns sadistic when another melancholic identification goes down. According to this scenario, it's up to the ego to get off—through couplification of the melancholic self-reproach. The caricaturist charge that turns animals into humans and vice versa inhabits the S/M porno novel—like another, twice-externalized, "life in the woods":

It was only a short time after that, I remember, that I had an experience that has haunted me ever since.

Fortunately it has only ever happened to me once, but that was once too often. A fat, elderly man approached me and said that he wanted a quick, stand-up session. I went with him to the wooden fence that surrounded the little fairground. I raised my skirts for action and he laughed in a nauseatingly slimy way. "Wait a minute. There's something missing," he said in a slimy voice. He took something from his pocket, but I could not see what it was because he kept it concealed in his hand. Then he slid his arms around me and, with one push, entered me. I was already mistrustful of him. "What have you got in your hand? What is it?" I asked anxiously. "You'll soon find out," he sneered in that same cloying tone. Then he began to thrust powerfully into me, driving me back against the fence, and suddenly I screamed with pain as something sharp and cold dug into my back between my shoulder blades. I saw his fat, sweating face swimming in a fog of pain before my eyes. His eyes were narrow, squinting, and his nose was broad, like a snout. He looked exactly like a pig. He giggled and mocked me aloud; "Just a little something to tickle you with. Just tickling you a little bit. Got to have a bit of a tickle with it. Can you feel it bleeding, eh? Feel the trickle of blood running down your back, eh?" (2:72)

The porky turn-on brought to us by the broken fragment of a metal comb turns on the disclosure of sexual difference which aggression instantly closes off. The resulting wired or charged (or caricatured) encounter and enclosure: the S/M master mixer of adolescence.

"I'm no Baron, my darling jockey, but your highness's stallion. My name is Black Star." With that he threw back his head and whinnied. . . . He knelt down before me and began to lick my supple leather boots, whinnying constantly. Then he asked me to mount him for "the great race of love.". . . "My lovely jockey has not got a whip," he said. "Who needs a whip?" I retorted. "My stallion hasn't felt the full weight of my hand yet." With that I gave him half a dozen slaps on the bottom, which really must have stung. His reaction was altogether childish. He whinnied and neighed and gurgled and then set off around the room again on all fours. . . . I seized his erection between the two soft leather sides of my boots and began to caress him slowly. . . . I slapped his bottom and stuck my finger in him. (2:102)

These two episodes replay both sides of the missing relation to father. By age twelve Josephine had slept with father, priest, and schoolteacher: "I could hardly believe what was happening to me. There I was, in a classroom full of children, being speared by my teacher . . . yet even as I felt the flow within me, he continued with the lesson. When he had finished, he slipped out of me" (1:114). Although, "even as a child" Josephine "would never let anyone get away with hitting" her (2:105), libidinal binding of the aggressions accompanying sexual and generational differentiation had to be admitted:

In the portrait gallery another man was playing "schools": . . . "What?" he thundered. "Twenty-seven? will you never learn your tables, you stupid girl? . . . I'm sorry, but I have no alternative but to punish you. Jeanette give your lazy sister two smacks on her backside. . . . And what about you, Jeanette? Is it right that you should treat your sister so cruelly?" . . . "But please, sir," whined Jeanette, "you told me to do it, sir!" "Oh, answering me back now, eh. Well, I'll soon knock the cheek out of you, my girl. Come on over my knee this instant." (2:114)

Our Friend the Atom

N	*ow, however, under the rule of economic, political,
and cultural monopolies, the formation of the mature superego seems to skip the stage of individualization: the generic atom becomes directly a social atom. . . . As
early as the pre-school level, gangs, radio, and television set the
pattern for conformity and rebellion; deviations from the pattern are punished not so much within the family as outside
and against the family. The experts of the mass media transmit
the required values; they offer the perfect training in efficiency,
toughness, personality, dream, and romance. With this education, the family can no longer compete.*

—Herbert Marcuse, *Eros and Civilization*

The Disney cartoon-portrait of machines as playthings
which metamorphose into automatic creatures that are then
tortured into operation (television alone tunes in a safety
zone within caricatured or abused childhood) advertises an

identification with machines which admits the father's censure. The machine is only the outer—paternal—limit of anthropomorphic metamorphosis. The machine represents the maternal bond realized p-unitively under the superego's direction: "You wanted control of relations with mother? Go ahead and *be* a control panel attached to some machine."

In the case of the cartoon of a bull named Ferdinand (a totemic stand-in for father), Grotjahn describes the laugh track of the paternal comeback:

> Ferdinand is not only the son who successfully avoids the fate of Oedipus; he is also the depreciated father about whom the son laughs before he identifies himself with him. . . . After depreciation of the powerful father and after laughing at him and his defeat, we can like and love him again.[1]

D. turned to the animation of *Bambi* at the time of his father's death; but the guilty commemoration was held back until its delayed (controlled) release in 1943 alongside *Dumbo* (where the father, already beating a retreat in *Bambi*, can only be found missing). D. compulsively rewatched *Bambi*, which he favored above all his other productions (each time unreservedly weeping).

Convinced that urban design had, through television's challenge, become the next great frontier and set of technology, D. spent the last phase of his life—the fifties—planning and building Disneyland. This frontier town was not only the set of the new TV show but also a place of ancient pedigree: Disneyland is a city of the dead (to this day dying children request a trip to Disneyland as last wish). D. had to hock his life insurance to finance the early stages of the park's construction. At the late stage of development D. not only collected dollhouse-sized furniture but also enjoyed (and thus we come full circle within the circuit of traumatic shock and quake preparedness) playing the uniformed engineer of a scale model train with which he had encircled house and property.

The detour around the father has been documented in

detail. D. named the family-controlled company that ran the empire Retlaw, which spelled Walter backwards (20). But even the retro-law D. observed spelled out the law of the father's name (which indeed returned, in a sense, in WED enterprises). Remarriage to the name propelled moving sidewalks or "WEDway People Movers" (21), the conveyer belt of "ageless" egos modeled after Mickey Mouse. (The D. trademark signature was—just like the figure of Mickey Mouse—drawn by some generic other.)

In the case of D., Freud brought into focus his view of the coupling of sadism and masochism in the topological pair-off or face-off of superego and ego—*the* S & M couple. At this atomic level, relations with father can be played back from all sides or angles (video-monitor style). In 1956, the head of D.'s science department published *Our Friend the Atom*, the story, in effect, of his majesty the ego who, via technology, seeks a way out of mortality and biological generation.

Sergei Eisenstein[2] recognized in D.'s conjugation of Darwinism and Totemism a "rebirth of universal animism" (43)—a born-again connection that (according to David Hamburg)[3] inhabits psychoanalysis, which "has long been concerned with the ways in which man's basic nature might reflect his evolutionary heritage, as transmitted both through genes and through customs" (185–86). Genetic evolution and cultural evolution combat or complement each other within the couplification of masochism and sadism (of ego and superego). Simply put, the superego is the delegate of the id and guarantor of a double generation which conjoins tradition and procreation. The ego, in contrast, just doesn't want to go.

According to Eisenstein, D. wins back the tribal sense of oneself as simultaneously human and totemic animal— as at once ego and superego. Animism or totemism is always based on movement or animation—on the movement, for example, of glancing and sketching (46, 52). In turn, metamorphosis, as advertised both by animistic beliefs and by D.'s animations, is always evolutionary. *Bambi* represents a "return to pure totemism" which accomplishes on the rebound the shift-down or reverse drive of evolutionary history: Bambi is a "re-deerized human." "Already a shift towards ecstasy," a revelation of "the repeating circles of lives," *Bambi* represents, in Eisenstein's estimation, D.'s ultimate achievement (56). But the "five-minute 'break' for the psyche," which is thus won, doubles, according to the logic of breakdown, as the time span "during which the viewer himself remains chained to the winch of the machine" (32).

But D.'s world, which undermines and disembodies the anthropomorphic grounding of subjects in order to admit sadomasochistic relations with machines, invites the "viewer himself" to attend his own evolutionary extinction. Thus the atomic egoic phantasm D. cosigned—for example in the film *Victory through Air Power*—was recognized by James Agee as revealing the otherwise missing link between the "sexless sexiness of Disney's creations" and "victory-in-a-vacuum which is so morally simple a matter . . . of machine-eat-machine" (Schickel, *The Disney Version*, 233).

As Ariel Dorfman and Armand Mattelart have demonstrated, in D.'s arsenal of "*automagic* antibodies" (29) both the ego ideal or superego and the gendered, generational body have been relinquished. There is no parental guidance in this network of relations—only, for example, avuncular arrangements. "Since they are not engendered by any biological act, Disney characters may aspire to immortality: whatever apparent, momentary sufferings are inflicted on them in the course of their adventures, they have been liberated, at least, from the curse of the body" (34). The separation from the body of reproduction—from mother—has been held in place by Mickey Mouse, whose perpetual "childish innocence" amounts to "a defiance of evolution" (98), just as his "false permanence is a symbol for a false mother" (92).

For Fritz Moellenhoff, too, the "symbolic meaning of Mickey's figure is obvious:" he is a desexualized phallus or, as Dorfman and Mattelart prefer to describe it, a false mother. In other words, MM is the tech-no-body, the egoic-atomic replacement of womb to tomb generation. The ego (or MM) is allowed to triumph uninterrupted only because it is still in perverse, that is, one-sided but insatiable accordance with the "ideologies of the superego." The tubes of biological evolution can be tied because another evolution in front of the tube and in the service of the ego is underway. On this cartoon evolutionary scale, the ego otherwise deleted from the biological scenario that promotes continuation of the generic is promised a comeback: the ego is always only temporarily separated from its new body. This is what every science fiction is about: every ego is on the lookout for the point of entry into the automatically evolving technobody.

The evolution of genes is rivaled, on a parallel track that is also the fast track, by a nonprocreative evolution of units of memory or tradition which—and this is where the super-egoic guard is dropped—can be most efficiently conveyed by machine-fed body-ego narcissism. Before the advent of the independent machine, the body could receive or transmit tradition only via torture, castration, self-abnegation. With gadget, however, what was each time lost in transmission—the immortal part—comes back fully technologized. As Peter Canning puts it: "We humans are the reproductive organs for the evolution of the technical object."[4] Individual immortality disappeared (according to every myth of paradise lost or regained) into the emerging gap of sexual difference. Generation and death are required as the synchronic laboratory where the rapid turnover of lives rehearses or repeats evolutionary diachrony or history. Like the amoeba Freud considers in *Beyond the Pleasure Principle* when he considers the outside chances of one's not dying—or like the friendly atom featured by D.'s science department—the ego would, on its own (in sync, that is, with an evolution of machines modeled after the transmission of memory or tradition) regenerate itself continually through a self-replication that would throw an S-turn around sex-generation.

But the ego must alternate its projection of the body with identification with the missing body. The work of mourning always follows the automatic expansionism of technologies. Insofar as it has so far been brought to us by the advancing fronts of warfare penetrating the deepest recesses of relations between self and other, techno-growth drops and downs a remainder and thus reverses itself to mark the spot of return of consumer relations. It was because corpse disposal was the issue that Freud modeled every identification on the totem meal. This, from the egoic point of projection—of the body as machine, plays back a scene of loss (to the ego) of immortality. The superego mocks the egoic attention span of techno-metamorphosis: "Just when you thought it was safe to be dead."

The atomic-egoic phantasm of technological evolution in the service of an immortality that circumvention of the womb alone can vouchsafe is a symptom—always—of melancholia. (Even in *Robocop* the projection was sprung from the sidelines containing the cop widow's rapid remarriage and refusal to mourn.)

Invasion of the Body
Snatchers

Géza Róheim links ongoing adolescence to a principle of evolution that still works in stereo, biological on one side, cultural or psychological on the other:

The reason man remains dependent for a relatively long time is not that he requires so much time to adapt himself to his culture, but rather that his culture—the interaction of generations through the medium of language and tradition—has evolved because of man's prolonged and never quite discarded infancy. Man is swayed by conflict. The demands of the id and the superego are most often conflicting. If it were not for the adaptive intervention of the ego, mankind would soon perish. Because of man's prolonged biological and psychological infancy, sex has become independent of its original goal of procreation. Dependency has been prolonged far beyond the limits found in all other animals. Fantasy and

memory—the past—determine man's actions. Man
has become a much confused primate.[1]

From the Stanford University research lab in Tanzania
where observation of chimpanzees and baboons endorses a
conjunction of evolutionary and developmental theories of
childhood, David Hamburg reports the discovery of the
missing link bonding child abuse to superego formation:

> This is an example of what ethnologists refer to as
> redirected aggression. Animals with similar domi-
> nance status rarely fight. More commonly they break
> off threatening encounters and attack a vulnerable
> animal—the small, weak, or relatively immobile.
> (189)

The aggression redirected (along bioevolutionary and
developmental psychological lines) toward children turns
on the society-wide phenomenon of "depersonalization"—
which, in Richard Lower's rendition,[2] functions as a screen
which the ego, in order to get off, starts tuning in and turning into within a household of abusers, losers, and loss.

> The child who experiences repeated humiliation at
> the hands of the sadistic parent has little recourse but
> to libidinize the experience, so that future shameful
> or painful experiences generate not only defense but
> also gratification. (595)
>
> The various subjective descriptions given by our
> patients may be manifestations of unconscious
> sadomasochistic fantasies, ultimately expressing the
> child's ego state in his passive-masochistic relation-
> ship with the sadistic parent (598).

Depersonalized patients who play dead or dumb play back
the crucial scenes of their sexual self-assertion in which the
parents treated them as though dead. But depersonalization
can also defend against object loss by enacting zomboid
reunion "with lost objects, particularly the mother" (599).
According to the cinematic epic of Californian depersonalization, *The Invasion of the Body Snatchers*, "epidemic mass

hysteria" (as the local psychiatrist diagnoses rampant charges that loved ones are look-alikes or impostors) cannot "explain that body"—the corpse that can replace you (in your sleep). The capacity for love has absconded from the group formation which this vegetarian invasion from outer space spreads. What horror films and science fictions try to cover over, in the one genre via the symptom formation of sexual repression, in the other through the fantasy of machine eat machine, is the rapport of mourning or unmourning with the primal machine, the superego. The internal relations featured in science fiction take libidinal charge via the critical disorders American psychoanalysis in the fifties discovered and diagnosed on the person of the adolescent group.

Gadget Love

When the quake struck, Serina Johnson, 13, and her sister Corina, 11, were alone in their small apartment across from Oakland's city hall. "The food started flying off the refrigerator, . . . the TV started knocking over . . . ," said Serina. . . . Said Corina: "It was like being in a blender."
—*Time,* October 30, 1989

Adolescence is a kind of converter or blender. The teenager rebounds back and forth between extremes and short attention spans (for example, between asceticism and sexual or self-destructive excess) because the two segregated sides of parental identification—the mother, the father—must be mixed into the assimilated identity of the ego or group member. Adolescence is an age of twist, quake, and shock. The building blocks of development—early identifications, sublimation, and superegoic sadism—must be libidinally bound up between couplification and group processes.

The group permits teenagers to get around their parents, who are too out-of-it or off-limits to give them their sexual license, which they receive, instead, from the group. (Being "with it" is thus the regular application of the family romance. One's real origin lies in the in-group.) But the sexual couple must therefore share its circuitry with conversion and the adolescent pack. Adolescent lovers take orders from the group (and not from their parents) to reproduce or reduce themselves. As Otto Kernberg puts it:[1]

> The "pairing" assumption leads a group to focus upon
> two of its members as a couple . . . that symbolizes
> the group's hopeful expectation that the selected pair
> will "reproduce itself" and thereby protect the group's
> identity and survival. (AS, 36)

But in the case of Romeo and Juliet, Kernberg witnesses a sexual union that at once fulfills the group fantasy of being moved by love to a double beyond (of Oedipal prohibition and primitive aggression) and gives the group unconscious satisfaction over the lovers' deaths. The only way out of the (Oedipal and pre-Oedipal) jealousies which the group reserves for the couple, which always withdraws from the masturbating child or the group-of-one like parents into the master bedroom, is a "projection of superego functions" and "submission to external leadership." This "protection against violence and against the destruction of the couple" must be paid to the superego in installments of total desexualization (AS, 40).

The couple must "overcome the Oedipal prohibitions separating sex from tenderness" (LCG, 97) which constitute the sexuality of the social group. But the perpetual adolescence of the group unceasingly infiltrates and erodes the couple's bond. Even "stable triangular relationships" (82)—which include, at the point where company becomes a crowd, masturbation to pornography, excessive telephoning, and the keeping of journals—not only re-enact aspects of unresolved Oedipal conflicts but, more to the point, represent, again, invasion of the couple by the group. Thus monogamy is not just the boring artefact and after effect of convention. Boredom is never the transparent sign of a repression produced by social constraints. Monogamy is what one wants—as in the one-on-one with mother which, owing to group protection, one never gets (to enjoy). The boredom that weighs down the couple is a symptom of the repression of a pleasure which the social group finds suspicious. Since on its own it ever verges on its potential for destructiveness and auto-destructiveness, the group requires the sexual love and futurity of the couple; but the group also regards the couple with the Oedipal and pre-Oedipal envy reserved for the secret prerogative of parents.

The group *does* provide protection via a controlled release of mutual aggression inside the couple (in other words, before witnesses). If overisolation of the couple leads to unwitnessed releases of hostility, the internal bonds guaranteeing the pleasure of couplification grow malignant—and the couple dissolves, again, within the group. Predominance of aggression and "deterioration of internalized object relations and sexual enjoyment" follow from this absorption and reversal of the couple (of, that is, the overcoming of the Oedipus complex). The pre-Oedipal bond with mother presses for release—for instance, via the one-way polymorphous perversity of group sex (which always admits female homosexuality while radically quarantining the prospect of male homosexuality). The ambivalence binding group to couple produces the resexualization of the group, group sex, or the idealization of the leader. But projections of the Oedipal superego onto the leader guarantee (Charles Manson style) that regression from adult to childhood morality will grow—perpetually adolescent. As in the development of a psychosis, the group moves forward or goes for it—*aggresses*—only to protract and protect identifications with the immediate family: sexual love remains the outside or outgroup activity (LCG, 106).

Unlike the group, sexual love does not need a future or any other guarantee; it *is* the future. The couple is the genitals of the group and not of another couple (the parents).

The group's need for the couple advances the desire of that which is not desire. It is identification (or the group) that wishes to join in in the love of the couple. It is up to the wife (the representative of the father function and protector of the couple) to set limits to identification's group participation in the couple. In the invasion of the couple which vampirism launches and shares with adolescence (immortality and undeath are teen fantasies), the outcome is determined by the already installed mode of responsibility or altruism, which is at stake.

According to Edward Carroll,[2] during adolescence the increase in self-awareness (the happy-face side of suicide) admits, but within the still-operative make-believe sensorium of childhood, "questions of" social and sexual responsibility, identity, and independence which the internal and eternal child acts out. "The failure to distinguish clearly between 'make believe' and reality facilitates acting out, which is so typical of adolescence" (524). If the adolescent attains a testing rapport with the outside via increasing facility with and range in language, then transference prospects open up for him. "The person who habitually acts out, however, does not complete this last step. He remains the perpetual adolescent with faulty distinctions between 'make believe' and reality" (525). What is acted out, of course, is the complete identification with an object. Rather than select some detail for symbolic representation, the teenager instead acts out complete dramatic sequences. Deliberation, anticipation, and prolongation are ruled out as sources of enjoyment or creation. The acting-out teenager is always "on"—"live":

> The person who acts out has a low tolerance for tension and anxiety; he must discharge such tension at once. He is likely to be passive, dependent, and conforming except in the area of his acting out, which is often a counter-phobic tempting of fate. (526)

The teenage blender thus did not do the job Carroll calls "language integration" (526). The delinquent adolescent who acts up acts out the vicarious expressions of unconscious conflicts of the parents (526). The perpetual adolescent picks up and transmits all the diseases of total identification; even those secret aspects of the psychological organization of the parents never on public display get aired in the juvenile delinquent.

Already a kind of multiplication of personality inheres in protracted or perpetual acting out, a psychological profile shared equally by channellers or mediums and the (real or alleged) victims of child abuse. Indeed the fantasy is shared at this end too: mediums of long-distance and long-dead voices almost invariably pack a charge of abuse in their backgrounds.

The power structure of the group inserts another rotating device into the blender of adolescence. Edith Buxbaum adds the twist:[3] in adolescent groups she finds a "repeated change between submission and opposition toward the leader, joining and leaving the group, alternating between being obedient member and active leader" (360). The importance of the "repeated experience of breaking away from the leader and of being allowed to assume his place, makes the adolescent less afraid to do in every respect what adults do":

> It seems to be easier to make the step into adult sex life from the group than from home. The child's fear of being left alone when he leaves the family proves unwarranted. He finds a new family. While in the original one it was forbidden to take the father's place he now discovers that it is possible to take the leader's place without being in any danger of punishment. (362)

But the way to adulthood prepared in adolescence is also stalled by the short attention span installed in relations between leaders and group members; rapid turnovers of identification produce and attract always only "new friends."

While turning around in the blender, the teenager also adopts (according to Roy Schafer)[4] a series of "fateful primitive psychological assumptions about the nature of feelings, self, identity, and his relations with other people" (46). The teenager (like the psychotic, for example) assumes that mental processes are substances (oral, sexual, or fecal in nature) which can be withheld or expelled or destroyed, just as they may fill one up and explode or leak out. "And, along with his fantasy of ridding himself of his dangerous substances, he will think of himself as being emptied out, disconnected, and perhaps as having lost or thrown away something he calls a self or identity" (47). The unconscious becomes a toilet that must be kept clean and sterile to avoid infection. But once the substances have been flushed, the adolescent feels empty and dead; he accordingly adopts "the dropping-out, rock-bottom, non-negotiable mode" (50). Erik Erikson[5] addresses the first emergence of long-term scheduling (or periodicity) in adolescence in terms of this teenage legacy of psychoticizing spatializations and splittings of self: "This fear of being left empty, and, more simply, that of *being left*, seems to be the most basic feminine fear, extending over the whole of a woman's existence. It is normally intensified with every menstruation" (366). The flow of the back-to-the-future channel is mixed via the unisex periodicity of drinking and drug taking: the body image or body ego is still under construction. Moses Laufer describes the disturbed end of this bodybuilding requirement:[6] "The adolescent patient . . . experiences his body as constant proof that he has given in or surrendered passively—and unconsciously surrendered it to the mother who first cared for him" (310). The sexual body that persecutes the adolescent refers, thus, to the mother as persecutor (315). In turn, the occasion and rationale for aggression must eternally be some supermaternal or feminine principle to which one pays the protection one gives it.

According to Erikson, the body count of teen pathologies rises with the identificatory requirement of killing time which draws adolescence eternally and internally onward: "These, then, are some of the basic intolerances, fears, and resulting anxieties which arise from the mere fact that human life begins with a long, slow childhood and sexuality with an attachment to parental figures" (367). But prolongation in place of progressive development has often been billed as the good news regarding adolescence. Erikson again: "Man's childhood learning is characterized by prolonged dependence. Only thus does man develop conscience, that dependence on himself which will make him, in turn, dependable" (361). Kurt Eissler goes so far as to credit delay in maturation with giving the grounds for all culture:[7] "I would speculate that if mankind matured fully directly after childhood instead of going into latency, it would have evolved tools but hardly anything that would have gone beyond facilitating physical biological survival" (510). In accord with Goethe's belief that genius relies always only on its connections to some primal and ongoing teen age, Eissler concludes: "all cultural achievements by great minds are in a direct genetic connection with their adolescence" (510). But Goethe also wrote the first chapter of Jonestown when *Werther* caused the teen blender to churn unbearably in a readership internally commanded to commit suicide in mimetic or epidemic manner.

But suicide only appears to follow from the crush of teen love; "love," crushed by identification, is only promotional part of the adolescent's overriding concern with occupational identity. (Goethe's *Wilhelm Meister's Apprenticeship* colonized what *Werther* kept inside: the internally projected emigration to America and job security.) The adolescent's one-track quest for the fitting job protects against the phantasmic threat of role diffusion. Erikson: "To keep themselves together they temporarily overidentify, to the point of apparent complete loss of identity, with the heroes of cliques and crowds. This initiates the stage of 'falling in love,' which is by no means entirely, or even primarily, a sexual matter—except where the mores demand it. To a considerable extent adolescent love is an attempt to arrive at a definition of one's identity by projecting one's diffused ego images on one another and by seeing them thus reflected and gradually clarified" (228).

Even that favorite villain in the standard psychocom of

the American family—the mom or momster—turns out to be, in Erikson's reckoning, the retro-causality, casualty, and coverup of what is in fact active in every family member: the constant pull of perpetually adolescent groups. "Mom" never gives up "such external signs of sexual competition as too youthful dresses, frills of exhibitionism, and 'make-up'" (249). But her own membership in a friendship culture based, like some beach town, always on the adolescent body or group, preserves the independence of American teenagers. (In California extended families inhabit only ethnicity or psychotic delusion; "grandparents" are senior citizens in youthful sportive attire who socialize within their own peer groups of friends.)

"Momism," Erikson suggests, is "only misplaced paternalism" (254). Rather than fight it out with father, the American adolescent includes father as "more of a big brother": "The adolescent swings of the American youth do not overtly concern the father, nor the matter of authority, but focus rather on his peers" (272). Father, in the Oedipal or European sense, is so far out of the picture that "the troubled American (who often looks the least troubled) blames his mother for having let him down" (255). The mother holds in reserve the only individualist or paternal model: the American "myth" of the mother's father (279). But the logic of adolescent independence, as it organizes or segregates each age group in denial of generational difference, shows this blame to be reversible: "we find at the bottom of it all the conviction, the mortal self-accusation, that it was the child who abandoned the mother, because he had been in such a hurry to become independent" (255).

The adolescent group's dehierarchization of the transferential rapport with leadership—and thus with "following" or understanding—brings Erikson to the point of *Childhood and Society:* the point of articulation of a parallelism of two case studies, of the American and the Nazi adolescent. In both cases their fraternal images are machine-fed. The antequated superego has been replaced by widespread identification with gadgets sealed or revealed (as in the insider's view of a Nazi propagandist) by an "instinctive pleasure which youth finds in the power of engines" (310). But once the superego withdraws from the combat zone of identifications, the remaining contest between id and ego alone gives the cartoonesque (that is, psychotic and perverse) rendition of relations with the Nazi fighting machine or the lean machine of California.

Approaching this identification from both sides of its ambivalence, Peter Giovacchini examines the hostile defensive impulses revealed by the aversion on the part of certain of his patients to (typically "American") gadgets, gadgeteers, and gadget lovers.[8] "These patients for the most part objected to two aspects of these devices which may be classified as follows. First, the regulation of time as in switches with either an automatic control or a feed-back mechanism to interrupt a circuit and turn something off or on. Second, enhancement of passivity" (330). TV appeared to be their most formidable enemy—to which they periodically succumbed.

The patients were regularly turned off by gadgets when their relation to the ego ideal was on. But the direct link to the primary process which the gadget-free phase promoted invariably led to ego disruption. The psychotic state that always followed featured absorbed interest in the gadgets the patients collected in buying sprees. For example:

> Also, during this phase, he reported no dreams, was unable to give free associations, and acted in a rigid, obsessive-compulsive fashion. He gave detailed photographic descriptions of what went on around him. (332)

The revolt against gadgets is directed against parents, specifically, against one's resemblance to them. "Denial and projection operate to re-establish harmony between ego and ego ideal" (335). Thus for Giovacchini's patients the gadget was, in each case, the means of disguise, displacement, and control of death wishes against the father.

In contrast to most machines, gadgets (which range

from TV sets to computers and back again) give the illusion of operating independently. According to the patients, a gadget's function is secondary to its operation: gadget lovers are fetishists who in the first place derive pleasure from the operation of the gadget itself. But when the patients turned to gadgets to re-establish ego integration against the id's bid for control, their own concentration on a gadget's operation led to an enhancement of reality-testing functions.

Unacceptable id impulses are countered by the ego's alliance with automatically operating machines. Threatened defense mechanisms are reenforced through emerging externalization. But these alliances in the struggle between ego and id reflect extra-normal imperatives: the ego wants immortality now (thus opting for aggression or power over sexual difference or anxiety). The ego finds unacceptable the id's and the superego's affirmation of reproductive or generational immortality—of the eternal return of "life's" difference from any individual, that is, egoic life or attention span.

In the thirties the German adolescent rapport with machines was symptomatic both of exclusion of father and of adherence to some entity of matricentric appeal. On the American side, the systematic teenagerization of everyone as peer group member independent of family ties was, for Erikson, good news: the American is an "emancipated adolescent who refutes his father's conscience and his nostalgia for a mother, bowing only to cruel facts and to fraternal discipline" (258). In America the adolescent "offers less of a problem and feels less isolated because he has, in fact, become the cultural arbiter; few men in this country can afford to abandon the gestures of the adolescent" (298).

But in both habitats, the American and the Nazi, "fraternal images step into the gaps left by decaying paternalism" (273). Erikson thus already subscribed to the bicoastal logic of this special report on California by paralleling but keeping out of phase the Nazi German collaboration with adolescence—which, loud as denial, only turned up the paternal, superegoic speaker full blast—and the upbeat American worship of teenager and friend. Typically, Erikson argues in his profile of German adolescence prior to the Nazi takeover, a firmly established patriarchal superego guaranteed that when it came time for the individualistic rebellious phase, youths did not have far to go before embodying disillusioned, obedient, "mere" citizenship. This comprised the "political immaturity of the German" which the Nazis readily exploited (293). The Nazi rebellion of "youth leading youth" advertised images of emotional adolescence" which invited father too to join fraternally in Nazi teen worship of maternal ideals (although remember, job placement *was* the issue) (302).

> Both fathers and sons now could identify with the Führer, an adolescent who never gave in. . . . He was the Führer: a glorified older brother, who took over prerogatives of the fathers without overidentifying with them. . . . He was the unbroken adolescent . . . a gang leader who kept the boys together by demanding their admiration, by creating terror. . . . And he was a ruthless exploiter of parental failures. (294–95)

ZAP: Depersonalized

Owen Renik explores depersonalization (via analogy with Freud's notion of the "screen memory") as a restriction of attention through hypercathexis of an unthreatening program.[1] As early as the *Project* and in more developed form in the seventh metapsychological chapter of *The Interpretation of Dreams,* Freud addressed a "primary thought defense" which consisted in withdrawal of attention from a disturbing preconscious content. (When an instinctual urge which through association with a perceptual residue—the memory of an auditory perception or word—has become "capable of being attended to," it is preconscious; with an investment of attention, it can turn conscious.) As in gadget love the depersonalization that allows one to observe oneself from a distance (as on monitors) and thus disclaim responsibility for one's actions or acting out preserves reality testing while altering the sense of reality even in the waking state. "In depersonalization, reality testing is preserved at the price of the sense of reality. The symptom is a kind of emergency measure. When it occurs, it protects against an action or a disorder of reality testing that would otherwise take place to the detriment of adaptation. In some cases, this may mean the emergence of poorly repressed perverse or psychotic trends" (598).

The concept of resistance first arose with Freud's observation during self-analysis that he found himself repudiating dream elements and associations he knew to be significant. Renik: "Hypercathexis (concentration of attention) of nonthreatening preconscious material abets and fortifies the defensive operation of withdrawal of attention from disturbing preconscious thoughts" (590). Thus when a parent threatens to interrupt the TV attention span of the children, this word from their sponsor is violently refused or must violently penetrate—outblast—the concentration of TV viewing and acting out.

The feeling of unreality—of observing oneself at a distance—tends to be accompanied by a change in how things look. Scopophilia and exhibitionism are implicated, as in any beach town, in the pathogenesis of depersonalization: to become one's own monitor is to be always "on" and opened up (or closed) to view. That the feeling of strangeness so often advertised by the depersonalized turns on a visual phenomenon reveals a hypercathexis of perception. But depersonalization is ultimately subjectively experienced less as a perceptual phenomenon than as judgment: Everything seems unreal; I'm not all there. "The outer line of defense consists of attention being withdrawn from a perception and concentrated upon the judgment, an abstract thought. It is not uncommon for patients to state this judgment aloud or internally to themselves, repetitiously insisting upon it in hardly varying form. There is an obvious parallel to induction of a trance state" (595). Recalling or fixing only on the gloss—"it was a dream," "it was this or that show"—lets one forget to say what can be recalled of the situation itself. Unlike the defensive operation of isolation, depersonalization permits endless attention to or viewing of whatever is on (or has escaped repression) inside a border zone between preconscious and conscious thought which the preoccupation with ideas of unreality reveals. But this endlessly "on" attention is not free: hence, again, the sense of unreality. "Disturbances in the sense of reality, as in depersonalization, indicate that, due to the presence of some danger (a threatening preconscious thought process) the scanning function of attention is interfered with" (596). The scanner is what TV superseded. The isolationist defenses of obsessional neurosis (like photography and cinema) create preconscious derivatives permitting attention to continue to range freely. "Depersonalization indicates that repression and its auxiliaries have failed to keep tolerable contents from preconsciousness; defensive maneuvers involving the distribution of attention must be brought into play, and an undisturbed sense of reality is sacrificed" (597).

Just as an obsessional symptom is often elaborated around a hysterical one, so the hypercathexis of perception inhabiting symptoms of depersonalization remains, Renik concludes, a conversion mechanism. Thus one patient's hypercathexis of a visual perception distracted attention from and defended against transference feelings. At bottom one should reach in the course of analysis a memory in which looking away, while it had a defensive purpose, also permitted (like the fetishistic object) the partial gratification of a scopophilic impulse. Back to the beach? No: TV, by being always on, even in the corner of the eye, covers the scanning of attention that would look away.

The erotic quality of symptoms of depersonalization reflects partial satisfaction of regressive instinctual urges expressed in the wish to sleep. This introduces another definition of prime time viewing:

> Thus, restriction of attention by means of hypercathexis of perception can be viewed as a compromise in which the sleep state is approached but at the same time warded off. A similar compromise can occur in daydreaming, when one stares fixedly, or while listening to music, both of which involve hypercathexis of perception. (601)

The Impostor

*"It's hard to explain how I did it; you would have to see me.
It's the way I* carry *myself. I'm so friendly."*
—Lionel Finkelstein, *"The Impostor"*

*My patient, who after some analysis came to characterize him-
self as a "closet Nazi," whose fiancée's tears left him dry-eyed
but full of hate-filled sexual excitement, would week copiously
at sentimental movies and plays, especially when parenthood
was being celebrated.*
—Leonhard Shengold, *"The Effects of Child Abuse as
Seen in Adults"*

On the other side of depersonalization—on the side of set
responses which refuse to be ignored—the "impostor" was
discovered. In 1925, in sync with Freud's application of the
second system to group psychology and female sexuality,
August Aichhorn and Karl Abraham guided psychoanalytic
attention to the impostor channel. The impostor whom

Helene Deutsch reports on in 1955 is, like the schizo, a group of one, but unlike the schizo requires at the same time countless "friends."[1]

> His narcissism did not permit him to be one of many; his self-love could be nourished only by feeling that he was unique. This desire for "uniqueness" did not, however, make him a lonely, schizoid personality. He was oriented toward reality which to him was a stage on which he was destined to play the leading role with the rest of humanity as an admiring audience. There were for him no human relationships, no emotional ties which did not have narcissistic gratification as their goal. His contact with reality was maintained, but it was not object libido which formed the bridge to it. He was always active and he surrounded himself with people; he sent out "pseudo-podia," but only to retract them laden with gifts from the outside world. (491)

The group phantasm of friendship which supports this mutual admiration society permits each member in turn to occupy the impostor's central position without removal of the other impostors. In the one-on-one, the impostor finds the one who wants to be fooled—and rips him off. The impostor, like the adolescent leader or member of the pack, cannot tolerate authority since he lacks the capacity for sustained effort and deferral required for any success other than the immediate or instant kind. The impostor flips from situation to situation, from role to role.

Our relationship to the ego ideal guarantees that anyone can fill or fall for the impostor role: "As one's ego ideal can never be completely gratified from *within,* we direct our demands to the external world, *pretending . . . that we actually are what we would like to be*" (503–4). According to Deutsch, the prepubescent girl, who is always acting out what she'd like to be like, serves as the standard on which defensive identifications both in puberty ("acting out" proper) and in schizoid personality (where they express pathological emotional states) are based (496).

The most aggrandized version of acting out belongs to the impostor; but he is also ultimately *the* group member merely recast in individual format. According to Lionel Finkelstein, those who have studied impostors (and, he adds, homosexuals) "often comment on how many can be observed once one has become aware of their existence" (85). But their number doubles and expands on contact precisely because they remain unanalyzable and often untreatable. "Their dishonesty and superficiality, their poor tolerance of frustration, their tendency toward action, and their deep underlying pathology tend to nullify any attempts to help them" (86).

Finkelstein bases his case study on the composite picture of the impostor which Phyllis Greenacre shot and assembled in the fifties.[2] According to Greenacre's wanted description, impostrous roles act out unresolved Oedipal conflicts in family romance fantasies. What further gives away the impostor is a disturbed sense of reality which destabilizes his identity—as if two identities were opposed inside him (in the one corner the impostrous roles, in the other the poorly constituted identity from which the roles emerged). Also part of the package, the impostor contains a defective superego which does not come with instructions or principles for the use of reality testing (86–87). Because he is without shame or guilt the impostor also sheds, like every make-believer or actor-out, the protective anxieties—whose absence renders the Californian the ready casualty of abuse that ultimately hits the streets, from drunk driving to mass murder.

Greenacre also excavated the family set on which impostors tune in. The relationship with the ambivalent, possessive mother was too close. Relations with an absent or ineffectual father never took on (or took in) the complete format of identification. With regard to mother the child supersedes father even though maturationally unable to do so. As in perversion's etiology, impostorship begins with this intensification of infantile narcissism which makes the

Oedipal conflict sharp and insoluble. In his impostures the product of this family (which, analysts in the fifties and sixties agreed, was the generic American nuclear family) will repeatedly kill the father or steal his penis (rip it off) to cover a sense of helplessness and incompleteness fixed in place when he was typecast too early in life in the manly role. The mother created the impostor's "cute" ego ideal by admiring and mirroring the two-year-old's heightened use of mimicry and gestures in his imitations of adult behavior.

The issue of job placement, which Erikson stressed in his bicoastal case study of the primal teenager, also directs the roles of imposture (according to Greenacre) which provide shortcut and short circuit of making it or getting ahead. The impostor gets this far because his victims, whose losses and wants asked to be made off and out with, were already (unconsciously) lined up and waiting at the impostrous role call. The impostor is driven by an urge to perpetuate fraudulence (or friendliness) which he pulls off on his consumers. In this regard his sense of reality is perceptive and responsive. But off screen he can be obtuse, brazen, and stupid. Although he is never found out in time to be unmasked or punished (but only when it's time for him to move on), he never makes it (career-wise, for example); he makes only guest appearances in the success stories of his conspirator-victims. Greenacre:

> The impostor has, then, a specially sharpened sensitivity within the area of his fraud. . . . The unconscious drive heightens his perceptions in a focused area and permits him to ignore or deny other elements of reality which would ordinarily be considered matters of common sense. It is this discrepancy in abilities which makes some impostors such puzzling individuals. Skill and persuasiveness are combined with utter foolishness and stupidity. In well-structured impostures this may be described as a struggle between two dominant identities in the individual: the temporarily focused and strongly assertive

impostrous one, and the frequently amazingly crude and poorly knit one from which the impostor has emerged.[3]

In the case of Finkelstein's patient, narcissistic self-enhancement defended against feelings of emptiness, worthlessness, and defectiveness while unresolved Oedipal conflicts (which stayed tuned to a faulty superego) caused him to falsify identity and background in the course of acting out hypercathected family romance fantasies. What Finkelstein discovers in addition to Greenacre's fifties' model is a certain feminine dimension or dementia of imposture. Finkelstein's patient, for example, made people happy—like a mother—by giving them what they wanted. Even the impostrous masculine (or paternal) roles which predominated within his repertoire defended against acknowledgment of the underlying femininity that emerged whenever he stopped being an impostor. In one period of remission or settling down he started caring for (even spoiling) his roommate as though he were the dude's mother-wife.

Finkelstein's patient is a "beautiful boy" and body builder who seduces the other into mutual admiration via a language of sincerity and friendliness.

> When he spoke he used such expressions as "really" . . . in an attempt to appear sincere. Later, as he found that in using these phrases he was revealing his essential dishonesty and wish to deceive, he was embarrassed to find that it was difficult to stop saying "really." . . . He was unsure whether he was trying to convince the other person or himself. (89)

Perpetual friendliness serves to reduce the transference to a vehicle for the right role.

> I was beginning to exist in his mind as a highly idealized figure. . . . Although he professed to idealize me as a perfect man and father and began to give lip service to values such as honesty and dependability, it

> became apparent that this was chiefly a new way . . .
> to flatter and please me by being a good patient. Even
> though his behavior had scarcely changed and he had
> not yet suffered any deep guilt or remorse, he acted as
> if he were a changed man and as if I were the finest
> analyst imaginable for having helped him so greatly.
> He let me know how often he praised me to his
> friends. In effect, he was playing an impostrous role
> of "the good patient." (102)

The friendship circuit into which Finkelstein's patient tries
to plug him was wired for castration. Although the patient
bragged about Finkelstein to his friends and clearly felt en-
hanced by their association, the bond of idealization is always with the dead. Like a child acting out in front of the TV,
the impostor acts out with his friends the transference he
watches via something like depersonalization on the Finkelstein set.

The fooled audience that asked for it was first modeled
by the parents who wanted to be taken in to the extent of
sharing with their offspring the at once desexualized and
phallic—the cute—ego ideal of mutual admiration. The impostor is "drinkable nectar"; everyone likes him (he's popular!) and he has a million friends. And yet the child who has
it all (as long as he can reflect back parental self-deception)
tends to be excitable and hyperactive (in other words, overstimulated); always needing attention and developing little
self-control or tolerance for frustration (just as at school he
remains too restless to be educable), the kid cruises for
bruises. The cycle of child abuse overlaps with the etiology
of the impostor.

Leonard Shengold locates in the charges of child abuse
the overstimulated child's need to escape an excess of libidi-
nization (and the rage and murderousness it brings forth);
the child identifies with the tormentor and thus turns the
rage on self and others. Via the case of George Orwell Shengold interprets child abuse as abuse of power and as contemporary pathology complimentary to depersonalization

and imposture: "child abuse has a particular resonance with, and relevance to, the twentieth century—to the world of *1984*."

> A young man in analysis for several years complained of having difficulty with his memory and with disruptions in his thinking that interfered with his professional achievements. . . . He lived a life of disconnected and largely unacknowledged sado-masochistic fantasy which he occasionally expressed in action that was quickly disavowed. So much was disavowed that his functioning sometimes suffered because of a discontinuity in his memory; this affected his sense of identity, and he had little feeling for himself as a child. He insisted on the façade of being regarded as the decent, helpful, kindly-but-feckless friend of the family—of so many families. His specialty was seducing the wives of his "good friends." He was a compulsive and successful seducer. This was part of a secret life that he covered by competent impersonation. He had been engaged for many years to a masochistic young woman who worshipped him and whom he treated very badly. He seemed to despise her for loving him, yet felt he needed her dependable affirmation of his "lovability." (21)

Identification and seduction corner the abuse charge. The patients regularly identify with the aggressor (who was also the only guardian figure around to turn to for protection from other, external threats): "To identify means to *be* and *not to see* someone. It follows that when these people . . . find their own victims they do not empathize with them" (27). While children are easily seduced because they want to be seduced, one also readily identifies with abusive parents because they so desire to inhabit their charges: "But getting inside, body and soul, is just what the parent who abuses his child can do. And it is exactly his ability to feel that gets interfered with" (43, n. 4). When Orwell describes his early inner habit of journalistically packaging and dispensing with experience ("'This was the making up of a continuous 'story' about myself, a sort of diary existing only in the mind'") as "'a common habit of children and adolescents,'" Shengold diagnoses instead a split between observing and experiencing egos (as in depersonalization or imposture) common only to those "who have to ward off the over-stimulation and rage that are the results of child abuse" (42).

Camp Counselor

The desublimation Herbert Marcuse recognized as the necessary accompaniment of technical progress and massification of sociality finds its counterpart in sublimation's provenance as melancholic addiction or iden-tification.[1] Sublimation's programmed withdrawal into re-pression gives more personal space to the impostrous invita-tion to identify, which rules absolutely. Whereas eros was supposed to reject group influence, technological de-sublimation has installed mutual identification inside groups as the only libidinal alternative to government by terror. No longer "haunted by father images" (52) the mod-ern citizen models his behavior on peers, gang leaders, stars of screen, music, or sports. At the same time he submits "to the exigencies of total administration, which include total preparation for the fatal end" (59).

Because the "massification of privacy" gives the exter-nalized ego ideal direction over "aggression toward the external enemies of the ego ideal," the ego-based individuals are perpetually "predisposed to accept and to make their own the political and social necessities which demand the permanent mobilization with and against atomic destruction" (51). One's privacy is thus coordinate (via the media) with that of all others. The "ego conscience" belongs to the kids, the peer groups, the friends; "the rest is deviation, or identity crises, or personal trouble," which the support groups discuss and work through.

Skipping the beat of the superego, the injunction to feel good about oneself instantly replays the ego ideal on the side of the group ideal (embodied by the leader of a group of friends or impostors bound and bonded on all sides by the mutual identification one likes and becomes like).

> The shrinking of the ego, its reduced resistance to others appears in the ways in which the ego holds itself constantly open to the messages imposed from outside. The antenna on every house, the transistor on every beach, the jukebox in every bar or restaurant are as many cries of desperation—not to be left alone, by himself, not to be separated from the Big Ones, not to be condemned to the emptiness or the hatred or the dreams of oneself. And these cries engulf the others, and even those who still have and want an ego of their own are condemned—a huge captive audience, in which the vast majority enjoys the captor. (49)

According to Marcuse, classifiable and recognizable perversion is only the effect of repression editing an originally polymorphous perversity into bit parts. Thus through the playback/erase of tapes which Marcuse calls desublimation, the regained original state or set of perversion would tune in the completely charged or "live" body while advertising a nonrepressive mode of sublimation. The body restored to a simulcast of zoning prior to genital centering could no longer be distributed and parceled out as object of labor or thought control. The fully eroticized (or perverse) body would model a different reality principle based on primary narcissism (or the utopian impulse).

On the pre-TV side of Freud's reception, Chasseguet-Smirgel situates the figure of perversion and imposture within an internal (or eternal) adolescence that already asserts itself as pregenital.[2] But in flipping through all the channels, the teenager or pervert uses the ego ideal as his published/public guide. As the recovery projection of the narcissistic perfection of one's own childhood, the ego ideal remains at bottom pregenital, perverse, and precious (cute!). Indeed, once a connection to the genital father can be made or observed, the ego ideal has already been superseded by the superego, just as idealization and mimicry (mechanisms in the service of a "cute" ego ideal) have, by then, already yielded to sublimation. To avoid within a mutual admiration society of friends recognition of the difference between (and the extended family across) the generations, "pregenital sexuality, with its erotogenic zones and its part-objects, must be submitted to a process of idealization" (350).

Whereas idealization, like the perverse act, covers the parts (including part instincts) comprising the predilection for objects, sublimation concerns in the first place the drive. But idealization of perverse acts and part-objects helps the pervert "to drive away and counter-cathect the perception—which would give rise to a feeling of total dereliction—that the genital father possesses powers which he lacks" (351). Both sublimation in the service of the superego and its ego-idealist simulation seek the release of creativity and art. But the creative works of perverts only pull one off and over their material or subject (which cannot vary). Like Mickey Mouse, the other works of perversion are also imitation original phalluses.

> The impossibility of identification with the father (or with the father-substitute) leads the subject to "make" rather than "engender" his work, which, like himself, would not bend to the principle of ascendancy through a "family line." . . . The originator of creative

work will therefore be the ego-ideal, but the raw material that is used will not have been fundamentally modified. (352)

The work of perversion produces a fictitious phallus or fetish by merging ego and ego-ideal and thus "short-circuiting the process of sublimation" (353). As pathological solution, then, the pervert's work "may be considered like an acting out miraculously destined to fill the space separating . . . the pregenital penis from the genital penis, the child from the father" (353).

"Faults in identification dispose to acting out" (353). These faults resounding within "a deep disturbance of the process of sublimation" bring up *Beben* destined for the perpetual groupification or imposture of adolescent friendship. Chasseguet-Smirgel addresses via Helene Deutsch and Phyllis Greenacre the group need for this con-art:

> The more painfully individuals feel the separation between ego and ego-ideal, or the more they fear its being revealed, the more they will be tempted to exploit creativity to make up for what feels like a very deep wound. (353)

The creativity of group members—journal keeping, acting, sketching, dancing—has the immediate goal of filling in this separation through imitation. Imitation remains "tied"—as in the S/M session—"to unconscious fantasies of omnipotence" (354). The magic of imitation thus produces the spell of being (rather than becoming) "great" or "nice."

The homosexual is perverted to the extent that he models a group membership of interchangeable parts of the perfect body that, friendly, helps you out. The campy, cute, awesome, and false work inspires infatuations or crushes which often exceed the emotive bond with "genuine achievements." Every impostor and pervert embodies the attractions of his minor art: "in imposing the pregenital penis of a little pubescent boy he displays an almost diabolical seductiveness and power of conviction" (356).

Go for It

Gustav Bychowski's title, "The Ego and the Intro-jects,"[1] doubles as the band or bond of acting out that links homosexuals, as its advance guard, to mass adolescence or group psychology. The homosexual reflects back—psychosis-style—unresolved bisexuality (his own and that of his parents).

> This lack of resolution of the bisexual conflict is but a part of the general lack of synthesis of the ego. All possible ambivalent and pregenital attitudes toward the object retain their primitive aims; archaic mechanisms such as narcissistic object choice, incorporation, turning against the self, the change from activity to passivity and vice versa remain as basic endowments of this ego organization. Rapid shifting from activity to passivity is a trait which the homosexual shares with the latent schizophrenic. (25)

The situations which prompt and promote homosexual acting out offer libidinal gratification, to be sure, but also eventually set off "primitive defense mechanisms and some form of primitive, undifferentiated aggression" (26). Upon impact with these stimulating situations, the barriers of countercathexis separating dissociated sections of the ego's sensorium release the drive power which had originally been withheld for their erection. Thus a sudden release of an undifferentiated libidinal-aggressive charge can be used for an instantaneous conquest ("in brief thrusts toward the object") but does not have staying power: the establishment of an object relationship cannot be maintained (26). This splitting of the egoic sensorium gives the central ego the typical feeling of deprivation. The result: compulsive searching for maternal tenderness and paternal strength via pseudo objects modeled after externalized introjects. The "true object relationship" is further threatened (as in all perversion which comes unprocessed by sublimating socialization) in the demand for an expenditure of libido beyond the ego's means to postpone. Whereas mature heterosexuality is designed to rotate perpetually on low like some libido lawn sprinkler, perverse libido goes under (unchecked) only to emerge periodically—wasted. "The task is abandoned, and the individual instead compulsively seeks gratification in thrifty short-lived acts of rapid discharge with pseudo objects" (28).

The strong charge of the introjects unchecked by the weakened countercathexis lets roll the projection. The weakening of the countercathectic encasement lets go or expels the dissociated introjects from the ego boundaries and refastens them onto "momentarily idealized chance encounters" (26). But each appointment with the "real object" is always another dis-appointment. The impulse rapidly to discharge the libidinal battery turns on in synchrony with the charge of aggression which often turns against the self. Acting out, whether adolescent, transplantational, or homosexual, is self-destructive. When aggression detached from the introjects is directed against both the pseudo object and the self, the punishing superego is subserved.

California Transplant

T he sister made an immediate and unqualified decision to be the donor and spontaneously stated that even if donating meant that she could never become pregnant because of having only one kidney, this was the least she could do for her brother. Her brother would owe her nothing; however, if she were the recipient of her brother's kidney, she might feel forever grateful, as if she would have to do something for him in repayment.

—Samuel Basch, *"The Intrapsychic Integration of a New Organ"*

Marilyn Monroe was a native Californian body-genital (of technical media). MM kept diaries, took notes in preparation for heavy conversations, was intellectual and supersensitive, did drugs, made suicide pacts, and kept busy with interesting activities (yoga, jogging, working out, nonsexual massage, politics, group sex). "Nobody ever got cancer from sex." MM's couplification attempts were turned on by a guy's friendliness and disappointed when discovering the partner's own diary coverage of the marriage. MM was a loyal friend but, when it came to the one-on-one, was not high fidelity. Hence, although MM was not into the reproduction or reduction of couplification, she plugged into another lifeline. "Do you know who I've always depended on? The telephone." Downing sleeping pills (every night was Jonestown), she dialed her support group of friends on her suicide hot line. MM fell asleep with the phone at her ear open to the switchboard. When the operator heard stertorous breathing, MM was saved once again.[1]

The techno-invasion of the couple by the sex of the group—the overexposure to the other's death and, in other words, excessive organ transplantation—embodied a crisis in defense systems which Freud identified as the beyond of the pleasure principle and which today is termed AIDS. The literalization of sex as identification (which Spielrein theorized) requires some form of the drugs that transplant patients must stay on: immunosuppressants.

As Pietro Castelnuovo-Tedesco's California-based research confirms, whereas earlier body image alterations were administered only as external losses (i.e., amputations), organ transplantation introduces a foreign part into the body it penetrates:[2] "the psychological processes in organ loss are different from those that occur when a foreign organ is introduced *into* the body" (349). Amputations belong to the side of traumatic neurosis; transplantation takes a shortcut and produces outright psychotic reaction: "there is substantial evidence that the patient may be responding to the presence within him of what is to him psychologically a foreign body" (351). It follows that the range of sexual identity (or of bisexuality) has been technologized: "the patient was clearly distressed by the fact that he possessed not only a heart that was not his own, but one that had belonged to a woman. Later, in his psychosis, he had the distinct hallucinatory impression that the woman was calling him" (351). Another male transplant patient, who had received a woman's kidney, felt that now he too was a woman. Yet another patient who only referred to his transplanted organ, likewise of female extraction, as his "lady" nevertheless answered some questions about himself in the female gender. In every case the transplant patients thus feel reborn: "God had come inside" one patient, depositing, with the kidney, a "new wisdom." But if a woman's heart represents the stolen heart—the heart of mother—then the son was not licensed to accept it. Reactions of male to male transplantation are equally Oedipal. Born again via the new organ donated by a man, one male patient wished to become a donor in turn—but of his eyes only.

Joining and working for the cause of transplantation can reward "the patient's feverish effort to remain on good terms with his ambivalently held introjects and to keep them from becoming dangerous persecutors as a result of further regression"—which could manifest itself "by a disorganization of psychotic proportions" (359). For transplantations are life-extending rather than, as with radical acts of removal, life saving. With life-saving operations patients experience loss, depression, and "phantom phenomena" (the tendency to retain the lost part or organ in fantasy). Through the removal of diseased parts, a patient might approach his normal or allotted life span. But transplant operations imply that the deadline has been pushed back beyond one's time share; the patient has been born again. The two modes of radical rescue differ according to Freud's two systems, to which they respectively belong.

Electro-Cute

In 1933 Carl Schmitt (in *The Concept of the Political*) defended the need for the friend or foe distinction against more current forms of political "association" (sponsored, for example, by William James). In a sense, Schmitt thus strikes out against the Teen Age without realizing, however, in the paranoid mode, that he's one of the gadget-loving participants; nor could he recognize that James's vote for "association" approximates a deconstruction of the adolescent state James self-consciously inhabits (and which is, after all, here to stay). Thus Schmitt reserves a place separate from his argument-in-progress for Christian love of the personal enemy (which really defines Christian or adolescent friendship), arguing that the enemy *(hostis)* he is prescribing (and he's clearly less interested in making friends) is the public enemy (indeed, there is no place in adolescent thinking for a public enemy number one). His argument can be souped-up for where we're headed: the global rise of Christian-adolescent friendship has, while drawing on the same current that makes the teenager want to live forever, also pulled up a suicidal impulse which Schmitt ascribes to the *absence* of the public enemy (which means that war must be waged on war itself).

Drugs operate at the public/private intersections of the war against war where drunk driving and smoking in public open up bottlefields of a total war that goes down between self and other. But the ecstasy of warfare (one need only consult the sublime register) has always gone down as drugs. War has always been "on drugs." According to William Burroughs, modern total war is fought over the rights to one's own body—the rights to drugs. Drugs are at the same time the weapon.

Total war "on drugs" has accelerated and interiorized within the media-technologized sensurround of modernity (of the dialectic of Enlightenment). Drugs got us "wired." The path of war "on drugs" is concurrent with conversion, telegraphy, and occultism. Drug addiction—"getting wired"— literalizes inspiration or dictation. Drugs place a call—are a mode of technicity. They mark a preference, Derrida has recognized, for the simulacrum, bad remembering, techno-recording (the kind that simultaneously erases).[1] Drugs are charged with making a move against anamnesis or genuine remembering. Like the Cargo Cultists in anticipation of the return of the ancestors, the drug user gets wasted, making way (waves) for the future. But at the controls of both cults there's no ancestor but only the unmournably dead.

The drug you down is a foreign body. But even the intake of drugs, which technologizes the body at the heart, is an externalization of psychic processes which *have* technologized the body. Freud thus calls drugs mere reflections or imitations of the "libido toxin" man has yet to find.[2] The drug, the foreign body, goes the identificatory way down of love.

Drugs are sexual aids. They blast sexualizable personalized difference and lube and anesthetize the transplant operations of sex which reinsert identifications, dictations, organs. At the moment when the perverse organization of groups around the drug of a "war" on drugs breaks down onto its internal improvements on love and war, AIDS takes over. It's the blood bond all over again. AIDS is what was all along being denied. At the heart of every triad of transference (and of its imitation or imposture) the "possibility of AIDS is installed." Derrida comes to the conclusion:

> At the heart of that which would preserve itself as a dual intersubjectivity it inscribes the mortal and indestructible trace of the third—not the third as the condition for the symbolic and the law, but the third as destructuring structuration of the social bond, as social disconnection, and even as the disconnection of the interruption.

Dear Diary

*T*he best preface to this journal written by a young girl belonging to the upper middle class is a letter by Sigmund Freud dated April 27, 1915, a letter wherein the distinguished Viennese psychologist testifies to the permanent value of the document:

"This diary is a gem. Never before, I believe, has anything been written enabling us to see so clearly into the soul of a young girl, belonging to our social and cultural stratum, during the years of puberal development. We are shown how the sentiments pass from the simple egoism of childhood to attain maturity; how the relationships to parents and other members of the family first shape themselves, and how they gradually become more serious and more intimate; how friendships are formed and broken. We are shown the dawn of love, feeling out towards its first objects. Above all, we are shown how the mystery of the sexual life first presses itself vaguely on the attention, and then takes entire possession of the growing in-

telligence, so that the child suffers under the load of secret knowledge but gradually becomes enabled to shoulder the burden. Of all these things we have a description at once so charming, so serious, and so artless, that it cannot fail to be of supreme interest to educationists and psychologists.

"It is certainly incumbent on you to publish the diary. All students of my own writings will be grateful to you."

—*A Young Girl's Diary*

Beginning in the thirties (in the midst of *Joseph and His Brothers*) Thomas Mann's literary production increasingly opened up its family romances to admit contemporary connections, current references and events. But this suggests not so much a shift toward the political contest and context which the advent of National Socialism opened but rather Mann's own streamlining of production around the other line of defense—identification. The diary that had been Mann's record of the everyday (unfolding around and on his own person and folding out in newspapers and journals) now entered directly into the place reserved for literature. (Identification slid ahead of sublimation, which withdrew into repression.) The late work therefore allegorizes neither a past nor an emigré present but rather the anticipated future of Mann's own impostor-like posthumous publications.

The journal Mann kept was all along the terminal of bonding between Mann's writing and journalism (both of newspaper and academic provenance). Mann co-signed and borrowed for his auto-commentary and PR job the academy's standard reception of his work.[1] It was an inside job. The journalistic outside entered his output through the diary—the "live" organ that he had retained from adolescence and which remained the battery of an adolescent energy that was taken for genius.

In America he continued to absorb psychoanalysis, the popular philosophy not only of this place of exile. But the psychoanalysis thus inside Mann's fiction remains preconscious—as in Madison Avenue advertising—and hence impervious to psychoanalytic readings (which in Mann criticism tend to be as uninteresting as the insistence with which patterns of incest and narcissism already in place in the works assert themselves). Boredom and mediocrity are symptoms of repression's press release. From his essays, letters, and literature to his diaries (and back again), Mann's writing production endlessly recycled in on itself. It was television: the diaries are the guide. The decision to pack his journalism for posthumous release was reached in California.

Mann thus inhabited California, that deepest recess of Kafka's "Amerika," totally as teenager. California is where he came out—not so much as gay writer but as another case of D., another group member whose bisexual constitution guaranteed a sadomasochistic administration of his libido; and not so much as phantom telecommanding the legacy from beyond the grave (we're not talking Goethe or Nietzsche), but as teen ghost writer who was forever the double agent and true "ironist" keeping under cover dear-diary commentaries running within and against the family which "Thomas Mann" had in public/published circles made the very measure of civilization.

Gnarly

ollowing his glimpse of the grand opening of the Berlin Olympics on newsreel, Mann concludes Stevenson's *The Strange Case of Dr. Jekyll and Mr. Hyde:* "Finished Stevenson 'Mr. Hyde,' a very intelligent and good story which one should turn into a film—a film I should perhaps direct" (diary entry of August 12, 1936). The story, which thus holds the place of Mann's projections, delivered a model for Mann's recasting of the Faust legend around and within the diaries, which he only then, during the casting call for *Doctor Faustus,* destined for posthumous publication (see, e.g., diary entry of March 21, 1943).

Dr. Jekyll's own strange case moves beyond any charge of mere hypocrisy: both sides of his double life "were in dead earnest."[1] But, as always in doubling, the dead ringer is the sole survivor; the original pharmaceutical solution that links and separates the two sides of doubling cannot be reproduced; what Jekyll had taken to be the crucial ingredient had been, originally, impure. It is this impurity, then, that cannot be reproduced—or reversed. The impurity which the solution contained has now allowed "the thing that was projected" (85) to be "much . . . nourished": "my original and better self was becoming slowly incorporated with my second and worse" (88–89).

Stevenson turns up the volume on the homonymic doubles of Hyde: at one end "Mr. Hyde" is reliteralized through punning contrast with the "Mr. Seek" (38) who must find him; at the other end a certain Dr. Lanyon receives from his more adventurous colleague Dr. Jekyll the derogation "hidebound pedant" (43). Both meanings achieve simultaneous broadcast on the occasion of the first murder the double commits: "Mr. Hyde broke out of all bounds" (47).

The interchangeability of *y* and *i* also renders, on another side, Jekyll's extremity: kill. The death-wish pact between Dr. and double thus comes into focus. Indeed, within the series of metamorphoses that the doubling of Dr. Jekyll embodies, the first altered state is attributed to those who, seeing Hyde, "turned sick and white with the desire to kill him" (31). What goes by the name Mr. Hyde has been reanimated by what goes without saying: projected death wishes which belong, properly, to the Jekyll side of the pact. Candidates for the position of corpse on this target range will, therefore, not be found lacking.

On the premier occasion of his turning into Hyde, Jekyll passes on the inside through "the hour of birth or death": "within I was conscious of . . . a current of disordered sensual images running like a mill race in my fancy, a solution of the bonds of obligation" (83). On the outside: "I was suddenly aware that I had lost in stature" (84). When it comes time for Hyde to turn into the killer, he "struck in a . . . spirit . . . in which a sick child may break a plaything" (90). Thus the ghostbusters, upon cornering Hyde in the crypt, pick up sounds of weeping that belong to "a woman or a lost soul" (69). This sick child, weeping woman, or lost soul is, in Jekyll's account, his own "insurgent horror," which was, fittingly, "knit to him closer than a wife." "He heard it mutter and felt it struggle to be born." But: "This was the shocking thing: . . . that what was dead, and had no shape, should usurp the offices of life" (95).

Once the original incorporation of some impurity has stretched Hyde over the Jekyll side, which remains hidden, "each return to Jekyll," which the drug still, though only briefly, induces, represents "a temporary suicide": just as Hyde loathes Jekyll's "despondency," so he fears Jekyll's "power to cut him off by suicide" (96). In the end "Hyde is gone to his account" over "the body of a self-destroyer" (70).

Threatened by the suicidal melancholia Jekyll embodies, Hyde, on the manic side, can only vandalize with graffiti the walls of his cell: "Hence the ape-like tricks that he would play me, scrawling in my own hand blasphemies on the pages of my books, burning the letters and destroying the portrait of my father." His perpetual adolescence or "love of life is wonderful" (96). Immediately after the first or primal murder Hyde commits (which starts shifting the balance of the death-wish pact in Hyde's interest), Dr. Jekyll beams himself back to his good standing: "The veil of self-indulgence was rent from head to foot, I saw my life as a whole: I followed it up from the days of childhood, when I had walked with my father's hand, and through the self-denying toils of my professional life." Once the metamorphoses into Hyde which replace Jekyll begin taking place automatically, the doctor can always first diagnose his altered state by glancing at his hirsute, werewolfish hand. But like a name that cannot vary, the hand they give each other also remains the same. Jekyll, having thus turned on automatic into Hyde—who, now that their relationship has turned around, must find and take the drug to change into Jekyll—can obtain assistance in his own name only by writing a letter: "Then I remembered that of my original character, one part remained to me: I could write my own hand" (93). But the double hand does not guard the reminiscence of father: the primal antibody has not aborted the other incorporation, the solution's impurity or unmournable corpse. The hand's inner reach (or retch) belongs not to the mournable dad.

The protagonist of the narrative frame and Dr. Jekyll's heir (in place of Mr. Hyde, whom he replaces), the lawyer Utterson, defends always in earshot of his own name a proper routing of legacies. The monster-producing will of the Dr. genius is, literally, the will or testament that, since written in the one hand, harbors a 3-D or "holograph" phantom. As Jekyll remarks to Utterson: "I never saw a man so distressed as you were by my will; unless it were that hide-bound pedant, Lanyon, at what he called my scientific heresies" (43). Utterson in turn is haunted by "the strange clauses of the will" to the point of brooding "awhile on his own past . . . lest by chance some Jack-in-the-Box of an old iniquity should leap to light there" (42).

The will that originally handed the legacy over to Hyde already holds the place of the monstrous confession that lives on hide-bound: "it provided not only that, in case of the decease of Henry Jekyll, . . . all his possessions were to pass into the hands of . . . 'Edward Hyde'; but that in case of Dr. Jekyll's 'disappearance or unexplained absence,'. . . the said Edward Hyde should step into the said Henry Jekyll's shoes" (35). This transmission from hand to hand—this transformation of hand into hand and rematerialization of one in the other's shoes—already represents, for Utterson, a "presentment of a fiend" (36). When Utterson receives Dr. Lanyon's testament, also a chronicle of secrets, he encounters again the strange terms or clauses of the will: the enclosure within Lanyon's cover letter cannot "be opened till the death or disappearance of Dr. Henry Jekyll" (58). "Utterson could not believe his eyes. Yes, it was disappearance; here again, as in the mad will . . . here again were the idea of a disappearance and the name of Henry Jekyll bracketed" (59).

Bracketed or cornered (as the uncanny) inside Jekyll's own room, Hyde can communicate with the servants only via what remains "unquestionably the doctor's hand": but the butler cannot be deceived about his master's voice, which has changed. Jekyll goes down with his voice; Hyde remains what he had already doubled as: the uncanny living on of the corpus. Thus Jekyll has already signed off at the moment he brings his memoirs to a close in anticipation of his imminent changeover and takeover: "this is my true hour of death . . . as I lay down the pen, and proceed to seal up my confession, I bring the life of that unhappy Henry Jekyll to an end." That which can no longer hide lives on: the memoirs bearing the signature one double always supplies the other one.

Hyde's double identity and signature first emerge around his abuse of a child he knocks down in passing: a vigilante crowd collects instantly around the charge of child abuse. Only a check, written in Jekyll's name, can stay the mob by paying it off. For Utterson this is the primal scene of Jekyll's delegation, according to the strange clauses of his will, of his hand. Thus Utterson discovers, with a certain Mr. Guest's assistance, that a handwritten note from Mr. Hyde and an invitation from Dr. Jekyll are each the other's mirror image: "there's a rather singular resemblance; the two hands are in many points identical; only differently sloped" (55). Abuse of the hand and abuse of a child prove the contamination of the legacy—which, if it stays in the family, can be handed down only to a suicide.

The child abuse charge, which doubles as the first recognizable link between Jekyll and his projection, forces Jekyll's hand; he opens a bank account in Hyde's name: "and when, by sloping my own hand backwards, I had supplied my double with a signature, I thought I sat beyond the reach of fate" (87). Both ends of Jekyll's monstrous will are conjoined in Utterson's nightmares as double feature. Utterson dreams over and again of the scene of child abuse and then of the fiendish child abuser who has the upper hand: "there would stand by his side a figure to whom power was given, and even at that dead hour he must rise and do its bidding. The figure in these two phases haunted the lawyer all night" (37).

The paternal hand job failed. Even the haunted state, the projection onto an impurity or corpse of the wish to kill, does not, once busted, hand it to father. The diary lives on.

The projection opened with a scene of child abuse—the perverse enactment of paternity and affiliation. Father is charged with abuse or neglect just as he is the target of every diary. Every diary is a deferred/deterred suicide note. (In the year following the story's publication, Stevenson's father dies, giving RLS financial independence. The already haunted and grief-stuck metabolism shoots up with the father's death; but the other life of postponed adolescence had already, beginning with RLS's trip to California, come out and taken over.)

Monstrosity fictions play back the history of psychoanalysis; their spooks rebound all the way from the missing place of the seduction theory. In Whales's *Frankenstein* and Browning's *Dracula*, for example, child abuse is what monstrous beings perpetrate outside the wedding night which then comes at the end to offer problem-free exit for the audience from this mock-phantom realm of sexual repression.

Split the Scene

*I*t was in San Francisco that the two Energy Forces met and coalesced. Together, Brother Jud and Even Eve set out to found the world's next great religion. Group sex metamorphosed itself into the more elevated concept of poly-fidelity. This novel sexual institution became the heart of the Kerista life-style. Its instrument was the BFIC, the Best Friend Identity Cluster. Each BFIC was composed of up to twelve women and twelve men. Sexual gratification was shared by— but not limited to—the members of the BFIC. Polyinfidelity— BFIC hopping—was not allowed: sexual relations were to be strictly endogamous. . . . The atmosphere in Kerista was said to be partylike because polyfidelity permitted the appreciation of many types of human beings, all of whom could be sampled and fully experienced within the BFIC. . . . As far as Kerista was concerned, you could be heterosexual, homosexual or bisexual. It just so happened that most of the monks at the *moment seemed to prefer heterosexual interpersonal relation-ships.*

—Shiva Naipaul, *Journey to Nowhere*

Jekyll and Hyde, Freud and Fliess: in both cases the privacy of letter and journal writing develops the double agent concept as cover for the charge of child abuse. In the midst of yet another return of the seduction theory—converging this time around with the bicoastal phantasm of missing and abused children—Jeffrey Masson has reloaded the charge: the concept of bisexuality was forged out of displacement of Freud's repeated discovery of traumatic seductions in early childhood; it was originally invented, in fact, to cover up Fliess's sexual mishandling of his young son Robert.[1]

The transfer of the bisexuality theory between Fliess and Freud rebounded beyond them onto the pinball game called, Back East, anxiety of influence. It hit and lit all the counters when Otto Weininger, under Freud's analysis, walked away with the bisexuality thesis. But his *Sex and Character* did not represent auto-analytic breakthrough; it left itself behind as suicide note.

Fliess was into symmetry. He was convinced that there was a predetermined timeplan, a given "mechanism," which lifespan and substance embody. But the mechanism did not tell clock time: the segments, events, or advents of lifetime are noninterchangeable each time they come up suddenly and with a jolt. Everything happens nonsuperimposably and in a flash.

So Fliess consulted the biological time-keeping mechanism of menstruation which, over time, is never regular. This irregularity reflects, it turns out, the effects of two periodic processes which do observe constant intervals. This discovery started him counting. Soon he was able to determine onset, length, and end of every lifespan. The irregular "days" or periods which Fliess was able to refigure in terms of their double constancy were the vital spans of substance units. The conclusion Fliess's obsessing calculations come to: "Wherever nature forms groups of 28 or 23 similar individuals (for example human beings) and binds them together through a common destiny, these groups are always given the same amount of vital substance. And within a natural group of individuals, the sum of vital substance is equally constant, as is the sum of energy in a closed system." The "substance-equality of natural groups," which the periodicity-blender extracted from temporal irregularities, will, Fliess forecasts, become the organizing principle of biology.[2]

Fliess's thesis casts masculine and feminine dispositions as each the other's seduction or repression; the process of repression, Freud objected, would thus, in theory, be sexualized, biologized, or, in short, couplified. But in practice the concept of bisexuality was, always and originally, the product of a couplification, *and* of a repression, having been transmitted by Fliess to Freud. Freud's feigned excitement over Fliess's bisexuality thesis, like the promise to accept it into his own work, reflects Freud's anxious attempts to reassure Fliess within their correspondence that Freud was getting something out of an exchange which in German must also always bear the senses of *Verkehr*.

Fliess's view of sexual difference as double-or-nothing reenters the already overdeterminedly gendered categories of aesthetic psychology which Freud dismantles at the start of "On 'the Uncanny.'" Freud would always grant that the others got "the unconscious" right. But only symptomatically, partially, or via phantom teleguidance—only because they (Fliess, Staudenmaier, Trotter, McDougall, Hall, Ruths, Adler, Jung, Reich) missed the repression connection, which Freud considered the most primal piece or block *(Stück)* of the construction of psychoanalysis (*SE* 21:153). In other words, Fliess built another Olympia, the android recording device or blowup dolly. But it's the Sandman figure returning on the repression track (events or advents come up, at the same time, always also in flashback) that brings us the uncanny. Since on each person one gender would be the unconscious of the other gender, the bisexuality thesis requires an at once personalizable (likable) and decidable (unambivalent) difference (the uncanny reverse of this view, according to Jentsch, was the *uncertainty* surrounding Olympia's animate or inanimate status). "Such a theory as this can only have an intelligible meaning if we assume that a person's sex is to be determined by the formation of his genitals" (*SE* 17:201). How else could one be sure which of the two sides of a personality belongs to which sex? Without biological decidables, investigation of a patient based on the symmetry thesis alone would, Freud concludes, reach "results" which should have served as the investigation's point of departure (*SE* 17:201). And yet the bisexuality axis of prepsychoanalytic psychologies (which include the unconscious but leave out repression) is the layout of institutionalization or technologization, psychoticization or massification, on the basis or person, always, of "sexual identities."

On two occasions which double-dated the openings of political fronts within psychoanalysis, Freud rejected Stekel's application of bisexuality to dream analysis. Stekel had obscured both the continued influence of archaic or childhood interpretations of sexuality and the always one-way identification with the outcome or coming out of sexual identity:

> It is true that the tendency of dreams and of unconscious phantasies to employ sexual symbols bisexually betrays an archaic characteristic; for in childhood the distinction between the genitals of the two sexes is unknown and the same kind of genitals are attributed to both of them. [1911.] But it is possible, too, to be misled into wrongly supposing that a sexual symbol is bisexual, if one forgets that in some dreams there is a general inversion of sex, so that what is male is represented as female and vice versa. Dreams of this kind may, for instance, express a woman's wish to be a man. [1925.] (*SE* 5:359)

Like group sex, "bisexuality" remains unidirectional (straight). The hard-bodied members of the group's sex (cheerleaders and swimmers alike) band together to re-phallicize mother. In 1912 and 1925 the theory of bisexuality presented, via the backfire of its untenability, the building blockages of postmodern Pacmen. At bottom: the childhood take on difference (which makes no difference); on top: the adolescent body—at once hard and feminine.

While Freud left "unsolved" the "problems of perversion and bisexuality" (*SE* 5:606–7, n. 2), their solution, once swallowed, transformed followers like Dr. Adler into teenagers who, with their own ideas, split Freud's scene. Adler's notion of "masculine protest" was yet another theory of bisexuality which sexualized the repression process (*SE* 17:201). Like the concept of bisexuality, the doctrine of masculine protest "represents the struggle between the two sexes as being the decisive cause of repression" (*SE* 17:201). But the protest doctrine diverges from the bisexual one in its introduction of an asymmetrical or antidialectical tension: every individual "struggles towards the 'masculine line,' from which satisfaction can alone be derived" (*SE* 17:201). But the thesis of masculine protest does not distinguish between character formation and the formation of neuroses, nor does it admit the "fact of repression" except as one-way backup support of the protest. "The repressing agency, therefore, would always be a masculine instinctual impulse, and the repressed would be a feminine one" (*SE* 17:201). The symptoms, however, owing to their displaced (but still substitutive) relation to that which gets repressed, would reflect the feminine impulse.

Both the bisexuality and the masculine-protest theories, "which may be said to have in common a sexualization of the process of repression," fail the test of the beating pageants. The bisexuality thesis is disqualified from the sexual-difference contest which, given the limited libido pool of applicants for the first object positions, is asymmetrical in focus and formation. Little boys and little girls alike must put father in the position from which they beat a retreat, just as they are equally unisex in their designs on mother. That's why the masculine protest gets and goes further when submitting to the S/M test. But the conclusion built into the one-way "repression" of the feminine line (which serves, according to the protest, as the background or backside of the beating fantasy) is that only the girl fulfills the terms of masculine protest with complete success. The boy relates to the masculine protest (both in fantasy and symptom) only in the mode of failure. But what also fails at this point is the distinction between fantasy and symptom. How can the girl's fantasy, which in fact completely achieves the conditions of masculine protest, also have the value and meaning of a symptom (*SE* 17:203)?

But as Freud advised Fliess in a letter dated May 25, 1897, if repression goes the (one) way of identification (to identify with someone is no longer to see him), then the feminine is the repression-free *agency* of repression. (If father gets repressed, then mourning goes the way of the father. The motive force of group cohesion [or repression] is internally and eternally feminine.) "It is supposed that the element essentially responsible for repression is always what is feminine. This is confirmed by the fact that women as well as men admit more readily to experiences with women than with men. What men essentially repress is the pederastic element." In another letter to Fliess (July 23, 1904), and thus at the close of the correspondence or *Verkehr* that had been the original context of the bisexuality-theory contest, Freud acknowledged that he had never followed the symmetrical or biological trend set by the bisexuality thesis, but only that provocative one-sidedness of the theory, which was the other side of his own theory (of repression). His introduction of "bisexuality" to his patients in the course of the transference was restricted to the explanation "that a strong homosexual current is found in every neurotic."

Freud could always show that, contrary to what Adler's protest advertised, the males who protested (too much) revealed and revelled in their masochistic attitude or bondage to women. "If the masculine protest is to be taken as having satisfactorily explained the repression of passive phantasies (which later become masochistic), then it becomes for that very reason totally inapplicable to the opposite case of active phantasies" (*SE* 17:203). If what gets repressed, moreover, is not passivity as such but only passivity toward men, then castration anxiety alone leads the protest. But in that case, Freud announced in 1914, in the midst of his discovery of narcissism and ego ideal, masculine protest cannot be the kernel of every neurosis: "Incidentally, I know of cases of neurosis in which the 'masculine protest,' or, as we regard it, the castration complex, plays no pathogenic part, and even fails to appear at all" (*SE* 14:92–93).

When asked in 1926 about this provocative aside, Freud could no longer recall the connection (*SE* 14:93, n. 1). But the enigmatic assertion was in fact made at the same time as Freud's admitted discovery that there could be bona fide neuroses of mourning. Although the melancholic context of the exception Freud takes to the rule of castration anxiety was forgotten or repressed, the connection itself was put through in Freud's second system where melancholic identification became the model of (always faulty or doomed) sublimation and superego formation.

Bisexuality is the constitution of adolescence (or California). The equal rights it bills homosexuality give teen dating and groupification the charge. The European artifact intelligence that brought us the couple is, in the case of Mann, the lookout post of an interiority that has remained teenage. The dead child (or sibling) fills the crypt that gives the battery charge to adolescence (to which Mann retained equal rights).

Smiley

Like the conversion mechanism, the "theory of bisexuality is still surrounded by many obscurities" (*SE*
21:105–6, n. 3) which lend their "enigma" to woman (*SE* 22:131). It also forwards woman to a busy intersection of pathologies. In the context of female sexuality, melancholic identification and conversion hysteria are the two
out-of-phase mechanisms of loss management which both
require the bisexuality thesis. (As Sarah Kofman puts it:
"Hysteria is the neurotic analogue of melancholic psychosis, since both are caused by a loss, in the one case that of the
erogenous zone, in the other that of an object."[1]) The hysteric, for her part, appears to be playing masculine and feminine roles: "This simultaneity allows what is at stake to be
both concealed and displayed."[2] Indeed, Freud writes in
"Hysterical Phantasies and Their Relation to Bisexualilty,"
the hysteric mimics the bisexuality thesis to produce symp-

toms that can only be read in stereo, that is, as confirming the thesis:

> We need not then be surprised or misled if a symp-
> tom seems to persist undiminished although we have
> already resolved one of its sexual meanings; for it is
> still being maintained by the—perhaps unsuspected
> —one belonging to the opposite sex. In the treat-
> ment of such cases, moreover, one may observe
> how the patient avails himself, during the analysis
> of the one sexual meaning, of the convenient possi-
> bility of constantly switching his associations, as
> though on to an adjoining track, into the field of the
> contrary meaning. (*SE* 9:166)

In the little girl's development a change in object must take place, a clearing must be made for the "transference" (onto father and husband) of love originally addressed to the mother. The girl must achieve disconnection from the mother by keeping her everywhere on the line: any trouble she later has with husbands she in fact has with mother (beginning with the change from initial love to hate). In "becoming" woman, the girl invents the "father." Hence the "wife" is always the father's delegate; the "other woman" is always the mother (in other words, the group). On March 20, 1930, Freud summarizes for his American training analy-sand Smiley Blanton girl-psychology's invention of the father function:

> In the case of the boy, he becomes attached to his
> mother and remains attached. But in the case of the
> girl, she becomes attached to her mother and then
> must break away and become attached to her father.
> In the case of the girl, it is a broken line that her de-
> velopment follows. It is only in the last few years that
> we have begun to realize just how complicated is the
> development of the girl.[3]

What cuts along this dotted line in the "last few years" of the twenties is the discovery of group psychology in which paternal support systems can only be found in withdrawal (reactions). The father function faces the problem of a group growing coextensive, at least in theory, with female sexual development. Child, peer group member, or groupie must share and bind the mother's wounds and restore to her an intact body.

The group restores the maternal body and absorbs the menstrual cycle, the dating and diary keeping of reproduction-preparedness—the heart beat, in short, of adolescent metabolism as it moves back and forth between the group and the couple. But that's why father gets repressed. Girl-psychology (which cheerleads group psychology) invents the *repressed* father function. But at the same time the only representative of father around, the only defender and guarantor of the couple, is "the wife." Hence, as Freud assures Smiley: "Picking a wife is one of the most difficult things in this civilization."[4]

Venice Beach

A lso declined the Marburg military school students, who requested a lecture of me even though an audience of caps and sticks might have been something new and delightful, indeed the ironic-erotic ideal of an audience.
—Thomas Mann, diary entry of February 21, 1920

In his 1925 essay "On Marriage,"[1] Mann defused Hans Blüher's charge that institutions outside the family (the university, scout organizations, and the state) are not only masculinist but in fact homosexual in origin. Mann set straight this inversion of institutional desire: though homosexuality may be found at the origin of the state, it cannot found the state, since that foundation or invention which homosexuality can only conceive once and for all must be born again in the family—so that the state can catch its citizens where they breed. Is Mann surprised that the state condemns as ultimate transgression the absolute desire within its transferential precincts? The Marquis de Sade wasn't. Unconscious homosexual or incestuous commissions fund guilt-*Geld* accounts to which family-unit thought control bills and binds its charges.

The reintroduction of homosexuality into safety zones of sublimation left Kafka, upon finishing Blüher's book, "strangely dissatisfied": "Psychoanalytically of course easy to explain: express repression. The imperial train is the one most rapidly dispatched."[2] Once again the sexological produces via its alliance with repression diversions that protect a cryptological Cargo. Closeted within the unsublimatedness and unprotectedness of "warm" or reanimated brotherhood, Kafka kept in touch with two dead brothers, whose teledictation he took down. The suicide of Mann's sister and declared double Carla was deposited in the background of the trip Mann took to Italy: traveling from the other direction this double loss slid beneath and ahead of its commemoration as Cholera.

In "Death in Venice" a side effect of the death Cholera fastforwards is the release of homosexuality from its unconscious academic habitat. Together with the advancing plague (with which they share a melancholic identification), Aschenbach's homosexual advances must be contained not so much via the death the epidemic brings but through a Death the novella summons to deliver the news: "And before nightfall a shocked and respectful world received the news of his death" (or: "from his Death").

It was on July 4, 1920, that Mann sought clarification and declaration of independence from his hot novella. It was the foundation day of a bi-zonal text which Mann's diaries, the anti-family pack he packaged in California, totally tube. July 4, 1920, was the date—of a letter—in which Mann shared with the homosexual poet Carl Maria Weber the genesis of "Death in Venice." Back from the beach, his original impulse was to go for it: he was stoked to write the "hymnic affirmation" of his "personal-lyrical travel experience."

(By October 16, 1911, as he confided on that date to

Ernst Bertram, another homosexual correspondent, the positive attitude had become "an impossible conception": "eine unmögliche Conception." He therefore conducted an "experiment" on the "bizarre thing" he had picked up on the beach. The boy in Venice, who was drinkable nectar, was now mixed with Hermes, on whose person writing, deception, doubling, and death have ever occupied interchangeable places.)

On the day he began writing down the bisexual constitution of his work Mann gave Weber the "artistic reason" for taking out homosexual desire: "the distinction between the Dionysian spirit of irresponsible-individualistic lyrical effusion and the Apollonian spirit of epic with its moral and social responsibilities and objective limitations." Within the recycling system he shared with the journalistic side of academia, Mann delivered or lip-synched the standard interpretation of his novella: when Aschenbach, an Apollo fan, suddenly develops a crush—on a young dude—he wipes out riding a virus called Dionysus. Mann's advance reservations in Venice anticipated their bi-coastal confirmations: contrary to what such psychoanalysts as Bergler would argue, homosexuality is not a "defense." Nor is it granted a defense: the bisexual constitution helps homosexuality *out*.

But when Mann showed Weber the way homosexuality undermines the defense systems which the opposition between Apollo and Dionysus guarantees, he at the same time addressed the "break down" of another opposition and defense. In the cases of Michelangelo, Frederick the Great, Winckelmann, Platen, and George, the polarity dividing and attracting the masculine and the feminine had been weakened by the exceptional and untenable place homosexuality holds (according to Goethe) inside and against nature.

> Obviously the law of polarity does not hold unconditionally; the masculine need not necessarily be attracted by the feminine. . . . Here one sees the po-

larity simply failing and we observe a masculinity so
pronounced that even in erotic matters only the masculine has importance and interest. I am not at all
surprised that a law of nature (that of polarity) breaks
down in an area which, despite its sensuality, has
very little to do with nature, but much to do with
mind.

Blood Drive

*I*t is a courageous, ruthlessly probing book, uncovering
without a trace of speculative frivolity the difficulties,
embarrassments and fears of marital and sexual life in
general, and never denying the knowledge we have attained of
the socalled perversions and aberrations in this sphere, namely
above all the homosexual component, a phenomenon which,
as Goethe says, is in nature, although it seems to be directed
against nature. (7. 4. 1830 mit Friedrich von Müller) The relationship between Professor Johnny and the young marine cap-
tain is observed clearly and accurately, and you act as a poet by
making the reader regard it as something quite human, and not
as a monstrosity. This work is characterized by the same hu-
mane frankness which, in your preceding book, served to make
the problem of dipsomania an artistic experience to the informed and uninformed alike. . . . The case holds my special
interest, because such a relationship plays a certain role in my
own new novel. Those involved are a lonely artist, a figure

*somewhat like Nietzsche whose clinical fate he also shares, and
a young man of impish traits to whom every human relationship becomes a flirt, and who courts this loneliness for so long
and with such boundless and uninhibizable confidence until
he overcomes and seduces it. However, he does not then grab the
poker, but is very proud of his conquest. It is the other man who
takes deadly revenge for his defeat. You see, everything is quite
different from your story.*

    —Mann to Charles Jackson, October 5, 1946

By the time Mann composed the essay "On Marriage," his
understanding of bisexuality absorbed and covered for his
exclusions of homosexuality; the meeting and exchange of
sexual traits in transit were reserved for the heterosexual
bond of marriage. Mann transferred the return or late arrival of bisexuality (advertised by certain popular receptions of
psychoanalytic research and the advent of boyish unisex
fashions) to the marital or joint account. Thus by 1925
Mann had publicly entrusted his every transmission only to
the institution of marriage. At the same time he projected
homoeroticism (or "erotic aestheticism") to the outside—as
the outside—of the "originary institution" *(Urinstitution)*:
"All that is marriage—namely, duration, foundation, procreation, progeny, and responsibility—all this homoeroticism is not."

    In the year of his marriage, 1905, Mann first conceived
the plan of rewriting the Faust legend. Looking back in 1943
on his first *Doctor Faustus* synopsis, Mann erroneously
dated its conception 1901, thus putting it right next to *Buddenbrooks* within his collected works. He synchronized the
collection of these works with the delay of *Doctor Faustus*'s
(controlled) release. "Have carried this idea about with me a
long time. . . . It is really a desire to escape from everything
bourgeois . . . into a world of drunken release, a life of bold,
Dionysian genius, beyond society, indeed superhuman."
The Dionysian high cops "self-abandonment to the instincts
and unrestrained 'Life,' which in fact is death and, insofar as
it is life, only the *Devil's work, product of infection.*"[1]

On the sidelines of the foundation and duration of his marriage—and at the same time (according to his double dating) on the side of *Buddenbrooks* and subsequent works—Mann advertised a remake of the Faust legend which featured the extramarital affair of "erotic-aestheticism." But while this affair condemned the artist to die of a sexually transmitted disease, it at the same time (once the artist's diagnosis was positive) sponsored the "posthumous" production of "works of genius." *Doctor Faustus* belongs, then, to what Mann (in the essay "On Marriage") promoted as the "metaphysical" side of his works which could be folded out and turned away from "the idea of the family." He took a turn (on the outside) by taking detours via Venice and Venice Beach. On the inside (whenever Mann looked back) it was already in place. Thus by 1920 Mann could turn up the volume on the metaphysical, anti-family ecstasy swelling Thomas Buddenbrook's decision to abandon identification with his sick effeminate son. That's no way to go: instead the perpetual teenager and abusive father looks forward to riding and merging (upon his death) with the future packs of blonde, buff dudes through whom he will return. (Mann really gets into it in "On Marriage.") But, he continues, despite the original connection inside art between homoeroticism and aestheticism, between death and beauty, artistic genius, while wiping out over the "abyss," always also carries its own "antitoxin." By simply living on upon completion of each of his works the living artist turns around the narrated events of Werther's suicide and Thomas Buddenbrook's death: "And the youthful author of Thomas Buddenbrook married a few years later, after he had guided him to death." But once literary works commence surviving their author (as when the writer Aschenbach dies on the beach), the authority over these works is conferred on the author's death, which now survives him. Mann thus counts down (identifies with) two corporeal deaths: the one he summoned to complete and compete with the conception of his literature; and the other one which, during the publication of the diaries, has survived the corpus. The first one was paternal and "boring"; the other was awesome and fun, friendly and cute.

His father's death, which he recognized in back of everything he had ever written, sponsored Mann's original rapport with his deadlines. One of Mann's first stories, entitled simply "Death," was composed, as Heinz Kohut suggested, in the year following his father's decease.[2] Thus Mann's first—primal—submission of "Death" was to a contest for the "best novella in which sexual love plays no part."[3] But, looking back, we can make out one death arriving in the place of another one, whose anticipated coming out was reserved for the diaries. Written in fact in diary format, "Death" is the record a journal writer keeps of his ongoing anticipation of the date and hour of his own Death's arrival.

> Oh what a constant bond there is between man and
> Death! With determination and conviction you can
> . . . attract Death such that he will approach you at
> the hour you appointed. . . . How anxiously I await
> the final moment, the very last one. Shouldn't it be a
> moment of rapture and of ineffable sweetness? A mo-
> ment of highest voluptuousness. Only three more
> short autumn days and Death will enter my room—
> now how will he behave! Will he treat me like a
> worm? . . . But I imagine him great and beautiful and
> wildly majestic.[4]

When Death turns out to be a dentist and not the trick he hoped to turn, the disappointed journalist keeps the appointment with father. In Mann's case, the paternal dental work—of mourning—always prescribes isolation and extraction of diseased elements to push back the threatened cholera-like spread of their melancholic identification or infection. Yes it's a different way: to bust your ghosts and have them too.

Mann first published under the quasi-pseudonym Paul Thomas—actually his two given names: the father's disapproval of any of his sons choosing a writing career stopped delivery of the co-signature. Since it would otherwise fall into incompetent hands, Mann's father provided in his will for the liquidation of the family business. Post mortem this proviso subsidized the literary careers of the Mann brothers. The father's death (by blood poisoning) was the credit line which backed Mann—into putting an end to the end of a line. The star of Mann's series—the artist figure—always had to go. He played in the finale of what had been, before the maternal blood donation, ongoing male-to-male transmission. Maternal blood poisoning terminates the family line (the father inside the son) and engenders the artist (the son as savior) who rather than sons, counts fans. (The diaries hit the fans, whose body count has been on the rise.)

But Mann had to accept what had been in his case, too, a maternal gift of writing. Hence the turn to his first names under which he originally published: every name-change amounts to the feminization and juvenilization of a name which rejects paternal association. His father's death restored Mann's patronymic; dread of contamination of this name left him unable to become a woman and conceive. Instead one poison, death, or theft was contained by and within another. His father's poisoned blood—the credit line along which death co-signed each completion of Mann's works—inoculated Mann's system against contamination by that degenerescent "'Life' which in fact is *death*" carried by his mother's foreign blood. But what went down in Venice was the repeatable requirement. To dislodge his writer's block—or, as he preferred to address it, the "momentary collapse of the central nervous system"—Mann accepted the "gift" of writing. His Venice gift or souvenir—his "travel experience"—was a ready-made complete with "innate symbolism."

> Nothing is invented in "Death in Venice." . . . Everything was given, had strictly speaking only to be arranged, and thereby demonstrated in a most extraordinary way a capacity for being used and interpreted as elements of composition. And perhaps it

was for this reason that, as I worked on the novella—as always it was a long drawn-out affair—I plumbed at moments the feeling of a certain absolute transformation, a certain sovereign sense of being borne up as I had never before experienced.[5]

The shrouded camera abandoned on the beach at the close of "Death in Venice" holds the place of Mann's voyeuristic reception of the gift of writing. Mann went to Venice as part of a primal band made up of his wife Katja and big brother Heinrich. The trip reunited brothers out of touch since Mann's marriage. But since the model of the one-on-one for Mann was sibling incest, his brother could represent the heterosexual libido for which Mann's marriage of Oedi-pals was the preservative, the impervious other side. The married Mann had grown increasingly fascinated with and repulsed by the endless "streaming" of his brother's writing; and yet, although his own writing tended to be more of the "dribbling" variety, it had originally poured out in symbiotic relation with his brother's stream. The source of their streaming had been in Italy where Mann, while sharing one address with his brother, delivered *Buddenbrooks*. But since that time of cohabitation Mann had not been able on his own, as though in palimony payment, to produce follow-up hits.

Mann's wife and brother remained hidden from view by the cabana he rented in Venice. With the family pack in the background, Mann eyeballed the cutest boy on the beach. Back home Mann developed the shot (by developing inoculations against it); at the same time his wife was away at the sanatorium under treatment for tuberculosis. Mann's relation to the "impossible conception" of homosexuality always required a familial or marital context kept hidden in some other place. To contain the gift or *Gift* ("poison") of writing, Mann required citational doses of decontextualization which his habit of "reading with a pencil" injected.[6] In "Death in Venice" Mann separates from Aschenbach at the point of injection: although Aschenbach trashes his immunological poetics to make the buff boy on the beach, Mann shoots up into the corners of the suicide scene paraphrases of *Phaedrus*. According to Terence Reed, this move Back East from the beach scene to Platonic paraphrase and propaganda was the inaugurating divide and drift of an "art of ambivalence" which continued only under cover to communicate with the Coast via the internal fault of the diaries.

On April 27, 1912, Mann wrote to Heinrich that he was still unable to conclude "Death in Venice." He summoned or cited marital and Platonic contexts. But in the end only Death, which superseded the other contexts, took. The Hermes figure and delegate of the death which absorbed homosexuality was summoned by Mann not only as god of thieves but also as citation's presiding deity. As appropriation which can never be reappropriated, citation (like the technical mediatization it models) kept open a direct line to Death. (Whenever Mann borrowed a character from life, he could not help himself: he included that figure's death in his rendition.)

California Antibody

Reflecting on the composition of *Doctor Faustus*, Mann in California proclaimed the artist to have become transmitter, seismograph, and medium both in the technical and occult senses.[1] The technologization Mann admitted in California was advanced by his claim to have completed *Doctor Faustus* posthumously. The prophecy Mann had made to himself that he would die at age seventy (the age his mother attained just before departing) was "allusively fulfilled" via his lung operation, which represented the "lowest point of his vitality."[2] The return of the death wish against the father which this kind of p-unitive merger with mother or medium always special-announces tunes in episodes of heavy or blocked breathing with which *The Genesis of Doctor Faustus* punctuates accounts of the technologization (and posthumization) of Mann's reception.[3] Immediately upon surviving himself as he awakened post-op from the anesthesia, he first had to organize his thoughts around the sudden realization that, on an unconscious range, the body continues to be susceptible to pain even after death (154). These are still a son's guilty assumptions. But the posthumous mode, which his auto-technologization rehearsed, would be realized through his diary publications, which must be kept separate from paternal economies of pain or denial of pain. In turn his double existence as diary writer and perpetual adolescent had been the placeholder for Mann's mediatization.

Mann's return from the grave (via the diaries) was simulcast with an occult medium's transmission of his thoughts "live" in California.[4] Mann's spirit interrupts the medium, Eva Herrmann, only once in the course of dictation to ask the time:

> "How long is it, dear, since I died?"
> "In August it will be twenty years."
> "Twenty years!" (183)

The cover of Herrmann's *From the Beyond* advertises that her book of messages comes complete "With a postmortem afterword by Thomas Mann."

> I am honored to append a short afterword to this book. For a long time now I have waited for a chance to describe what one commonly views as the end. Although I cannot bring it to paper, it is still possible for me to clothe my intention in words and to transmit it telepathically to a woman still living on earth who has for a long time been friend to me and my family. (179)

Shortly after her emigration from Europe in 1939, Herrmann, already renowned as caricaturist and cartoonist, found herself attending a seance: the Californian medium called her by name and gave her news from her dear departed. She was converted. The mediums whom she could not stop visiting and interviewing assured her that she too was "medial." After ESP training in LA she could sense that her deceased friend was now always nearby. After another twenty years she was hearing voices and writing down their dictation. But soon she discovered that the voices lied. They either mimicked her guardian spirits or came out with obscenities; their hellish laughter revealed them to be demons. She risked madness. But she was able to figure out that authentic messages were always accompanied or announced by a light. Next she started picking up toneless words and typing them out. "Perhaps one could describe the process in this way: it is as though someone thought through me, the way a hand works through a glove" (24).

She is *not* under the remote control of the unconscious. In the sequel, *From the Beyond II*,[5] Freud "confesses" that he is working his way out of hell: his hatred, which found systematic form in his fraudulent science, extended across the ages. Freud's ghost thus knows nothing about a superego: instead he confesses to the propagation of the belief while he was alive that one's childhood determined one's subsequent development. Freud's ghost knows nothing from identification.

Herrmann (like Staudenmaier and Spielrein) feels more comfortable with Jungian surfer speech (than with Freudian valspeak). Even Freud's ghost—like the phantom-like anticipations of his system—would delete identification from psychoanalysis. And yet the deletion is psychotically acted out. Thus (in the first volume) Herrmann discovers that we ourselves have selected our own parents, who are at best responsible, in the other direction, for our corporeal side (74).

> While you are incarnate, your guardian angels and other helpful spirits reach you via your subconscious, which is noticed only by sensitive types and by a few children, who are receptive to extrasensory influences from the beyond, that is, until one talks them out of it. You might receive hints and signs and come up suddenly with ideas or reach decisions in your sleep, all of which appears to emerge from your own ego but can at the same time be attributed to external influences. (60)

Because spirits are effective through the "subconscious," the illusion is created "that whatever has been received reflects the medium's own thoughts" (70). The dependency of the spirits (including Freud's) on Jungian structures serves, as was the case with Spielrein, a likeability principle:

> The information received from the subconscious may come from the spirits or from what Jung called the collective unconscious. But this latter notion is misleading: thoughts as well as feelings are attracted to each other and to individual souls according to the attraction of likes—this explains mass movements and the low niveau of the ideas picked up by individual souls. (71)

Together with the other anticipators of psychoanalysis, Herrmann sizes up the endopsychic competition; now that Freud has been taken out, proper understanding of hypnosis or electricity can be claimed on her side: "The way hypnosis is practiced today reminds one of an electrician who, while he knows how to bring about this or that effect, has no sense of the actual essence of electricity" (92–93). But the current worldwide problem, against which she and her spirits militate, is posed by drugs and their cure—which she forecasts as the final theater of total war. Via drug culture and the war against drugs, mankind will be decimated and civilization will slide into Atlantis-like disappearance (82).

Drugs, suicide, immortality, adolescence: in sync with the time-release of the diaries, Mann's ghost dictates, after twenty years of silent death, a reunion (beyond the death wish) with his dead children, a new-found rapport which the diaries also remake by turning around the alliances constituting the household or economy of Mann's name and reputation.

> My children Klaus and Erika were both here; Klaus went ahead of me, Erika followed a few years after my death. Klaus, as is well known, took his own life. Erika died of a long painful illness. Both were not doing well. . . . Klaus still suffered the consequences

of his act. . . . As soon as I had worked my way up from the twilight zone in which I originally found myself, a twilight inside and around me, since the degree of illumination of a soul determines the immediate environment (they correspond one to the other, are two aspects of one and the same reality), I was in a position to concern myself with the children. One might think that such concern is the most natural thing in the world, but things are different here than on earth. Family ties have value only where there is at the same time an inner bond, and since the newcomer to the beyond is usually busy dealing with his own needs and the demands of his newly awakened and now wide-awake conscience, seldom is he inclined to deal with something other than the solution of his own pressing problems. That's the way, at least, it was with me: yet one tells me that not all souls share this course of development. In our world the veiling of feelings is an impossible thing since they express themselves immediately. One cannot hide them behind an untrue word or a meaningless smile or a silence that would conceal the true purpose. The often brutal honesty which results from this is for the new arrival at first a surprise until he gets accustomed to this condition as to many other aspects of our world. It is curious how much the living earthling does not know and does not want to know of that which goes down behind the surface of interpersonal relations. Here, by contrast, wherever true inclination is lacking, parents and children encounter each other coolly, husband and wife ignore each other, and friends pass each other by. . . . All conventions go to the devil and one is so free as one often wished to be while alive. . . . This explains a certain preliminary distance between me and my children. . . . Perhaps I saw my son here for the first time, after I had sloughed off that which came between us in life. Only here was I at last free to devote myself to him and did so with the love of one spurned. In the end everyone can only deliver himself, but it helps when certain things, that were problematical on earth, are cleared up and it also helps when one is offered a love the depth of which one has no grounds in the hereafter to doubt. . . . And finally, after seemingly endless years he too took a first step, which brought him in a sense to my side, so that he too participated in those joys which I described at the beginning. (185–189)

Ecce Mann

D oes one [man] *live, when others are alive?"*
            —Mann, citing Goethe

At the same time that Mann hyped Weber with declarations of his heterosexuality—"I am a family founder and father by instinct and conviction"—Mann's diaries were recasting this paternal position along a shifting divide. Alongside his public announcements as sponsor or father, Mann was writing down adolescent journalism which would reveal, twenty years after his death, the fragility of a commitment to marriage and progeny that had been forged out of renunciation at age thirty of homosexual involvement. According to the other sex fiction which Mann's diaries held back and now unfold, in the year 1920, after fifteen years of faithful marriage to his wife, Mann stopped having relations with her, though he continued to maintain his marriage. In the year 1927, however, Mann was involved, according to the diaries, in a love affair with a certain seventeen-year-old boy.

Mann situated this crush within the switching registers of his rapport with Goethe. What now appears unforgivable to the writer of the diaries is that Goethe was straight: "Thought back on that time and its passion, the last variation of a love that probably will not flare up again. Strange, the happy and fulfilled man of fifty—and then *finis*. Goethe's erotic life continued into his seventies—'always girls.' But in my case the inhibitions are probably stronger and so one wearies sooner, apart from the differences in vitality" (September 14, 1935).

"Death in Venice," according to the letter to Weber, was Mann's ironic inversion of the seventy-year-old Goethe's affair which gave place, as another last resort, to *The Marienbad Elegies*. Mann was totally into writing about the gnarly old poet's infatuation with a seventeen-year-old ("always girls"). Forget about that smoker and queen on Venice Beach. The original high Mann copped when he did "Death in Venice" turned on the larger teen issues of passion, fame, immortality.

> Passion as confusion and as a stripping of dignity
> was really the subject of my tale—what I originally
> wanted to deal with was not anything homoerotic at
> all. It was the story seen grotesquely—of the aged
> Goethe and that little girl in Marienbad whom he was
> absolutely determined to marry. . . .—this story with
> all its terribly comic, shameful, awesomely ridiculous
> situations, this embarrassing, touching, and gran-
> diose story which I may someday write after all.

When he did get around to writing *The Beloved Returns*, however, Mann gave humbled recognition of Goethe's ability to become a woman in the act and thus conceive his writing. Yet at the same time that "Goethe" is asked to affirm (in *The Beloved Returns*) his ability to become impregnated with an art of androgynous provenance, he must admit that all art is essentially parodistic citation. In his understanding of Goethe, and of himself as Goethe's heir, Mann cannot but confuse conception with theft or adoption.

In the letter to Weber, Mann secured for Goethe (and for himself) safety zones which would be up there, untouchable, and displaced with regard to the "impossible conception" of "Death in Venice." It was recommended that Weber consult *Elective Affinities,* which the author of "Death in Venice" had read and reread some five times in order to come down off his beach high. The "equilibrium between sensuality and morality" which *Elective Affinities* achieved acknowledges the artificiality of the institution of marriage—the natural affinities lie not between the married partners—and at the same time ascribes all-importance to the contractual bond itself (and to the need to sublimate). But Goethe's account of "double adultery" and "double resemblance of the son" models another equal but separate "equilibrium" which Mann achieved within his own marriage (at least according to its serialization in the diaries).

Buff

W *hy do I write all this? Only so that I can destroy it in time before I die? Or is it that I desire that the world know all about me? I believe it knows more in any case—or at least its more perceptive people do—than it lets on to me.*
    —Mann, diary entry of August 25, 1950

Although wife and children, friends and biographers were forbidden access to his diaries, Mann made provisions through a clause in his will that they be published twenty years after his death. We can only speculate on the friendliness of the author's intentions in scheduling the coming out of these sex revelations for as early as twenty years after his death.

    Why this delay of only two decades in the publication of Mann's diaries? Does the comparatively early release of private documents indicate, as the editor and translator of

Mann's diaries suggests, that Mann was certain of his posthumous fame? Or is this publication of confessional work a timebomb programmed to detonate in the midst of his family and immediate readership? (Or was it just another one of Mann's firecrackers?) Michael Mann, who founded a short-lived career lecturing on the diaries he had opened and now guarded and interpreted, and who at the same time began to drink himself to death, was the first casualty of Mann's posthumous publications.

Is this publication of confessions, then, a suicide of sorts directed against the handing down of the legacy, the apocalyptic ending of the line by the over-Mann? Or had Mann foreseen that his legacy would require sensationalist reinterpretation and revitalization? Does Mann, then, in posthumously introducing into his corpus an unresolvable tension which ever calls for reinterpretation of this corpus, finally accede to the Nietzschean irony he had long hoped to claim for his writing, "the loftiest, most erotic and slyest irony playing between life and mind?"

As testimonial to his own double life, Mann's diaries come out in the missing place of a conclusion to the *Confessions of Felix Krull, Confidence Man,* Mann's most "autobiographical" work. In 1911 the first version of Mann's case study of an impostor had come to a standstill as part of the writer's block which the trip to Venice dislodged. Published shortly before Mann's death, *Confessions of Felix Krull, Memoirs Part One* casts the double life of a trickster-thief and perpetual adolescent as the simulcast of bisexuality (that is, with the division edited out). Krull's erotic ideal, which he refers to as the "double image," is a "penchant for double enthusiasms, his fascination by the double-but-dissimilar" which would embrace "what is beguilingly human in both sexes." Thus he could, in effect, make love not to two individuals, male and female, but rather to a singular duality. Fascination with this double image, with an originary bisexuality, traverses Mann's works, having already guided, for example, Tonio Kröger's and Hans Castorp's erotic attachments. But though the masculine and the feminine would have thus been made superimposable onto each other, the doubling of sexual preference (rather than difference) remains essentially a moment of arrest for homosexuality, which has been accommodated only to be assimilated and isolated within a potentiated heterosexuality.

Once Mann discovered that, before he could complete *Doctor Faustus*, he had already survived himself, a new death, the bearer of revelations, began controlling Mann's legacy. While concluding *Doctor Faustus* in his new phantom role, Mann determined the shape and schedule of his posthumous revelations. Certain diaries he burned; the 1918–21 diaries, which he had consulted in the course of composing parts of his Faust novel, he placed in the same box with materials tagged 1933–51. This "accident" (as Peter de Mendelssohn puts it) increased the charge of repressions or revelations with which Mann had thus loaded the 1920 essay on marriage.

Mann's diaries turn on two biographies or autobiographies which cannot be confused—one being public, the other in its other place—and two legacies which, in contrast to the double sexuality advanced in *Felix Krull*, are kept apart along unbreachable lines of sexual preference. The waves Mann's posthumous sex revelations made were the offshore barrels "Death in Venice" already totally tubed.

Several years after the beach story's completion it was surf's up. Klaus Mann had turned fourteen, the same age as Tadzio. The author of the diaries displaces the wife into the background of his infatuation with the next available adolescent boy body, which his fourteen-year-old son embodies.

> It can scarcely be a question of actual impotence, but more likely the customary confusion and unreliability of my "sex life." Doubtless the stimulation failure can be accounted for by the presence of desires that are directed the other way. How would it be if there were a young man "at my disposal"? (July 14, 1920)

> Am enraptured with Eissi [Klaus], terribly handsome in his swimming trunks. Find it quite natural that I

should fall in love with my son. . . . lying tanned and shirtless on his bed, reading; I was disconcerted. (July 25, 1920)

I heard some noise in the boys' room and came upon Eissi totally nude. . . . Deeply struck by his radiant adolescent body; overwhelming. (October 17, 1920)

It seems I am once and for all done with women? (July 25, 1920)

And again, on July 5, 1920 (on, that is, the morning after giving Weber his artistic reasons for condemning homosexuality to death), Mann announces: "In love with Klaus these days. Beginnings of a father-son novella."

Klaus had decided to become a writer at fourteen, the age of Mann's own first commitment to writing. This commitment took the form of submissions to journals despite the father's dissuasion and disapproval (see July 11, 1920). Only "the wife" can penetrate or take the outside view of a reserve of adolescent interiority and journalism which fuels the writing of two perpetual fourteen-year-olds. On May 5, 1920, Mann records in his own diary how his wife violates the privacy and personal space of Klaus's diary. She is shocked to discover this teenager in their midst; all along he had been nice—as ice.

Yesterday evening a shattering episode. Katja found Klaus's diary lying open and read it. Though there was nothing overtly wicked in it, it revealed such an unhealthy coldness, ingratitude, lovelessness, deceitfulness—to say nothing of the callow and silly literary and radical posturing—that her poor mother's heart was deeply disappointed and wounded. Katja wept over the boy as she had some years ago when he lay at death's door. Myself sick at heart, I attempted to reassure and comfort her. I will never play the infuriated father. There is nothing the boy can do about his nature, which is not of his own making. (May 5, 1920)

The homoeroticism of Mann's posthumous father-son novella is also literally an attraction to the same or *homos:* to the same sex, certainly, but also to the same writing, conceived at the same age, and indeed, ultimately, to the same name or summons. In the first mention in his diary of his attraction to Klaus, Mann finds himself alarmingly aroused by his son's evident maturation, by Klaus's becoming-man, his *Mannwerden* (April 26, 1920). At the same time that Mann records his attraction to his son's *Mannwerden,* we find him, in his letter to Weber, justifying his seeming rejection in "Death in Venice" of homosexuality. But in his diary, homosexuality can be referred to, without disapproval, as "man-manly eroticism" *(mann-männliche Erotik)* (July 1, 1920).

This incestuous or homosexual attraction to the patronymic haunts, like some primal scene, Klaus Mann's writing, which opens onto a father's incestuous pursuit of his daughter and, at the other end, juxtaposes mature homosexuality with a sister's or mother's illegitimate offspring. In one of his earliest stories, "Father Laughs," Klaus Mann in 1925 ventriloquates a teenage girl's apprehensions about her father: "how improper he is with me, I cannot even tell you.—At night he comes naked to me, when I want to sleep." But like father like son: "every artistic man," says Klaus Mann, is ruled by "the deep desire for scandal, for self-revelation."[1]

Klaus Mann was a believer in the legendary coupling of homosexuality and death. In 1949 he killed himself while his father was still alive. Mann's posthumous father-son novella (a tribute to his son) qualifies a Romantic cliché (real popular within the standard reception of "Death in Venice") which associates homosexuality's desire for auto-engenderment or impossible conception with self-annihilation. In Mann's posthumously published diaries homosexuality keeps up association with death but not with the self-annihilation of Mann's heritage. The diaries make clear that homosexuality must be coupled and credited with the perseverance of Mann's heritage: the Eternal Return of the *homos*. The new Thomas Mann, the now publicly homosexual Mann, who was only playing or passing for dead, comes into his own posthumously in order to renew his legacy.

It has long been claimed that Mann's fictional and essayistic writings advertise the reality of bisexuality. But are critics playing it straight when they argue that reconciliation of homosexuality and marriage on the common ground of this bisexual constitution had been the ultimate aim of Mann's poetology and ideology?[2] Certainly homosexuality would remain left out of this family album. Mann's diaries come out with another aspiration; they seek to insert into the transmission of Mann's legacy (and thus into the institution of his marriage) both heterosexuality and homosexuality.

The institution in which Mann took the greatest pride, his own marriage, in which he had kept hetero and homo distinct, though he had also given them equal time, became the pattern which delineated his relation to his heirs. In the diaries Mann posthumously legitimizes his other line of descent represented by his three homosexual children. Fully twenty years after his death, then, Mann reverses himself, turns in his grave, giving now the other half of his legacy equal time and acknowledgment. Though not based on the alleged opposition between the feminine and the masculine, Thomas Mann's legacy nevertheless proceeds through segregation and strict sequencing of heterosexual and homosexual affiliations. And while "man-manly eroticism" can now be seen as affirming and promoting the handing down of the legacy from Mann to Mann, heterosexuality remains the dominant procedure within the institution of the Mann legacy. But this heterosexuality can only be conceived—impossibly conceived—as a division of sexuality where difference can meet without contamination or crossing over.

From the significant name of the protagonist to the way in which that protagonist's sexual preference is at once accommodated and isolated within the House of Representatives, is given equal but separate time, indeed accorded, after the fact, a certain advantage (over his dentist colleague), the journalistic coverage in 1983 of two incidents of sexual congress involving members of the United States legislative body with their pages could have been conceived by that Thomas Mann who in the eighties was completing the coming out of his collected works.

> Last week the Ethics Committee recommended that the full House "reprimand" two Representatives, Democrat Gerry Studds of Massachusetts and Republican Daniel Crane of Illinois, for having had sex with pages in 1973 and 1980, respectively.
>
> Both Congressmen admitted their misconduct. Studds' dalliance occurred a decade ago with a 17-year-old boy, just after the Congressman's election to the House.
>
> According to the special counsel's report, Studds first invited the page to his Georgetown apartment, and then later that summer took the boy on a two-week trip to Portugal. The ex-page testified that he bore no ill will toward Studds.
>
> In fact, many of his constituents seemed surprisingly supportive last week. Said Boston Political Consultant Michael Goldman: "Now that he is out of the closet, he could become even more effective." The prospects are less clear for Crane. . . .
>
> Crane, a dentist from Danville, came to Capitol Hill in 1979. A year later, he and a female House page, then 17, had sex four or five times at his suburban apartment.
>
> "This does not fit the image Dan Crane has tried to portray," says Danville lawyer Tom Lindley. "This makes it less likely he'll run for re-election."[3]

Mann's absorption in (or by) the course and circulation of institutionalization has been witnessed by his great postmortem success in guiding, through precisely timed revelations, the institution of his name and legacy. Mann's uncanny timeliness in these matters literalizes Nietzsche's telepathic rapport with the future of his signature. Mann gained another existence for his corpus by signing ahead of time and scheduling for posthumous publication confessional writings which would undermine (or revitalize) the once timely, now dated, public Thomas Mann. Unlike Nietzsche, Freud, and Goethe, Mann did not thus risk his signature; his release from the grave, which he was able to contrive in exchange for the future of his signature, follows Nietzsche's posthumous birth to the letter, while reversing it point by point. In Mann's case, a posthumous death, which the diaries pushed back, was part of the bargain. Alongside his published works, Mann wrote down and kept in a separate place another set of reflections which reversed, qualified, or exceeded his public views—which remain the standard of exchange of thought in what is called Germanistics. Only the spontaneity of Mann's double writing, the simultaneity of both texts, could have guaranteed the contextual integrity of his collected works. Through the publication schedule he adopted, Mann guaranteed instead that the context that each text required would remain in some other place. By thus disrupting his public reception of German culture—which perversely blends the philosophies of Schopenhauer and Nietzsche, Freudian psychoanalysis, and "Goethe" into one end product—Mann, or rather his phantom, would appear to have issued a vast rereading assignment. But according to the logic Freud situated within "the underworld of psychoanalysis," this ghostly assignment can be followed only upon locating the precincts of the corpus's at once sexological and cryptological concealment. This place belongs to a concept, that of sexual identity as bisexuality, which administers in and between Mann's two texts the group-psychological effects of a phantom. It is along the fantasmatic stereo track of Mann's own sexual identity that the release of his other text—his adolescent interiority—comes to be delayed, controlled, and segregated. By posthumously dividing and doubling his legacy along lines of sexual preference, the diaries can only project—as or at their conclusion—the at once double and simultaneously co-present bisexuality of teen phantoms.

And Then He Goes

I *keep dreaming of Asiatic journeys, of going overland to*
China, of impossibilities, of the Indies or of California—
the latter always excites me on the human side.
—Flaubert to Louis Bouilhet, November 14, 1850

What we need is a life politics, a politics without others.[1]
Knowledge is not the way to go. Any knowledge about the
environment is recycled back into the environment, which
comes complete with the prefab insights of the master discursivities. Knowledge about life is already consumed with
life. Freud called this journalistic reflexivity of our modern
era the endopsychic sensurround. According to the headlines, decisions made in Asia produce effects of homeless-
ness—of the uncanny—in California. Decisions belong to
networks of effects that must be interfered (invented) with
in the deconstructive mode.

"The tree of knowledge," Byron's Manfred pronounces

(and Nietzsche lip synchs), "is not that of life." After he has released the narcissistic object he constructed over the undead body of his twin sister, Manfred discovers that it's not so difficult to die. Is this the discovery Freud was preparing to share but (before he could release it in contiguity with his system, life, and name) was forced to relocate to the Coast? He tried to crack the crypt in *Moses and Monotheism* which he recognized as beaming up the "unlaid ghost" that had "haunted" him his whole life long (*SE* 23:103). That part of Freud which belonged to his undead brother Julius completely identified with "Moses." Please release me from unmourning the dead on maternal or group channels. There must be an end to unconscious politics.

Only on the Coast of his system could Freud go meglo and address the big issues, as though for the first time, of life and death. The experiment is on in California. Each morning we decide which cereal to try, which look to put on, when to schedule the workout. It doesn't matter if it looks like the same difference. We run through (again, for the first time, and for the time to come) decisions which are, in effect, inventions. We invent our lives with each morning (mourning).

But the segregation of (object) choices or differences to be had and made (the decision-making Mann's corpus progressively networks) opens onto the final set of a contest of identification which continues to build the body and corpus—the narcissistic object. This adolescent boy body, at once hard and feminine, is the legacy of California: the transplantational or segregational identifications which build around this body the body of the group fastforward phantasms of total or totaled defense (for instance, the "computer virus") to every outpost of the sensorium.

The adolescent likes to be different—like everyone he likes (to be like). The choices he flips through are thus kept under remote control. Only the group's greater body—its cause and future—can recover the projection and loss of each ego's (maternal) body. But the convergence of the "live" with the posthumous can be admitted only through the controlled release which a journal or a journalism admits: alterity is thus at once identified with, segregated, and given the go-ahead to "go"—in other words, to "disappear" but also, as the natives have it, to "speak" or publish. Within the double recesses of identification which adolescence prolongs and promotes we find another invention—and future—of "California."

It's the future that Hegel (who at the same time proved that there no longer is a future) reserved for America—and thus for California, the deepest recess of its closure or no-future. California could be seen thus as the opening of a frontier; but its simultaneous lack of future, its perpetual dread of the before, reduces the frontier onto which it opens to the zone of a theme-park. That which is both before and in the future is the native habitat of "savages" whose awesome physique (which Hegel cannot help but recognize) recommends them for anthropology.[2]

Between Hegel and Mann, between the before and the (no) future, Derrida has reopened the anthropological reserve of friendly natives to thinking: in 1987 he reclaimed California as the state of theory. The invention of California has placed a call and question to theory or thought: "What else am I going to be able to invent?"[3] Like adolescence (like journal-ism and like California) invention was invented in the eighteenth century.[4] The dialectic of the enlightenment turned on two types of invention: the invention of stories and that of machines. But since invention is always invention of oneself, as soon as the creator of either type of invention has to be identified (and identified with), the invention belongs to the other. At first invention implies illegality and the breaking of a contract (like the adolescent dear-diary break with the family pact). But like yet another inside-out mode of adolescence, invention can never remain private once its status as invention—its patent or parent—has to be certified and conferred. But dependence on the techno-media (which now program invention) reinstalls dreams of reinventing invention. The loud (as denial) identification with citation, on Mann's part, preserves invention in the mode of dream or make-believe. Invention, which was always invention of the subject, produces via its backfire (via depersonalization) the impostor, gadget love, the leader and the pack. But invention (like citation) still belongs to the other who's not new but who's the future, the time to come.

"If we spoke today of the invention of America or of the New World, that would rather designate the discovery or production of new *modes* of existence, of new ways of seeing things, of imagining or inhabiting the world, but not the creation or discovery of the very existence of the territory named America."[5] The experiment is on—in California—to seek an affirmation (a way in and a way out) of the Teen Age. Only within the (reinvention of) adolescent modes of existence can we survive what is in effect (since the other is always the first to go) our immortality, which at the same time comes complete (and for all the same reasons that brought us immortality) with the impulse to die, to die someone else. Only the time to come counts: it allows the adventure and event of the entirely other to come. Life Politics, Safe Text: it's time to come clean.

Notes

Fast Foreword

1. Cited in Andreas Huyssen, "Adorno in Reverse: From Hollywood to Richard Wagner," *New German Critique* 29 (Spring-Summer 1983): 15.
2. Cited in *The Essential Frankfurt School Reader*, ed. Andrew Arato and Eike Gebhardt (New York: Continuum, 1985), 18.
3. Sigmund Freud, *The Standard Edition of the Complete Psychological Works*, ed. James Strachey (London: Hogarth Press, 1953–1974), 13:59. Hereafter cited in the text as *SE*.
4. The cannibalizing conditions of the trek west, which went down as miniaturization and condensation (as in condensed milk, a German favorite), frame the installation of the telephone. See Avital Ronell, *The Telephone Book: Technology—Schizophrenia—Electric Speech* (Lincoln: University of Nebraska Press, 1989), 342–43.
5. Philippe Ariès, *Western Attitudes toward Death: From the Middle Ages to the Present*, trans. Patricia M. Ranum (Baltimore: Johns Hopkins University Press, 1974), 67–68.
6. Leon L. Altman, "'West' as a Symbol of Death," *Psychoanalytic Quarterly* 28 (1959): 239. Further references are given in text.

7. Ernest Jones, *The Life and Work of Sigmund Freud* (New York: Basic Books, 1955), 2:53ff.
8. Peter Gay, *Freud: A Life for Our Time* (New York: W. W. Norton, 1988), 562–70. Subsequent references in the text to Freud's aversion to America are documented in Gay's biography within this sequence of pages.

Let the Children Kodak

The title of this chapter was an early Kodak advertisement slogan. Epigraph: Edith Fiore, *The Unquiet Dead: A Psychologist Treats Spirit Possession* (Garden City, N.Y.: Doubleday, 1987), 5–6.

1. Freud's conception of endopsychic perception (or projection) is extensively rediscovered and rerouted in Rickels, *Aberrations of Mourning: Writing on German Crypts* (Detroit: Wayne State University Press, 1988). See, e.g., pp. 18–20, 41–43, 123–24, 147–48, 354–62.
2. See H. G. Wunderlich, *Wohin der Stier Europa trug. Kretas Geheimnis und das Erwachen des Abendlandes* (Reinbek bei Hamburg: Rowohlt Verlag, 1972). Evans unearthed a Mycenaean civilization that was instantly billed (and primalized) as matriarchal. It was the missing link. Thus the discovery of ancient Crete, complete with its delayed release detonations which traverse its westward migrations (to California), was analogized by Freud with the discovery, inside the second system, of the pre-Oedipal zone of feminine identity. The blood bond even had a place in history (it was already in place in every individual development) from which to return as vampire, mummy, or ghost.
3. Ernst Schneider, "'Experimental Magie,'" *Internationale Zeitschrift für Psychoanalyse* 7 (1921): 483. See also Silberer's review in *Imago* 2 (1913): 447–51; and the review (signed W. H.) in *Zentralblatt für Psychoanalyse und Psychotherapie* (1913): 252–55. Staudenmaier's discovery that the body rehearses its projective reach by overstimulating peripheral organs which are (as in ventriloquism) possessed of or by their own speech gets his case into Victor Tausk's study of Natalija A. and her "influencing machine." See Ludwig Staudenmaier, *Die Magie als experimentelle Naturwissenschaft* (Leipzig: Akademische Verlagsgesellschaft, 1912, 1st ed.; 1922, 2d ed.). On p. 135 (this and subsequent references in the text are to the 2d ed.) Staudenmaier refers (in passing) to connections between his results and those of psychoanalysis which, for the moment, he cannot go into (he credits Breuer with founding psychoanalysis and Freud and his students with developing it further). The point of comparison would have been with conversion hysteria.

4. Staudenmaier, 21ff. The *Projektionsfasern* or "rays of projection," which Flechsig discovered at the same time that Schreber recognized in their broadcast of castration and resurrection his own sensorium, once again double on contact when Staudenmaier applies them as the model of his own exploration of the psyche.

5. The genealogy of media that Staudenmaier recaps here on automatic gets the full treatment in Friedrich Kittler, *Aufschreibesysteme. 1800. 1900* (Munich: Wilhelm Fink Verlag, 1985).

The Disappearance of Childhood Is a Rerun

1. Philippe Ariès, *Images of Man and Death*, trans. Janet Lloyd (Cambridge, Mass.: Harvard University Press, 1985), 247. Incunabala, the earliest printed books, were also literally "infants."

2. Philippe Ariès, *L'Enfant et la vie familiale sous l'ancien régime* (Paris: Plon, 1960). For another scheduling of the decrease in child mortality rates, see Neil Postman, *The Disappearance of Childhood* (New York: Delacorte Press, 1982).

3. R. F. W. Diekstra and K. Hawton, eds., *Suicide in Adolescence* (Boston: Martinus Nijhoff, 1987), 8–9.

4. Renato J. Almansi, "On Telephoning, Compulsive Telephoning, and Perverse Telephoning: Psychoanalytic and Social Aspects," *Psychoanalytic Study of Society* 11 (1985): 222.

5. Diekstra and Hawton, *Suicide in Adolescence*, 156.

6. "The Woman from Tangu." Cited, in German translation, in Friedrich Steinbauer, *Melanesische Cargo-Kulte* (Munich: Delp'sche Verlagsbuchhandlung, 1971), 188.

7. Friedrich Kittler, "Draculas Vermächtnis," *Zeta 02/ Mit Lacan*, 103–33. See also Akira Lippit, "Phantographics," *Qui Parle* 2, 1 (Spring 1988): 142–149.

Kalifornien

1. See Friedrich Kittler's "Benn's Poetry—'A Hit in the Charts': Song under Conditions of Media Technologies," *SubStance* 61 (1990): 5–20.

2. Frances Hannett, "The Haunting Lyric: The Personal and Social Significance of American Popular Songs," *Psychoanalytic Quarterly* 33 (1964): 226–69. Page references are given in the text.

3. Gilbert J. Rose, "In Pursuit of Slow Time: A Psychoanalytic Approach to Contemporary Music," *Psychoanalytic Study of Society* 10 (1984): 363, 364.

4. Heinz Kohut and Siegmund Levarie, "On the Enjoyment of Listening to Music," *Psychoanalytic Quarterly* 19 (1950): 64–87. Page references are given in text.

Pact Rats

1. Ursula Mahlendorf lines up Kafka's noise phobia, the 1917 mouse invasion, and "Josephine the Singer" in the sixth chapter of *The Wellsprings of Literary Creation* (Columbia, S.C.: Camden House, 1985). For a reading of Kafka's tuberculosis in terms of psychic mechanisms of remote control, see John S. White, "Psyche and Tuberculosis: The Libido Organization of Franz Kafka," *Psychoanalytic Study of Society* 4 (1967): 185–251.
2. Franz Kafka, *Briefe 1902–1924*, ed. Max Brod (New York: Schocken Books, 1958), 205.
3. Gustav Janouch, *Gespräche mit Kafka* (Frankfurt: Fischer Verlag, 1968), 111–12.
4. Ibid.
5. Ibid., 83.
6. *Briefe 1902–1924*, 388.
7. *Briefe an Milena*, ed. Willy Haas (Frankfurt: Fischer Taschenbuch Verlag, 1966), 199.
8. See diary entry of December 13, 1914, and letter to Brod, dated July 5, 1922.
9. See Nicholas Abraham and Maria Torok, "Introjection-Incorporation: Mourning or Melancholia," in *Psychoanalysis in France*, ed. Serge Lebovici and Daniel Widlöcher (New York: International Universities Press, 1980), 15–16.
10. Diary entry cited in Mahlendorf, 130.
11. *Briefe 1902–1924*, 447.
12. See both the diary entry of February 11, 1913, and Janouch, 54.
13. See in this regard Rickels, *Aberrations of Mourning*, 286–88, 299–301. In the doubly, because deceptively, Oedipal "Letter to Father," Kafka attributed his hypersensitivity to sound to his father's perpetual noise track. From "The Judgment" to "Josephine the Singer," however, Kafka's apprehension of that threat to the future which his works signal shifts, along with the swing around of his "childish-disgusting but successful game," from the father to the child and sibling.
14. *Briefe 1902–1924*, 205.
15. Géza Róheim, *Magic and Schizophrenia* (Bloomington: Indiana University Press, 1970), 124, 151, 164–65, 173.
16. Theodor Reik, *The Haunting Melody* (New York: Farrar, Straus & Young, 1953).
17. Christoph Ruths, *Experimental-Untersuchungen über Musik-*

phantome und ein daraus erschlossenes Grundgesetz der Entstehung, der Wiedergabe und der Aufnahme von Tonwerken (Darmstadt: Kommisionsverlag von H.L. Schlapp, 1898), 106–7, 163, 174, 207, 232. Subsequent references are given in the text.

Grin and Bury It

1. Ruths, *Experimental-Untersuchungen über Musikphantome,* 151, 156. Subsequent references are in the text.
2. Ernst Kris, *Psychoanalytic Explorations in Art* (New York: Schocken Books, 1964), 213 n. 12.

Follow the Bouncing Ball

1. "The attraction a man feels for a foreign woman is often irresistible because it corresponds to his desire for the forbidden love object. . . . And it is because of this transfer of feeling from the incestuous love object to the foreigner that the latter can so easily become an object of intense jealousy, guilty fascination and repulsion. . . . Under Hitler sexual relations between Germans and Jews were qualified as incestuous and therefore strictly forbidden. Yet at the same time Hitler went to extremes to prove that the Jews were of a totally different race from the Germans. This contradiction is particularly revealing in view of the role played in Hitler's life by his unconscious attachment to his mother and sister." Rudolph M. Loewenstein, *Christians and Jews: A Psychoanalytic Study,* trans. Vera Damman (New York: International Universities Press, 1951), 73–74.

The Endopsychic Sensurround

1. Letter to Fliess dated December 12, 1897.
2. Walter Benjamin, *Gesammelte Schriften,* ed. Rolf Tiedemann and Hermann Schweppenhäuser (Frankfurt: Suhrkamp Verlag, 1977), vol. 2, pt. 3, 1005–06.
3. Ibid., vol. 1, pt. 2, 461–62.

The "Uncanned"

1. Fritz Wittels, *Freud and His Time* (New York: Grosset & Dunlap, 1932), 299.

2. Jacques Lacan, "Desire and the Interpretation of Desire in Hamlet," trans. James Hulbert, *Yale French Studies* 55–56 (1977): 36–66. I have by now also been referring to Lacan's "Kant avec Sade," in *Écrits* (Paris: Editions du Seuil, 1971), 2:119–48.
3. Theodor Adorno, "Über den Fetishcharakter in der Music," *Gesammelte Schriften,* ed. Gretel Adorno and Rolf Tiedemann (Frankfurt: Suhrkamp Verlag, 1973), 14:14. Its companion piece is "Über Jazz," in *Gesammelte Schriften,* vol. 17. Subsequent page references to these essays, abbreviated as F and J respectively, will appear in the text.

"Grateful Dead"

1. Jacques Attali, *Noise: The Political Economy of Music,* trans. Brian Massumi (Minneapolis: University of Minnesota Press, 1985), 36. Subsequent references are to this edition and are given in the text.
2. This is Friedrich Kittler's discovery. See his *Grammophon, Film, Typewriter* (Berlin: Brinkmann & Bose, 1986), 374 ff.

Mickey Mouse Club

1. Richard Schickel, *The Disney Version* (New York: Avon, l968), 151. Subsequent references are given in text.
2. Stephen Jay Gould, "Mickey Mouse Meets Konrad Lorenz," *Natural History* 88, no. 5 (1979): 30, 32, 34, 36. Gould's general pursuit of evolutionary revision of history admits the compelling impact of random incursions of new media upon the course of mankind's development which, as in neotenization, can be radically altered or arrested.

S-Laughter

1. Walter Benjamin, *Gesammelte Schriften,* vol. 1, pt. 2. Page references are given in the text.
2. See Lynne Kirby, "Male Hysteria and Early Cinema," *Camera Obscura* 17 (1988): 113–31.
3. Mel Gordon, *Grand Guignol: Theatre of Fear and Terror* (New York: Amok Press, 1988). On p. 2 Gordon sums up: "Here was a theatre genre that was predicated on the stimulation of the rawest and most adolescent of human interactions and desires: incest and patricide; blood lust; sexual anxiety and conflict; morbid fascination with bodily mutilation and death; loathing of authority; fear of insanity."
4. Hitchcock borrowed from Robert Bloch's novel on which the

film was based, its basis in the actual 1957 case of Wisconsin mass murderer Ed Gein: "A quiet but well-liked middle-aged farmer who was often called on by his neighbors to baby-sit for them, Gein was also a mom-fixated sexual psychopath who indulged in necrophilia, cannibalism, and finally murder—usually at the time of the full moon. His crimes were eventually uncovered by a local deputy sheriff who came upon the headless corpse of his own mother hanging on a hook in Gein's squalid farmhouse; the house was littered with the bones and flesh of Gein's victims, as well as parts of other bodies Gein had recently disinterred. . . . Gein often made waistcoats from the skin of his victims and wore them about the house." John McCarty, *Psychos: Eighty Years of Mad Movies, Maniacs, and Murderous Deeds* (New York: St. Martin's Press, 1986), 132.

Body Master Machines

1. David I. Berland, "Disney and Freud: Walt Meets the Id," *Journal of Popular Culture* 15, no. 4 (1982): 102.
2. Jean Laplanche, *Life and Death in Psychoanalysis*, trans. Jeffrey Mehlman (Baltimore: Johns Hopkins University Press, 1976), 102.
3. Ibid.
4. Ariès, *Western Attitudes toward Death*, 98.

Gag Me with a Tune

1. Cited in part in Elizabeth A. Lawrence, "In the Mick of Time: Reflections on Disney's Ageless Mouse," *Journal of Popular Culture* 20 (1986): 71–72. A more complete citation can be found in Schickel.
2. Fritz Moellenhoff, "Remarks on the Popularity of Mickey Mouse," *American Imago* 1 (1940): 31, 23.
3. Daniel C. Schuman, "False Accusations of Physical and Sexual Abuse," *Bulletin of the American Academy of Psychiatry and Law* 14, no. 1 (1986): 10.
4. *Time* (December 21, 1987), 61.

Good Mourning America

Epigraph: "Tuning In to the Departed," in *Spirit Summonings* (Alexandria, Va.: Time-Life Books, 1989), 144.
1. Stanley Cavell, *Pursuits of Happiness: The Hollywood Comedy of Marriage* (Cambridge, Mass.: Harvard University Press, 1981), 163–87.

2. Stanley Cavell, "Freud and Philosophy: A Fragment," *Critical Inquiry* 13, no. 2 (1987): 386.

3. Cavell, *Pursuits of Happiness*, 13, 16–17; Cavell, "Freud and Philosophy," 389–90.

4. See the survey of film-theoretical contributions collected and edited by Philip Rosen: *Narrative, Apparatus, Ideology*, (New York: Columbia University Press, 1986). Jean-Louis Baudry sees the mirror stage reflected back as a cinematic desire at least as ancient as Plato's cave parable; in Laura Mulvey's view, these reflections take shape close-range in Hollywood films which keep to the mirror orbit of male spectator and female spectacle. As is by now public opinion—and this tendency at the same time invites suspicion—Mulvey's exploration can be seen to succumb to the stage she discovers constraining popular films. But when Paul Willeman argues that her showdown of looks and spectacles leaves out—the gays—, he has in turn only spun once around the ocular orbit Mulvey successfully charted. Kaja Silverman's charge, however, that Mulvey excludes the nonvisualizable Other or gaze of the law, attracts conviction. This uncoupled gaze corresponds to the post-Freudian isolation of the apparatus (by Baudry and Walter Benjamin) as the unconscious side of cinematic representation and identification which produces, at the conscious end, identification with characters.

5. Bertram Lewin, "Sleep, The Mouth, and the Dream Screen," *Psychoanalytic Quarterly* 15 (1946): 421–22. Further references are given in the text.

6. Joseph Bierman, "Dracula: Prolongued Childhood Illness, and the Oral Triad," *American Imago* 29, no. 2 (1972): 186–98. In *The Telephone Book*, Ronell reorganizes the *Dreck-erinnerung* of media technology—and vampirism—around a maternal superego. Also see Ronell's "The Walking Switchboard," *SubStance* 61 (1990): 75–94.

7. Lacan, "Desire and Interpretation in Hamlet," 46.

Cute Buns

1. Sherry Turkle, *Psychoanalytic Politics: Freud's French Revolution* (New York: Basic Books, 1978), 238.

2. Janine Chasseguet-Smirgel, *Creativity and Perversion* (New York: W. W. Norton, 1984). Page references are given in the text.

Boobs Tube

1. Samuel Abrams, "The Meaning of 'Nothing,'" *Psychoanalytic Quarterly* 43 (1974): 115.

2. Bertram Lewin, "Phobic Symptoms and Dream Interpretation," *Psychoanalytic Quarterly* 21 (1952): 316. Cf. Lewin, "Metaphor, Mind, and Manikin," *Psychoanalytic Quarterly* 40, no. 1 (1971): 30–31.

3. Bertram Lewin, "Sleep, Narcissistic Neurosis, and the Analytic Situation," *Psychoanalytic Quarterly* 23 (1954): 487–510. Page references are given in the text.

4. Also see in this regard Lewin, "Dream Psychology and the Analytic Situation," *Psychoanalytic Quarterly* 24 (1955): 169–99.

5. Joseph Kepecs, "Observations on Screens and Barriers in the Mind," *Psychoanalytic Quarterly* 23 (1954): 65. Further references are given in the text.

6. Joseph Kepecs, "A Waking Screen Analogous to the Dream Screen," *Psychoanalytic Quarterly* 21 (1952): 168. Further references are given in the text.

7. Lewin, "Sleep, Narcissistic Neurosis, and the Analytic Situation," 504.

8. Angel Garma, "Vicissitudes of the Dream Screen and the Isakower Phenomenon," *Psychoanalytic Quarterly* 24 (1955): 372.

9. Lewin, "Sleep, Narcissistic Neurosis, and the Analytic Situation," 494, n. 3.

10. Ariel Dorfman and Armand Mattelart, *How to Read Donald Duck: Imperialist Ideology in the Disney Comic* (New York: I. G. Editions, 1975), 94.

11. In an interview, Heidegger admitted the analogy between television and the structures of his thought; see *The Telephone Book* on TV: 199–200.

TV Führer

1. This current Anglo-Americanism is the happy-face counterpart within contemporary psychoanalysis of the Lacanian dialectic (or antidialectic) of recognition.

2. Ernst Kris and Nathan Leites, "Trends in Twentieth Century Propaganda," *Psychoanalysis and the Social Sciences* 1 (1947): 395.

3. Friedrich Kittler has demonstrated the traumatic shock connection between World War I and film in *Grammophon, Film, Typewriter*.

4. This 1912 newspaper citation can be found in Lynn Spigel, "Installing the Television Set: Popular Discourses on Television and Domestic Space, 1948–1955," *Camera Obscura* 16 (1988): 13.

5. Raymond Williams, *Television: Technology and Cultural Form* (New York: Schocken Books, 1975): 9–14. The book was "mainly written in California" (7).

6. Ibid., 19.
7. See Rüdiger Campe's "The Rauschen of the Waves: On the Margins of Literature," *SubStance* 61 (1990): 21–38.
8. See Hanns Sachs, "The Delay of the Machine Age," trans. Margaret J. Powers, *Psychoanalytic Quarterly* 11, no. 3–4 (1933): 404–24. The deferral dimension of Derrida's *différance* gets us this far; the differentiation dimension allows Sarah Kofman to take up the challenge of Freud's analogues. At first sight these negative versus positive analogies are as ancient as any metaphysical opposition. But via a photo-analogue in *Moses and Monotheism* which *expressis verbis* advertises neither a necessary nor dialectical development from negative into positive, Kofman is able to dislodge Freud's arsenal of analogies from a doubly ideological turn to machines no newer in their metaphoric makeup than camera obscura or silhouette. See *Camera obscura—de l'ideologie* (Paris: Editions galilee, 1973), 37–46.
9. Hugo Münsterberg, *The Film: A Psychological Study* (New York: Dover Publications, 1970), 41. (This Dover edition is the republication of the 1916 work *The Photoplay: A Psychological Study*.) Münsterberg shares his insights at gun point: the use of a pistol on stage cannot compare in shock value to the close-up of a gun pointed at the movie audience: "Here begins the art of the photoplay" (37). By modeling perceptions of movement projected by film on the effects obtainable by looking out train windows, Münsterberg switches to the other conveyer of traumatic shock that contributed to the invention of film.

The Lang Goodbye

1. Marshall McLuhan, *Understanding Media: The Extensions of Man* (New York: McGraw-Hill, 1964), 91.
2. Ibid., 95–96.

1936–1958

1. Jacques Lacan, *Écrits. A Selection*, trans. Alan Sheridan (New York: W. W. Norton, 1977), 239.
2. Jacques Lacan, "Television," trans. Denis Hollier, Rosalind Krauss, and Annette Michelson, *October* 40 (1987): 40. While radio was pressed into the service of Nazi propaganda, television was reserved for the remote control or live monitoring of total war: scientists in Nazi Germany used TV to monitor stored bombs prone to auto-detonation and, in experiments, to guide missiles. (My thanks to Friedrich Kittler for this information.)
3. Richard Mandell, *The Nazi Olympics* (New York: Macmillan, 1971), 138. Klaus Landsberg was a gadget lover at heart who

auto-trained in short-wave reception before wiring the 1936 Berlin olympics for "live" transmission. In 1937 he emigrated to the United States after his invention of an electronic navigational aid (which in fact led to the invention of radar) was appropriated and suppressed by the German authorities as a military secret. By 1941 Landsberg was in charge of Paramount TV in Los Angeles. Based on the coverage capabilities of German TV in the mid-1930s, he systematically promoted mobility in the station's broadcasts. Remote telecasts would become the irrepressible feature of Paramount, which "was there." See Mark Williams, "Paramount's KTLA: Considering the Independent Station as a Factor in the Rise of Network Television," *The USC Spectator* 7, 2 (Spring 1987): 27.

4. L. R. Lawkes, "Historical Sketch of Television's Progress," *A Technological History of Motion Pictures and Television*, ed. Raymond Fielding (Berkeley: University of California Press, 1967), 227.

5. Lacan, "Television," 7.

6. Ibid., 31.

7. Lacan, *Écrits*, 259.

8. George Everson, *The Story of Television: The Life of Philo T. Farnsworth* (New York: W. W. Norton, 1949), 51.

9. Theodor W. Adorno, "Prolog zum Fernsehen," *Gesammelte Schriften*, ed. Adorno and Tiedemann, 10:507. Subsequent page references are given in the text.

10. "Television," 27–28.

11. Beverle Houston, "Viewing Television: The Metapsychology of Endless Consumption," *Quarterly Review of Film Studies* 9, no. 3 (Summer 1984): 183–95. Houston writes: "the promise of television lies in its flow, the uninterrupted filling of air time . . . producing the idea that the text issues from an endless supply that is sourceless, natural, inexhaustible, and coextensive with psychological reality itself. . . . It suggests the first flow of nourishment in and from the mother's body, evoking a moment when the emerging sexual drive is still closely linked to—and propped on—the life-and-death urgency of the feeding instinct" (184). Thus "the television also addresses the drive to incorporate" (184). Keeping the scanner on the side of translation, Houston writes also from the side of resistance and transference: "It's hard to resist talking about the television image itself as never completed, always requiring a scanning process at the unconscious level to assemble lines into a readable image" (188). On its own, however, the TV image "depends on its promise to provide for endless consumption" (189).

12. Friedrich Kittler pursued this exclusion in his 1987 graduate seminar at the University of California, Santa Barbara. The Hegel reference is *Enzyklopadie*, sec. 459. (My thanks to Mathias Rosenthal, my informant.)

13. Lawkes, 227–54.

14. See Herbert Marcuse, *Five Lectures: Psychoanalysis, Politics, and Utopia*, trans. Jeremy J. Shapiro and Shierry M. Weber (Boston: Beacon Press, 1970), and *Eros and Civilization: A Philosophical Inquiry into Freud* (Boston: Beacon Press, 1955). Joel Whitebook elaborates the connection in *Perversion and Utopia* (Cambridge, Mass.: MIT Press, forthcoming).

15. In "Some Thoughts on the Ego Ideal: A Contribution to the Study of the 'Illness of Ideality,'" Janine Chasseguet-Smirgel argues that in the pervert, as in the group, pregenitality and pre-generationality are promoted against the idea of development or evolution and (at the same time) against the 3-D perspective or received distance sponsored by the superego. What the superego cuts off or interrupts is what the ego ideal advertises: the child's fusion with mother. *Psychoanalytic Quarterly* 45 (July 1976): 345–73.

16. Sachs, "The Delay of the Machine Age," 421.

17. Ibid., 417.

18. In *Understanding Media*, McLuhan develops the notion of a subliminal veil which every technical medium supplies to maxi-shield us from direct awareness of the terrible pressure extension (and excision) of our senses exerts on us. The subliminal gets recircuited through sublimation and psychosis (or sublimation breakdown) in *Aberrations of Mourning*, 120–21, 294–317.

1912/1936

1. See Introduction to Bettina L. Knapp, *Machine, Metaphor and the Writer: A Jungian View* (University Park: Pennsylvania State University Press, 1989), in which Jung on the machine (*Collected Works*, 8:42) is presented. But Jung's notion of synchronicity, e.g., belongs to a post-transferential, postendopsychic—pure TV—machine or metaphor.

2. William McGuire and R. F. C. Hull, eds., *C. G. Jung Speaking: Interviews and Encounters* (Princeton: Princeton University Press, 1977), 93.

3. Ibid., 61–66.

4. Ibid., 13–24.

They Got Up on the Wrong Side of the Dead

1. Jung's published diagnosis of the Spielrein case can be found included in Aldo Carotenuto, ed., *Tagebuch einer heimlichen Symmetrie: Sabina Spielrein zwischen Jung und Freud* (Freiburg: Kore, Verlag Traute Hensch, 1986).

2. C. G. Jung, *Symbols of Transformation*, trans. R. F. C. Hull (London: Routledge & Kegan Paul, 1956), 328, n. 38.
3. C. G. Jung, "The Significance of the Father in the Destiny of the Individual," *The Psychoanalytic Years*, trans. R. F. C. Hull (Princeton: Princeton University Press, 1974), 116 and 116, n. 26.
4. Cited in Gerhard Wehr, *Jung: A Biography*, trans. David Weeks (Boston: Shambhala, 1988), 22. Immediately subsequent citations from Jung which can be found in Wehr are given in the text.
5. Nandor Fodor, "Jung's Sermons to the Dead," *Psychoanalytic Review* 51, no. 1 (Spring 1964): 74–78. Page references given in text.
6. Nandor Fodor, "Jung, Freud, and a Newly-Discovered Letter of 1909 on the Poltergeist Theme," *Psychoanalytic Review* 50, no. 2 (Summer 1963): 119–28. The subsequent page references given in text are to this article.

Bottom Turns

1. See Carotenuto's concluding essay in *Tagebuch einer heimlichen Symmetrie*, 257ff.
2. In "Jung's Sermons to the Dead," Fodor relocates Jung's Christ neurosis, as evidenced in a dream featuring the murder of Siegfried, within the relations to Freud which Spielrein sought to re-pair: "He dreamed that he was with an unknown, brown-skinned savage. It was dawn. They heard Siegfried's horn sounding over the mountain, and Jung knew that he had to kill the savage. As he drove down the mountain in a chariot made of the bones of the dead, he killed him with a rifle-shot. . . . On awakening, Jung felt a terrible urgency to understand the dream. He heard a voice shouting in his ear: If you do not understand the dream, you must shoot yourself. . . . Then, in a flash, an understanding came: Siegfried was the tyrannical will of the Germans and stood for Jung's own mental attitude; therefore he had to be killed. The interpretation was good as far as it went. But it missed completely that SIEGFRIED was SIG FREUD. Jung had to kill his death wishes against Freud on whose dead bones he wanted to rise into the status of the master" (78). But Fodor misses completely that also the SIEG (or "victory") was assigned to FREUD (over his dead body).
3. *Tagebuch einer heimlichen Symmetrie*, 301.
4. See Eva Meyer, *Autobiographie der Schrift* (Frankfurt: Stroemfeld/Roter Stern, 1989), 124.
5. In the same letter Freud reports on the slower progress of his own current project: "My paper on taboo is coming along slowly. The conclusion has long been known to me. The source of

taboo and hence also of conscience is ambivalence." In 1920 Spielrein was the happy medium reached by Freud. In a lecture she presented in 1920 on the origin of the child's first words, Spielrein was able to synchronize—*fort-da* style—the discoveries released (at last) in *Beyond the Pleasure Principle.* Sucking motions in the absence of the desired breast produce first verbalization: Mama. The lip-synching of breastfeeding produces the mother tongue: but father introduces desire in playful isolation from hunger. Papa is produced when the completely satiated infant mouths the nipple, playing with it and letting it go.

Is That All There Is?

1. Sabina Spielrein, *Die Destruktion als Ursache des Werdens* (Tübingen: Edition Diskord, 1986), 9. Subsequent references are to this edition and are given in the text.

Girl Talk

1. "Is it the object I love or do I love being loved by the object—or is it love that I love?" The endless conjugation of subject/object nonrelations in love, which gets searched by every popular song (love is radio-active), gave Spielrein pointers or hints to make the auto-analytic shift, in the course of double psychoticization (hers and Jung's), to theorization of the psychotic condition and thus to a first transference (a symbolization or biographization of love's body and biology).

Giving Grief

Epigraph: William McDougall, *Psycho-Analysis and Social Psychology* (London: Methuen & Co., 1936), 197. Quotation is from W. H. Sheldon.
1. W. Trotter, *Instincts of the Herd in Peace and War*, 6th ed. (London: T. Fisher Unwin, 1921 [1st ed., 1916]), 81.
2. Juliet Flower-MacCannell has analyzed the failure of the couple. In her reading the story of *1984* spectacularly reduces to the challenge that a couple of lovers can pose to Big Brother (*The Regime of the Brother* [London: Routledge, forthcoming]). Derrida has given the groundplan of fraternity's deconstruction in his (double)take on friendship: "What relation does this domination maintain with the double exclusion that can be seen at work in all the great ethico-politico-philosophical discourses on friendship, namely, on the one hand, the exclusion of friendship between women, and, on the other hand, the exclusion of

friendship between a man and a woman? This double exclusion of the feminine in the philosophical paradigm of friendship would thus confer on it the essential and essentially sublime figure of virile homosexuality. Within the familial schema . . . this exclusion privileges the figure of the brother, the name of the brother or the name of brother, more than that of the father—whence the necessity of connecting the political model, especially that of democracy and that of the Decalogue, with the rereading of Freud's hypothesis about the alliance of brothers" ("The Politics of Friendship," *Journal of Philosophy* 85, no. 11 [November 1988]: 642).

3. Joseph Wortis, *Fragments of an Analysis with Freud* (New York: Simon & Schuster, 1954), 98.

4. "A Short Study of the Development of the Libido, Viewed in the Light of Mental Disorders," *Selected Papers*, trans. Douglas Bryan and Alix Strachey (New York: Basic Books, 1960), 435–37.

5. "Nach dem Tode des Urvaters," *Imago* 9, no. 1 (1923), 113–18.

Teen Passion

Epigraph: Sigmund Freud, "Fragment of an Analysis of a Case of Hysteria" (*SE* 7:53–54)

1. G. Stanley Hall, *Adolescence* (New York: D. Appleton & Company, 1904), 2:282. Further references are given in the text.

2. William James, *The Varieties of Religious Experience: A Study in Human Nature* (New York: Modern Library, 1929). References are to this edition and are given in the text.

3. Gabriel Tarde, *The Laws of Imitation*, trans. E. C. Parsons (New York: Henry Holt & Company, 1903), 89ff.

4. Edwin D. Starbuck, *The Psychology of Religion: An Empirical Study of the Growth of Religious Consciousness* (London: Walter Scott, Paternoster Square, 1901), 27. Subsequent references are to this edition and are given in the text.

5. In the corner of this research projection we again find, in the book version, "Flechsig's associational centers" (152). The earlier article version does adolescence on its own, without Flechsig's centers. Page references to "A Study of Conversion," *American Journal of Psychology* 8 (January 1897): 268–308, are given in the text preceded by SC.

6. "The ecumenical movement is synonymous with electric technology" (Marshall McLuhan, *Understanding Media*, 280). The eighteenth-century English star of mass conversions, Reverend John Wesley, already wired this connection in 1759 when he published *The Desideratum or Electricity Made Plain and Useful By a Lover of Mankind and of Common Sense* (subsequent page

references are to the 1871 edition; London: Baillière, Tindall, and Cox). The current Wesley turns on jams the circuits from the nervous system to the soul: "Perhaps if the Nerves are really perforated (as is now generally supposed) the Electric Ether is the only Fluid in the Universe, which is fine enough to move through them. And what if the *Nervous Juice* itself, be a Fluid of this Kind?" (4). Or again: "Such is the extreme Fineness, Velocity, and Expansiveness of this active Principle, that all other Matter seems to be only the Body, and this the Soul of the Universe" (9). Fastforwarding these connections to electroshock therapy (and TV), Wesley thus sees electricity's useful application precisely in "nervous Cases of every Kind" (in particular those of Hysterics, Fits, and Epilepsy): "It will be easily observed that a great Part of these are of the nervous Kind; and perhaps there is no nervous Distemper whatever, which would not yield to a steady Use of this Remedy" (42-43).

Circle Jerk

1. The teenager, according to Hall, comes complete with a sense of being the victim of ancestral vice (in other words: child abuse) (309).
2. Gustave Le Bon, *The Crowd: A Study of the Popular Mind*, 6th ed. (London: T. Fisher Unwin, 1909 [1st ed., 1896]), 44. Cf. Mikkel Borch-Jacobsen, *The Freudian Subject*, trans. Catherine Porter (Stanford: Stanford University Press, 1988), 139. Borch-Jacobsen explores the same intertextual complex that gives me "teen passion"; but the collapse of differentiating theories of identification, which he tends to restrict to an internal fault only within Freud's drift toward group psychology, reflects rather the externalizing *Blitz* of Girardian reckonings with Freud. "Freud" is too massive and discursivitous not to be assumed always to be right—at some bottom or on a side that is up to the archaeological reconstructor to discover.
3. In *Cryptonomie: Le verbier de L'Homme aux loups* (Paris: Editions Aubier Flammarion, 1976), Nicolas Abraham and Maria Torok explore an "internal hysteria" set up inside as a kind of entertainment apparatus for incorporated guests. In Freud's final reference to—and dismissal of—the mechanism of conversion in *Inhibitions, Symptoms and Anxiety,* symptoms produced by conversion are treated as exceptional indeed "obscure" since not among the effects of repression: an initial act of repression is followed up by an interminable sequel in which the struggle against the instinctual impulse is prolonged into struggle against the symptom. This symptom and struggle the ego is able to "incorporate" as part of its overriding economy. But another kind of incorporation is conveyed by conversion. "An analogy

with which we have long been familiar compared a symptom to a foreign body which was keeping up a constant succession of stimuli and reactions in the tissue in which it was embedded. It does sometimes happen that the defensive struggle against an unwelcome instinctual impulse is brought to an end with the formation of a symptom. As far as can be seen, this is most often possible in hysterical conversion" (*SE* 20:98). In the 1893 "Preliminary Communication" coauthored with Breuer we find that the memory of the psychic trauma (that souvenir which turned the electrical system into a projector) "acts like a foreign body which long after its entry must continue to be regarded as an agent that is still at work" (*SE* 2:6). But already in the *Studies on Hysteria*, in 1895, the more complete coverage Breuer and Freud granted hysterical symptom formation required qualification of the analogy: "In fact the pathogenic organization does not behave like a foreign body, but far more like an infiltrate. In this simile the resistance must be regarded as what is infiltrating" (*SE* 2:290). In 1926 (in *Inhibitions, Symptoms and Anxiety*) the specific case of conversion survives—and doubly so—as foreign body.

Tubular

Epigraphs: Stanley Hall, *Adolescence: Its Psychology* (New York: Appleton & Co., 1924), 1:xvi. Subsequent references to vol. 1 are to this edition. Freud, *Totem and Taboo* (*SE* 13:23).

1. Hall, *Adolescence*, 1:xvi.
2. Michael Bálint, "A Contribution to the Psychology of Menstruation," *Psychoanalytic Quarterly* 6 (1937): 346–52.
3. See Pierce Julius Flynn, "Waves of Semiosis: Surfing's Iconic Progression," *American Journal of Semiotics* 5, no. 3–4 (1987): 397–418. When it came to menstruation, Marilyn Monroe went public, pubic, sublime: she "was there" on every occasion of her bleeding, the onset of which she always allowed to take her by surprise without any preparedness or deterrence on her part.
4. "The Problem of Melancholia," *International Journal of Psychoanalysis* 9 (1928): 420–38. References are given in the text.
5. George Gero, "Sadism, Masochism, and Aggression: Their Role in Symptom-Formation," *Psychoanalytic Quarterly* 31 (1962): 31–42. Page references are given in the text.
6. Poul Faergeman, "Fantasies of Menstruation in Men," *Psychoanalytic Quarterly* 24 (1955): 1–19. References are in the text.
7. Faergeman would admit this slant only in those situations where identification with the omnipotent mother can be established (3).
8. Tampax advertising supplement, "Boy—Am I Glad I'm a Girl," 1990.

Bitch Bunnies

1. Sigmund Freud, *Übersicht der Übertragungsneurosen*, ed. Ilse Grubrich-Simitis (Frankfurt: S. Fischer, 1985). Page references are given in the text.
2. J. J. Bachofen, *Myth, Religion, and Mother Right: Selected Writings*, trans. Ralph Mannheim (Princeton: Princeton University Press, 1973), 112ff. Further references are given in the text.

Honkies For Jesus

1. In German "Freud" is a near look-alike of "Freude" (joy or gaiety). But another near-miss and lapsus, which was often performed on Freud's name, was teleguided by death wishes: it was the German word, proper name, and concept "Freund": the "friend."
2. Theodor Reik, *Masochism in Modern Man*, trans. M. H. Beigel and G. M. Kurth (New York: Farrar, Strauss, 1941), 342.
3. In "The Dogma of Christ," trans. James Luther Adams, in *The Dogma of Christ and Other Essays on Religion, Psychology and Culture* (London: Routledge & Kegan Paul, 1963), Erich Fromm diagnosed a progression of the Christian phantasm in three steps which coincides, he guarantees, with that of a psychic illness (69). The founding belief in Christianity, the elevation of a man to God, expressed the "unconscious wish for the removal of the Divine Father" (35). An inward turn accompanies the next step: Catholic (as opposed to early Christian) dogma is no longer stressed out about the overthrow of the father but rather bummed on the self-annihilation of the son (49–50). After the down shift from identification with the suffering Jesus to masochistic expiation through self-annihilation, a third development of the same identification transforms the fatherly God (or what's left of him) "into the mother full of grace who nourishes the child, shelters it in her womb, and thus provides pardon" (68). This is the psychotic, uncanny or homeless end of construction of the narcissistic object—of the invention of California.
4. See, in this regard, Eva Meyer, *Autobiographie der Schrift*, 65–82.
5. Manfred Schneider, "Hysterie als Gesamtkunstwerk. Aufstieg und Verfall einer Semiotik der Weiblichkeit," *Merkur* 439/440, no. 9/10 (September/October 1985): 879–95. Whereas Freud saw demoniacal possession model for hysterical conversion symptoms, Schneider charts the hysterical sign back to Dante's *Inferno*—and the intertextuality (*Pamela*, for example) that follows from it. The historical shift from literature to visual media in the representation of femininity—whereby hysteria is left behind—is covered by Schneider's essay. In a letter to Benjamin

dated August 2, 1935, Adorno speculated on the far-reaching contemporaneity of psychoanalysis and art nouveau which together replaced interiority with sex.

6. Victor Tausk, "Über die Entstehung des 'Beeinflussungsapparates' in der Schizophrenie," in *Gesammelte psychoanalytische und literarische Schriften*, ed. Hans-Joachim Metzger (Berlin: Medusa Verlag, 1983).

7. Prado de Oliveira, "Schreber, Ladies and Gentlemen," in *Psychosis and Sexual Identity: Toward a Post-Analytic View of the Schreber Case*, ed. David B. Allison, Prado de Oliveira, Mark S. Roberts, and Allen S. Weiss (Albany: State University of New York Press, 1988), 171.

But Don't Forget to Breathe

1. Samuel Atkin, "Notes on Motivations for War: Toward a Psychoanalytic Social Psychology," *Psychoanalytic Quarterly* 43 (1974): 37. Subsequent references are in the text.

2. Leo Stone, "Reflections on the Psychoanalytic Concept of Aggression," *Psychoanalytic Quarterly* 40 (1971): 195–244. Page references are given in the text.

3. The jargon of infantile aggression—bite it off, rip it off, cut it off—has, by 1950, become wholly psycho-interrorized, projected, technologized (Stone 226).

Stoked!

1. Bertram D. Lewin, "The Train Ride: A Study of One of Freud's Figures of Speech," *Psychoanalytic Quarterly* 49 (1970): 71–89. Page references are given in the text.

Shanky Spaz

1. Sigmund Freud and William C. Bullitt, *Thomas Woodrow Wilson: A Psychological Study* (Boston: Houghton Mifflin, 1967). Page references are given in the text.

Toxic Shock

1. "These dreams are endeavoring to master the stimulus retrospectively, by developing the anxiety whose omission was the cause of the traumatic neurosis. They thus afford us a view of a function of the mental apparatus which, though it does not contradict the pleasure principle, is nevertheless independent

of it and seems to be more primitive than the purpose of gaining
pleasure and avoiding unpleasure" (*SE* 18:32).
2. Ernst Simmel, *Kriegsneurosen und "Psychisches Trauma"* (Leipzig: Verlag von Otto Nemnich, 1918), 25.
3. Tiedemann and Schweppenhäuser, eds., *Gesammelte Schriften*,
vol. 1, pt. 2, 614ff.
4. For a concise history of shock therapy, see Max Fink, *Convulsive
Therapy: Theory and Praxis* (New York: Raven Press, 1979), 5–11.
In the context of treatment of World-War-I traumatic neuroses,
Freud presented psychoanalysis as the alternative to shock therapy, which he took to be punitive in its logic and thus successful
only through overkill (*SE* 17:214–15).

Double Date

1. Barrie M. Biven, "A Violent Solution: The Role of Skin in a
Severe Adolescent Regression," *Psychoanalytic Study of the Child*
32 (1977): 350.
2. William Spring, "Observations on World Destruction Fantasies," *Psychoanalytic Quarterly* 8 (1939): 48–56.
3. *Gesammelte Schriften*, vol. 2, pt. 1, 218–19.

Laugh Track

1. Martin Grotjahn, "Ferdinand the Bull: Psychoanalytical Remarks about a Modern Totem Animal," *American Imago* 1
(1940): 40.
2. Theodor Adorno and Max Horkheimer, *Dialectic of Enlightenment*, trans. John Cumming (New York: Herder and Herder,
1972), 140ff.
3. The following references given in the text are cited in *Laughing
Gas (Nitrous Oxide)*, ed. Michael Shelin and David Wallechinsky
(San Francisco: And/Or Press, 1973).

The Other Reich

1. Wilhelm Reich, *The Mass Psychology of Fascism*, trans. Vincent
Carfagno (New York: Farrar, Straus & Giroux, 1970), 336.
2. Ibid.
3. For the details of Reich's psychotic breakdown, see Janine
Chasseguet-Smirgel and Bela Grumberger, *Freud or Reich? Psychoanalysis and Illusion*, trans. Claire Pajaczkowska (New
Haven: Yale University Press, 1986).
4. *The Mass Psychology of Fascism*, 336.
5. C. G. Jung, *Flying Saucers: A Modern Myth of Things Seen in*

the Skies, trans. R. F. C. Hull (Princeton: Princeton University Press, 1978), 66.

Bringing Up Beben

Epigraph: Time (November 20, 1989), "Letters," p. 12.

1. Ralph Waldo Emerson, *The Conduct of Life* (Boston: Houghton Mifflin, 1904), 140. There are direct funereal connections featuring a dead brother (who was his "best friend") between "Culture" and the essay "Friendship." The connections are, moreover, technologized. "Science with her telegraphy" must fine tune "dull nerves" so that the new free man can be received: "There is nothing he will not overcome and convert." Finally, the new man will be born (in America) out of the trajectory of travel to California (rather than to Europe, the "mental home" of American "invalid habits"). The "search after friendship" supersedes desire; everyone seeks an "equal" to "deal with . . . with the simplicity and wholeness with which one chemical atom meets another." My thanks to Eduardo Cadava for alerting me to the tremors in Emerson.
2. My thanks to Avital Ronell, my correspondent at the quake (I was in Berlin).
3. On the day of the unification of the currencies of the two Germanys, the "Painted Cave Fire" split Santa Barbara from the mountains to the sea.
4. William James, "On Some Mental Effects of the Earthquake," in *Memories and Studies* (New York: Longmans, Green, 1911), 212–13. Subsequent references are given in the text.
5. See the contributions of Werner Hamacher and Friedrich Kittler in *Positionen der Literaturwissenschaft. Acht Modellanalysen am Beispiel von Kleists "Das Erdbeben in Chili,"* ed. D. E. Wellbery (Munich: Verlag C. H. Beck, 1985). See also Wolf Kittler, *Die Geburt des Partisanen aus dem Geist der Poesie: Heinrich von Kleist und die Strategie der Befreiungskriege* (Freiburg: Verlag Rombach, 1987).
6. My thanks to Marc DeWitt, who called this passage (in *Journals* 1 [1838]: 120) to my attention.
7. C. G. Jung, "Psychic Conflicts in a Child," *The Psychoanalytic Years*, trans. R. F. C. Hull and Leopold Stein (Princeton: Princeton University Press, 1974), 124–51. References are to this edition and are given in the text.

Serfs Up

1. Fritz Wittels, "Unconscious Phantoms in Neurotics," *Psychoanalytic Quarterly* 8 (1939): 141–63. Page references are given in text.

2. Fritz Wittels, "Phantom Formation in a Case of Epilepsy," *Psychoanalytic Quarterly* 9 (1940): 103.
3. See Jean-François Lyotard, "Jewish Oedipus," trans. Susan Hanson, *Driftworks* (New York: Semiotext[e], 1984), and J. Starobinski's "Introduction" to the French translation of Ernest Jones's *Hamlet and Oedipus* (Paris: Gallimard, 1967). In what follows I also refer, again, to Lacan's "Desire and the Interpretation of Desire in Hamlet."
4. Theodor Reik, *The Compulsion to Confess: On the Psychoanalysis of Crime and Punishment* (New York: Farrar, Straus & Cudahy, 1959), 309.

Radical Ambivalence

1. Sándor Radó, "The Problem of Melancholia," *International Journal of Psychoanalysis* 10 (1928): 420–38. Page references are given in the text.
2. See, e.g., Miller's *The Untouched Key*, trans. Hildegarde and Hunter Hannum (New York: Doubleday, 1990).

Why WE THE PEOPLE Don't Get Off

Epigraph: Leo Stone, "Reflections on the Psychoanalytic Concept of Aggression," *Psychoanalytic Quarterly* (April 1971): 234.

Eating Bambi

1. Schickel, *The Disney Version*, 10; subsequent references are in the text.
2. Rudolf Kleinpaul, *Menschenopfer und Ritualmorde* (Leipzig: Verlag von Schmidt & Günther, 1892). Page references are to this edition and are given in the text.
3. During summer 1988 in Paris, Avital Ronell and I were regular guests at the Derridas': the topic to which discussion always returned was carnologocentrism, the topic of the ensuing paragraphs.
4. Paul R. Gagne, *The Zombies That Ate Pittsburgh: The Films of George Romero* (New York: Dodd, Mead & Company, 1987), 31–32.
5. See "Eating Well, or The Calculation of the Subject: An Interview with Jacques Derrida," trans. Peter Connor and Avital Ronell, in *Who Comes After the Subject*, ed. E. Cadava, P. Connor and J.-L. Nancy (New York: Routledge, 1990).
6. Cited in Jane Caputi, "Films of the Nuclear," *Journal of Popular Film and Television* 16, no. 3 (Fall 1988): 102.

Memoirs of a Viennese Whore

1. Anonymous, *Oh! Oh! Josephine* (London: Loxor Press, 1973), 2 vols. Page references are to this edition and are given in the text.

Our Friend the Atom

Epigraph: Herbert Marcuse, *Eros and Civilization*, 97.
1. Grotjahn, "Ferdinand the Bull," 37, 38.
2. S. Eisenstein, "On Disney," in *Walt Disney* (Venice: La Biennale, 1985), 25–61. References are given in the text.
3. David Hamburg, "An Evolutionary and Developmental Approach to Human Aggressiveness," *Psychoanalytic Quarterly* 42 (1973). References are given in the text.
4. Peter Canning, "The Mything Drive," unpublished manuscript.

Invasion of the Body Snatchers

1. Géza Róheim, "The Individual, the Group, and Mankind," *Psychoanalytic Quarterly* 25 (1956): 8, 10.
2. Richard Lower, "Depersonalization and the Masochistic Wish," *Psychoanalytic Quarterly* 40 (1971): 584–602: References are given in the text.

Gadget Love

1. Otto Kernberg, "Adolescent Sexuality in the Light of Group Processes," *Psychoanalytic Quarterly* 49 (1980): 27–47. Hereafter referred to in the text as AS. Kernberg's companion piece ("Love, the Couple and the Group," same issue, pp. 78–108) will be referred to in the text as LCG.
2. Edward Carroll, "Acting Out and Ego Development," *Psychoanalytic Quarterly* 23 (1954): 521–28. Further references are given in the text. Cf. S. Louis Mogul, "Asceticism in Adolescence and Anorexia Nervosa," *Psychoanalytic Study of the Child* 35 (1980): 155–75.
3. Edith Buxbaum, "Transference and Group Formations in Children and Adolescents," *Psychoanalytic Study of the Child* 1 (1945): 351–65. Page references are in text.
4. Roy Schafer, "Concepts of Self and Identity and the Experience of Separation-Individuation in Adolescence," *Psychoanalytic Quarterly* 42 (1973): 42–59. Page references are in text.
5. Erik Erikson, *Childhood and Society* (New York: W. W. Norton, 1950). Page references are given in the text.
6. Moses Laufer, "The Nature of Adolescent Pathology and the Psy-

choanalytic Process," *Psychoanalytic Study of the Child* 33 (1978): 307–22. Page references are in text.
7. K. R. Eissler, "Creativity and Adolescence: The Effect of Trauma in Freud's Adolescence," *Psychoanalytic Study of the Child* 33 (1978): 461–517. Page references are in text.
8. Peter Giovacchini, "On Gadgets," *Psychoanalytic Quarterly* 28 (1959): 330–41. Page references are in the text.

ZAP: Depersonalized

1. Owen Renik, "The Role of Attention in Depersonalization," *Psychoanalytic Quarterly* 47 (1978): 588–605. References are given in the text.

The Impostor

Epigraphs: Lionel Finkelstein, "The Impostor: Aspects of His Development," *Psychoanalytic Quarterly* 43 (1974): 85–114. Quotation is from a patient. Leonhard Shengold, "The Effects of Child Abuse as Seen in Adults: George Orwell," *Psychoanalytic Quarterly* 54 (1985): 37. Subsequent references are in the text.
1. Helene Deutsch, "The Impostor: Contribution to Ego Psychology of a Type of Psychopath," *Psychoanalytic Quarterly* 24 (1955): 483–505. References are given in the text.
2. I am following Finkelstein's review of the literature.
3. Phyllis Greenacre, "The Impostor," *Psychoanalytic Quarterly* 27 (1958): 363–64.

Camp Counselor

1. Herbert Marcuse, "The Obsolescence of the Freudian Concept of Man," in *Five Lectures* (Boston: Beacon Press, 1970), 44–61. References are given in the text.
2. Janine Chasseguet-Smirgel, "Perversion, Idealization and Sublimation," *International Journal of Psycho-Analysis* 55 (1974): 349–57. References are given in text.

Go for It

1. Gustav Bychowski, "The Ego and the Introjects," *Psychoanalytic Quarterly* 25 (1956): 11–36. References are given in text.

California Transplant

Epigraph: Samuel Basch, "The Intrapsychic Integration of a New Organ: A Clinical Study of Kidney Transplantation," *Psychoanalytic Quarterly* 42 (1973): 364–84.
1. Anthony Summers, *Goddess: The Secret Lives of Marilyn Monroe* (London: Sphere Books, 1985), 466, 223, 382, 403.
2. Pietro Castelnuovo-Tedesco, "Organ Transplant, Body Image, Psychosis," *Psychoanalytic Quarterly* 42 (1973): 349–63.

Electro-Cute

1. See "Rhétorique de la drogue," *Autrement* 106 (April 1989): 197–214.
2. See Freud's letter to Karl Abraham dated June 7, 1908.

Dear Diary

Epigraph: A Young Girl's Diary, Prefaced with a Letter by Sigmund Freud, trans. Eden and Cedar Paul (New York: Thomas Seltzer, 1971), i.
1. In his *Thomas Mann: Fiktion, Mythos, Religion* (Stuttgart: W. Kohlhammer Verlag, 1965), 120ff, Herbert Lehnert documented the extent to which Mann, in his interpretations of his own works, borrowed from critics and academics writing on his work—in fact often did so on the occasion of his having to explain his works in an academic context (e.g., when he was at Princeton). Jochen Hörisch demonstrates that in *Magic Mountain* Mann plays around with a pencil or crayon at a point of reception of psychoanalysis which remains external to Freud. Hörisch identifies Mann's pre-post-Freudian absorption in pencil circulation as Lacanian; see *Gott, Geld und Glück: Zur Logik der Liebe* (Frankfurt: Suhrkamp Verlag, 1983), 206–39. In "Pilgrimage" (*New Yorker* 63 [December 21, 1987]: 38–54), Susan Sontag describes her 1947 afternoon visit, at age fourteen, with Thomas Mann in Pacific Palisades. She went with her high school friend Merrill, who was chunky, cute, but smart (a loner). "I never told anyone of the meeting. Over the years I have kept it a secret, as if it were something shameful. As if it happened between two other people, two phantoms, two provisional beings on their way elsewhere" (54). The meeting came close to the release of *Doctor Faustus* which Mann automatically described to the kids in terms he was recycling in countless letters and would soon publish in *The Genesis of Doctor Faustus:* "'I regard this as the most daring book I have written.' He nodded at

us. 'My wildest book'" (47). Sontag: "I wouldn't have minded if
he had talked like a book. I wanted him to talk like a book. What I
was obscurely starting to mind was that (as I couldn't have put it
then) he talked like a book review" (48).

Gnarly

1. Robert Louis Stevenson, *The Strange Case of Dr. Jekyll and Mr.
   Hyde and Other Stories,* ed. Jenni Calder (Harmondsworth: Penguin Books, 1985). References are to this edition and are given
   in the text.

Split the Scene

Epigraph: Shiva Naipaul, *Journey to Nowhere: A New World
Tragedy* (Harmondsworth: Penguin Books, 1980), 194.
1. Jeffrey Masson, *The Assault on Truth: Freud's Suppression of
   the Seduction Theory* (New York: Farrar, Straus & Giroux,
   1984).
2. Wilhelm Fliess, *Vom Leben und vom Tod* (Jena: Eugen
   Diederichs, 1909), 109.

Smiley

1. Sarah Kofman, *The Enigma of Woman: Woman in Freud's Writings,* trans. Catherine Porter (Ithaca: Cornell University Press,
   1985), 125.
2. Ibid., 123.
3. Smiley Blanton, *Diary of My Analysis with Sigmund Freud* (New
   York: Hawthorn Books, 1971), 52.
4. Ibid., 41.

Venice Beach

1. "Über die Ehe," in *Gesammelte Werke* (Frankfurt: S. Fischer Verlag, 1960), vol. 10.
2. From a letter to Brod written upon finishing Blüher's *The Role of
   Eroticism in Masculine Society,* mid November 1917.

Blood Drive

1. Cited in Terence J. Reed, *Thomas Mann: The Uses of Tradition*
   (Oxford: Clarendon Press, 1974), 364–65. In a letter to Agnes

Meyer, dated October 11, 1944, Mann described *Doctor Faustus* as picking up again where his other modernist or Nietzschean works ("Death in Venice" and, before that, *Buddenbrooks*) had left off.

2. Heinz Kohut, in his "'Death in Venice' by Thomas Mann: A Story about the Disintegration of Artistic Sublimation," in *The Search for the Self: Selected Writings of Heinz Kohut, 1950–1978*, ed. Paul H. Ornstein (New York: International Universities Press, 1978), 2:107–30, suggests the link between Mann's father's death and this early story, maintaining that it was in fact written within a year of the father's death (120–21).

3. Cited in Richard Winston, *Thomas Mann: The Making of an Artist, 1875–1911* (New York: Alfred A. Knopf, 1981), 93.

4. *Gesammelte Werke*, 8:72, 74.

5. "Lebensabriss," in *Gesammelte Werke*, 11:124.

6. Throughout *Die Entstehung des Doktor Faustus* Mann refers to his serious reading, in other words, reading that went into his writing, in this case into *Doctor Faustus*, as "reading with a pencil." See Reed, esp. 156ff, where he shows how phrases, images, and ideas from works by Plato and Plutarch supplied the remedy for Mann's original intoxication in Venice, thereby enabling him to recover, alter, and write about his Venice trip.

California Antibody

1. *Die Entstehung des Doktor Faustus* in *Gesammelte Werke*, 11:126–27.

2. Ibid., 9–11.

3. See *Aberrations of Mourning*, 362 ff.

4. *Von Drüben: Botschaften, Informationen, Praktische Ratschläge*, transmitted by Eva Herrmann (Remagen: Otto Reichl Verlag, 1976). References are given in the text.

5. *Von Drüben*, vol. 2, *Weitere Mitteilungen und Gespräche*, transmitted by Eva Herrmann (Remagen: Otto Reichl Verlag, 1978).

Ecce Mann

Epigraph: See, e.g., Mann's letter to Agnes E. Meyer, dated March 8, 1944.

Buff

1. See Peter T. Hoffer, *Klaus Mann* (Boston: Twayne Publishers, 1978), 41–45, 53–58.

2. See, e.g., Hans Rudolf Vaget's "Thomas Mann und Das Tag-

ebuch: Aspekte der Sexualität in *Der Zauberberg, Joseph und seine Brüder* und *Lotte in Weimar,*" in his *Goethe: Der Mann von 60 Jahren* (Königstein: Athenäum, 1982), 140–73.

3. *Time* (July 25, 1983), 21.

And Then He Goes

1. At a 1990 Santa Barbara conference, Tony Giddens announced as coming attraction a life politics to which I here subscribe.

2. My thanks to Becky Comay for the coordinates of Hegel's "California."

3. Jacques Derrida, "Psyche: Inventions of the Other," trans. Catherine Porter, in *Reading de Man Reading,* ed. Lindsay Waters and Wlad Godzich (Minneapolis: University of Minnesota Press, 1989), 25.

4. After delivering a lecture on conversion ("Teen Passion") at the Johns Hopkins University, I got the surprise of my life! Werner Hamacher broke the news to me: he too had been working on the connection between diaries or journals and journalism. So I checked it out. Hamacher's article on Paul de Man's wartime journalism also covers the release of Paul T. Mann's dear diaries: "The diarist's every word could be his last. Thus in the form of the diary—and in every related form, from the aphorism to the newspaper article—the absolute skepticism about the durability of the written word and its meaning is intertwined with an astonishing optimism that demonstrates itself more in the compactness and conciseness of its linguistic expression than in its contents: since each entry could be the last, everything that comes together in it must appear under the aspect of its perfection, that is, of closure and finality. The world and language of the journal are finished. Its words are no longer intended for someone else, not even for the writer—thus the diary's appearance of empty interiority, thus the newspaper's merely formal, abstract public aspect, thus the pathos of the obsessively detailed realism of both. . . . Journalists and diarists are prophets of their deadline." See Werner Hamacher, "Journals, Politics. Notes on Paul de Man's Wartime Journalism," in *On Paul de Man's Wartime Journalism,* ed. Werner Hamacher, Neil Hertz, and Thomas Keenan (Lincoln: University of Nebraska Press, 1989), 438–39.

5. Derrida, "Psyche: Inventions of the Other," 47.

Index

Aberrations of Mourning
(Rickels), 4, 340 n. 1
Abraham, K., 154
Abraham, N., 4, 354 n. 3
Abrams, S., 92
Addiction, 190–91
Adler, A., 300, 302, 303
Adolescence. *See also specific*
topics
  body and, 260–62, 284–85
  childhood and, 20–24, 68, 79
  conversion and, 158–69, 222
  evolution and, 253–55
  Freud on, 8–10
  groups and, 150–53, 181, 185–
  86, 190–92, 260
  haunting and, 23
  homosexuality and, 280–82
  journalism and, 167–68
  media and, 68, 71–74, 344 n. 3
  psychology of, 256–65, 281–
  82, 336

psychosis and, 90–93
temporality and, 171–72
Adorno, T., 51–52, 56–59, 64,
  112–13, 221, 357 n. 5
AIDS, 288
Aggression, 76–77, 193–94, 230,
  254, 357 n. 3
Altman, L., 5, 6
Ambivalence, 9
Anality, 87–93, 129
Analogy, 133, 143
Animals, 40–41, 66, 239
Antisemitism, 44, 65, 81, 238–41
Archaeology, 198
Ariès, P., 5, 23, 77
Atkin, S., 191
Atomism, 247–51
Attali, J., 61
Autoeroticism, 146, 179

Bachofen, J. J., 182
Bálint, M., 171, 175

Deconstruction, 8, 222, 335
De Man, P., 366 n. 4
DePalma, B., 72–73, 178
Depersonalization, 267–70
Derrida, J., 84, 131, 242, 287–88, 337, 348 n. 8, 352 n. 2, 363 n. 1
De Sade, 76, 233, 234
Desire, 87, 259
Destruction as the Cause of Becoming (Spielrein), 124–49
Deutsch, H., 271
Diaries, 327, 328, 329, 334, 366 n. 4
Disney, W., 31, 40–46, 50, 66–67, 71, 74, 79, 97, 247–49. *See also* Mickey Mouse
Doctor Faustus (Mann), 312–13, 318–23, 329, 365 n. 6
Dostoevsky and Patricide (Freud), 224–28
Dreams, 6, 84, 85, 93–95, 102
Drugs, 31–32, 286–88, 363 n. 1

Earthquake, 219–23
Ego and the Id, The (Freud), 35, 231
Ego psychology, 109, 141, 261–64, 265
Eisenstein, S., 249
Eissler, K., 262
Elective Affinities (Goethe), 326
Electroshock, 207
Embalming, 77–78
Emerson, R. W., 219, 359 n. 1
Endopsychic function, 48, 103, 131, 150, 159, 321, 335, 340 n. 1
Epilepsy, 225–28
Erikson, E., 261–64, 265
Evolution, 251
Experimental Investigations of Music Phantoms (Ruths), 38–42

Facial expression, 40–42, 46
Faergeman, P., 176
Farnsworth, P., 112

Father, the. *See also* Mourning; Oedipus complex
archetypes of, 125–26
Christianity and, 81–82
family and, 180–81, 186, 226
guilt and, 76
Jung and, 125–26
leader as, 54, 89, 263
piety and, 44
projection and, 54
repression and, 186, 226, 307
Spielrein and, 129–30
the unconscious and, 186, 226–27
wife and, 175–76, 306–7
Films, 71–73, 84, 103
Finkelstein, L., 272, 274
Fiore, E., 12–13, 171
Fliess, W., 127, 196–201, 241, 299–303
Fort-da, 352 n. 5
Frankfurt School, 6, 100
Fraud, 272–75
Free association, 195
French Revolution, 150
Freudian theory. *See specific concepts, persons, works*
Friendship, 60, 88–90, 275, 352–53 n. 2, 359 n. 1
Fromm, E., 356 n. 3

Garma, A., 96
Gaze, 84, 346 n. 4
Gero, G., 176
Ghosts, 19–21, 37, 127, 196
Giddens, T., 366 n. 1
Giovacchini, P., 264–65
Goethe, J. W. von, 218–21, 262, 325–26
Gould, S. J., 68
Grand Guignol, 72, 344 n. 3
Greenacre, P., 272–74
Grotjahn, M., 210, 248
Grimace, 40–42, 46
Group psychology. *See also* Conversion
adolescents and, 150–53, 181–82, 260
Christianity and, 184–87

Popular music, 29–30
Possession, 14–21
Postmodernity, 10
Primal horde, 180–81
Primal scene, 61
Primitive groups, 23–27
Projection, 17–19, 39, 54
*Psychopathology of Everyday Life,
    The* (Freud), 47–48
Psychosis, 118
Pursuits of Happiness (Cavell), 83

Radó, S., 94, 174
Ratman case, 35–37
Reich, W., 213–17
Reik, T., 37, 227
Religion, 166–69. *See also*
    Christianity; Conversion
"Religious Experience, A"
    (Freud), 154–55
Renik, O., 267–69
Repression, 31, 136–37, 145,
    300–303, 354 n. 3
Resistance, 268
Reversal, 16, 44, 87
Riefenstahl, L., 110–19
Rock music, 62
Róheim, G., 37, 154, 253–55
Ronell, A., 339 n. 4, 359 n. 2,
    360 n. 3
Rose, G., 30
Ruths, C., 38–42, 47

Sachs, H., 74, 117
Sacrifice, 58, 61, 239–41
Sadomasochism
    bisexuality and, 146–47
    children and, 254
    death drive and, 243–46
    mourning and, 10
    music and, 57
    pain and, 18, 176
    pleasure principle and, 61–64,
        185
    sacrifice and, 55–66
    women and, 176–77
Schafer, R., 260–61
Schizophrenia, 37, 45
Schmitt, C., 286–87

Schneider, M., 189, 356 n. 5
Schreber case, 45–46, 49, 54–55
Schreiber, K., 82
Screen theory, 96
Seduction, 153, 276
Seven Sermons to the Dead, The
    (Jung), 126
Shengold, L., 275
Shock, 218–23, 358 n. 4
Simmel, E., 205
Sleep, 84–85, 94–95
Slips, 38
Speech, 340 n. 3
Spielrein, S., 124–49, 351 n. 2,
    352 nn. 1, 5
Spiritualists, 127, 318–23
Spring, W., 208–9
Starbuck, E. D., 159–65
Staudenmaier, L., 14–17, 131,
    340 n. 3
Stein, G., 77
Stekel, W., 147, 301
Stevenson, R. L., 292–97
Stoker, B., 86
Stone, L., 192–93
*Strange Case of Dr. Jekyll and Mr.
    Hyde, The* (Stevenson), 292–
    97
Studies on Hysteria (Breuer), 156
Subject/object, 352 n. 1
Sublimation, 143, 277–79,
    350 n. 18
Suicide, 24, 50, 62, 84–85, 208–
    9, 262, 331
Superego, 35, 70, 94, 230, 247,
    250–54, 350 n. 15
Surgery, 72, 154

Taboo, 351 n. 5
Tarde, G., 159
Tausk, V., 85, 86
Technology. *See also specific me-
    dia concepts*
    adolescents and, 264–65
    the body and, 76, 214–15, 252
    hallucinations and, 16–17
    invention of, 117
    memory and, 205

religion and, 353 n. 6
sublimation and, 350 n. 1
Teenagers. *See* Adolescence
Telepathy, 33, 39
Telephone, 101, 339 n. 4
Television. *See also* Media, the
analysis and, 95–97, 101–4,
110
conversion and, 164–65
Lacan on, 110–11
the mother and, 114
psychotic states and, 264
transference and, 113–14
Testament of Dr. Mabuse, The
(Lang), 105
*Three Contributions to a Theory
of Sexuality* (Freud), 165
"Timely Thoughts on War and
Death" (Freud), 152
Torok, M., 4, 354 n. 3
Totem and Taboo (Freud), 13, 19,
46, 50, 53–54, 115, 186, 238
Toxic shock, 204–6
Trains, 195–97, 199
Transference
the death drive and, 139–40
Freud on, 181, 195–96, 200
scene of, 135–38, 306
television and, 109–10, 114,
349 n. 11

Transplantation, 283–85
Trotter, W., 150–51

Vampires, 14, 19, 24–27, 87,
132–35, 254
Virginity, 175

War, 77–78, 100, 192
Wesley, J., 353–54 n. 6
West, image of, 5–6, 158–65,
335–38
Williams, R., 101–2
Wilson, W., 202
Wittels, F., 54, 224–25
Wolfman, 95–96
Women. *See also* Mother, the
American, 122, 153
conversion and, 164, 168–69
death and, 123, 133
family and, 122–23
hysteria and, 153
menstruation and, 170–78,
261
transference and, 135–38, 306
the unconscious and, 83–84,
122
writing and, 187–88
Wortis, J., 152

Zombies, 242, 243

Laurence A. Rickels is professor of German literature at the University of California, Santa Barbara, where he also teaches art and film studies. He is the author of *The Vampire Lectures* and the forthcoming *Nazi Psychoanalysis,* and the editor of *Acting Out in Groups,* all published by the University of Minnesota Press.